2198232060906062

A SIGN OF AFFECTION

3

suu Morishita

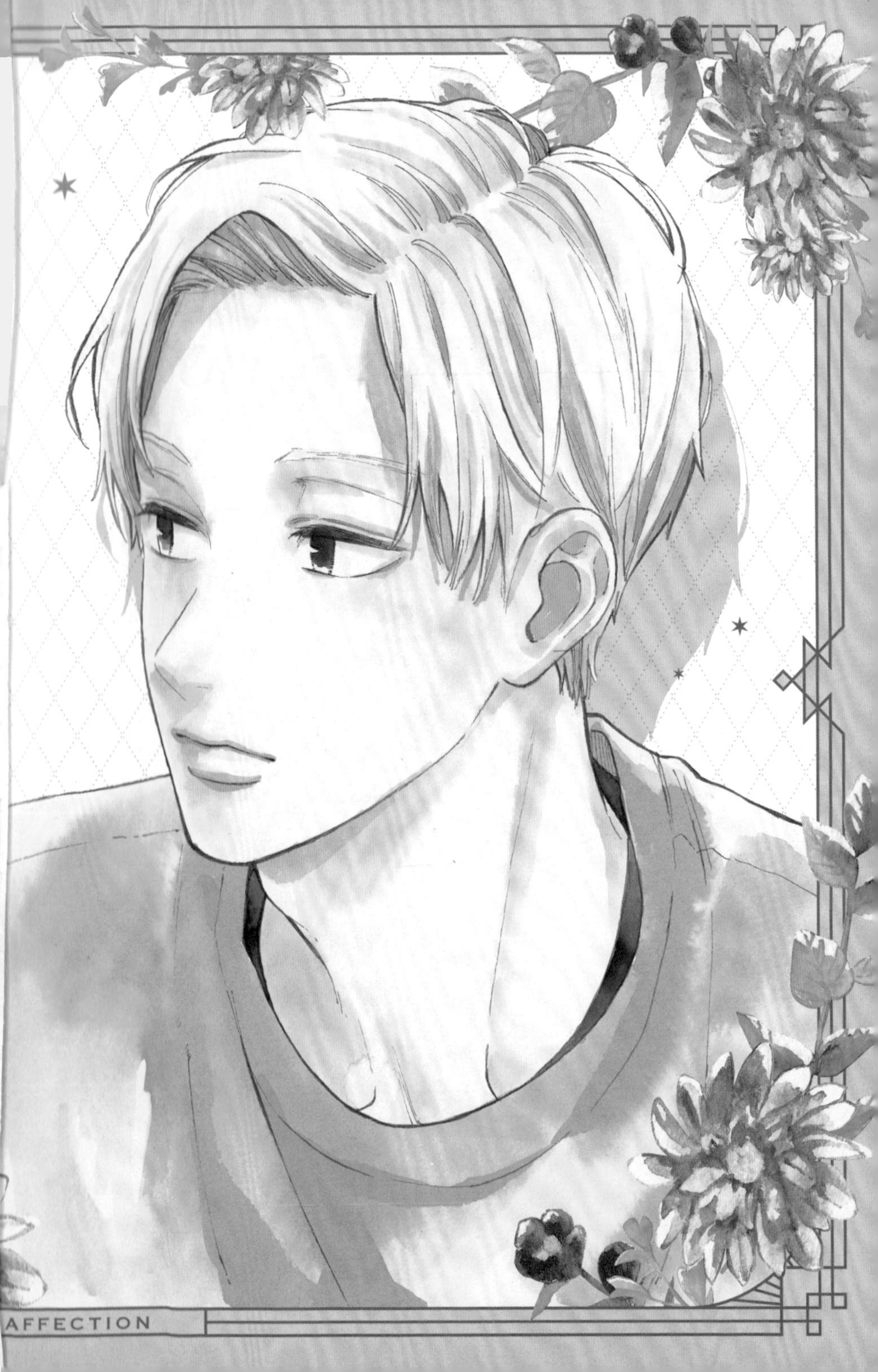
AFFECTION

Sign.9

I Always Thought I Just Wanted to Watch

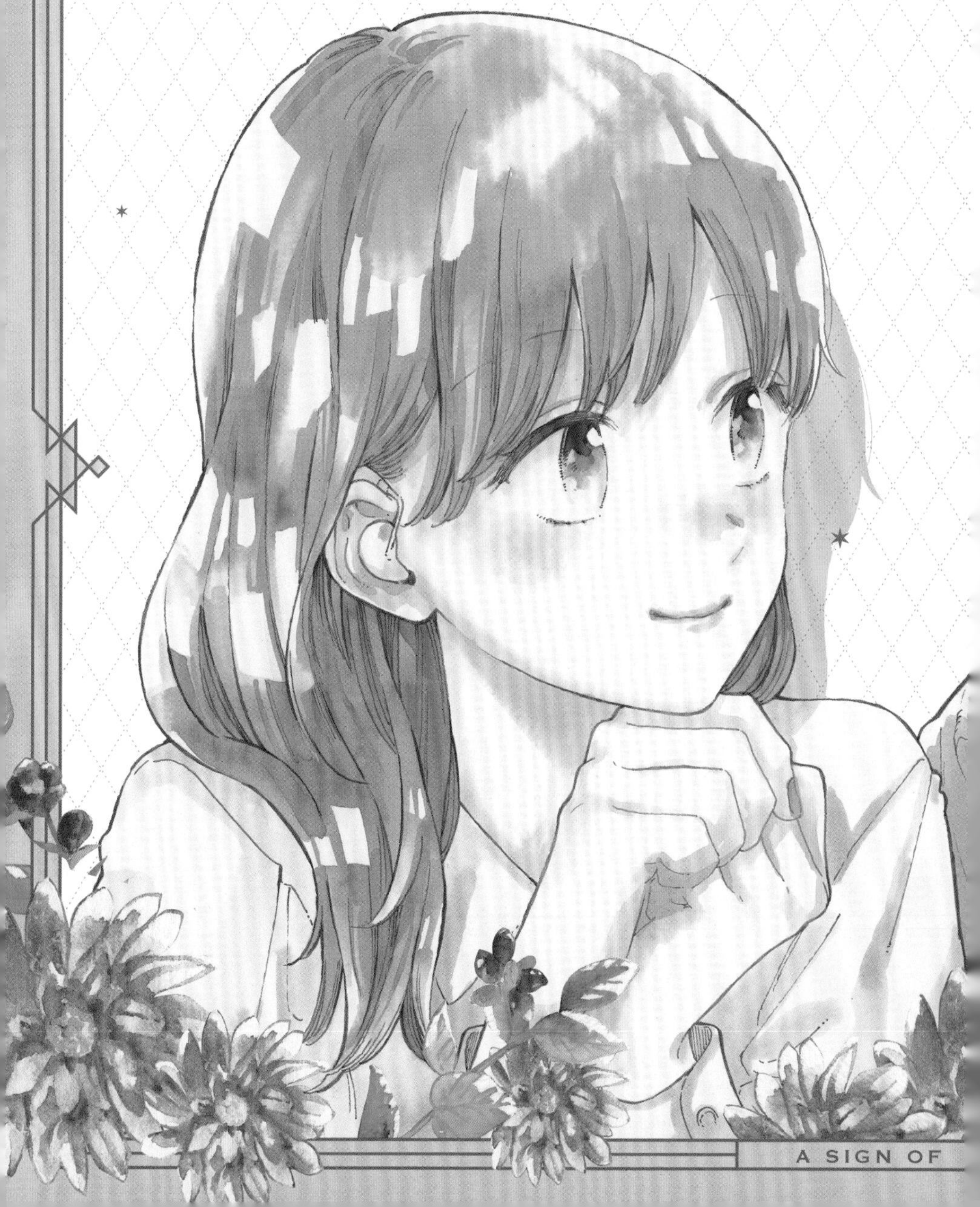
A SIGN OF

CONTENTS

*When the letters in the bubbles are washed out, it means that Yuki is reading the speaker's lips and discerning words from the context of the conversation. When the letters are shown sideways, it means she's having difficulty figuring out a word.

CHARACTERS

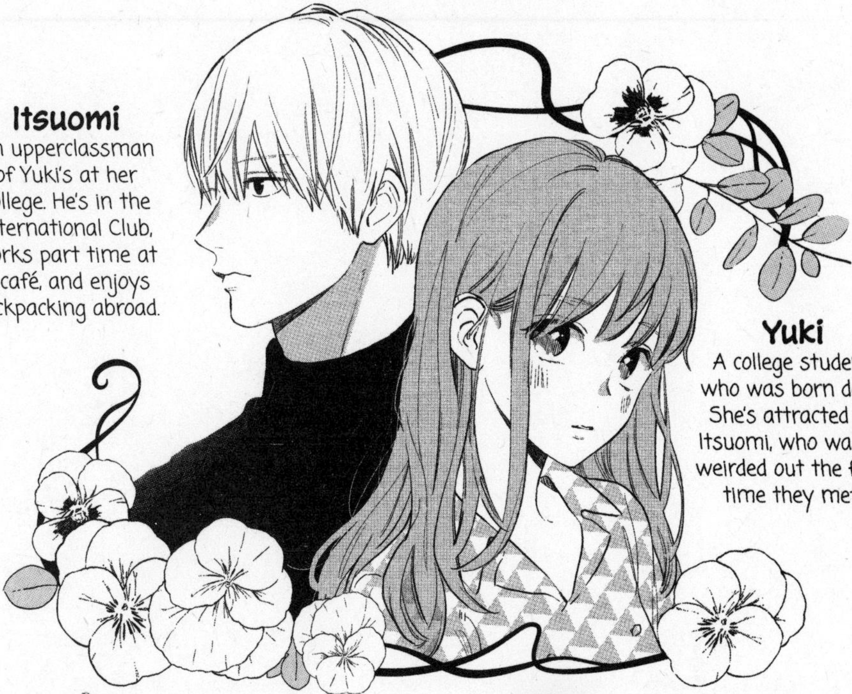

Itsuomi
An upperclassman of Yuki's at her college. He's in the International Club, works part time at a café, and enjoys backpacking abroad.

Yuki
A college student who was born deaf. She's attracted to Itsuomi, who wasn't weirded out the first time they met.

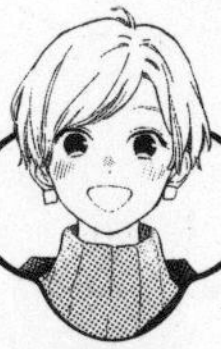

Rin-chan
A friend of Yuki's and a member of the same club as Itsuomi. She's crushing on Kyouya.

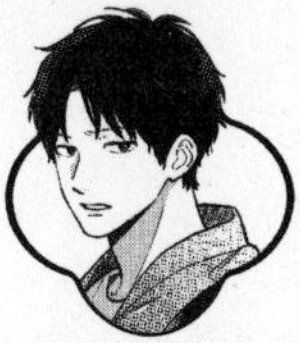

Oushi
A childhood friend of Yuki's. He can use sign language and somehow always ends up giving her a hard time.

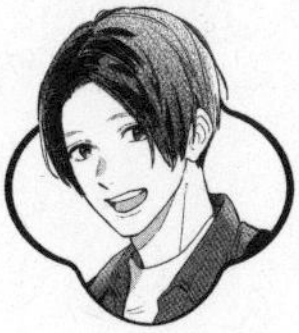

Kyouya
Itsuomi's cousin and owner of the café where Itsuomi works part time.

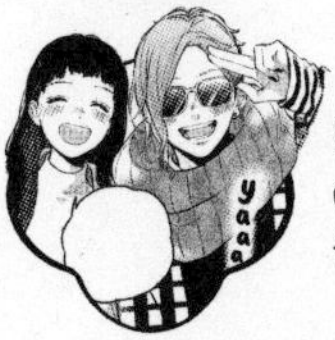

Emma & Shin
Classmates of Itsuomi from high school.

STORY

Yuki is a college student who was born deaf. One day, a foreign tourist asks her for directions on the train. Not knowing any English, she panics, until an upperclassman from her school, Itsuomi, comes to her rescue. Itsuomi doesn't treat her like a delicate flower so, every time they meet, Yuki is more and more enchanted by him, eventually realizing that she's in love with him. She decides to go after him seriously and is surprised to find herself invited to his place, where things heat up. On the way home, Yuki starts feeling insecure about Itsuomi's friend Emma, but then Itsuomi runs up and kisses her hand...

A SIGN OF AFFECTION

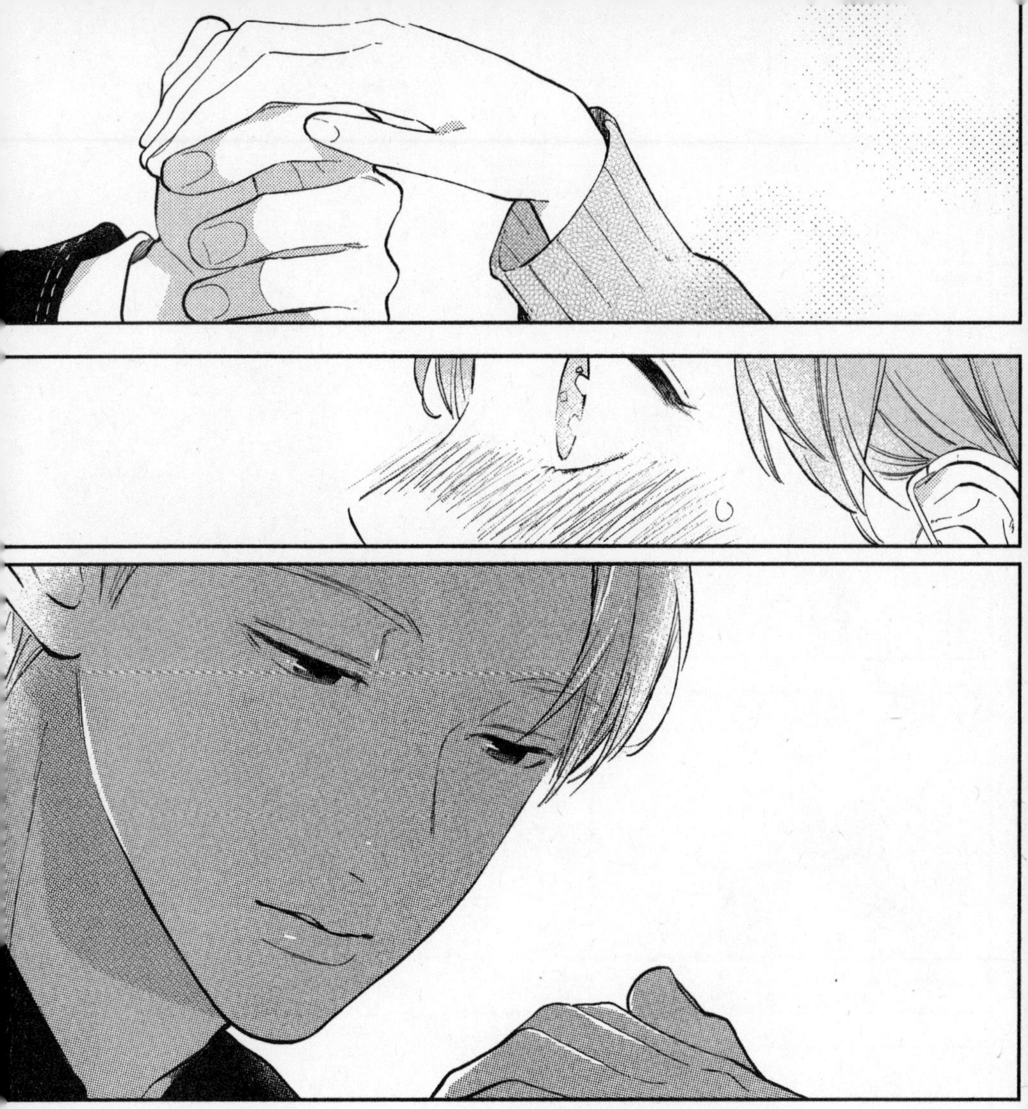

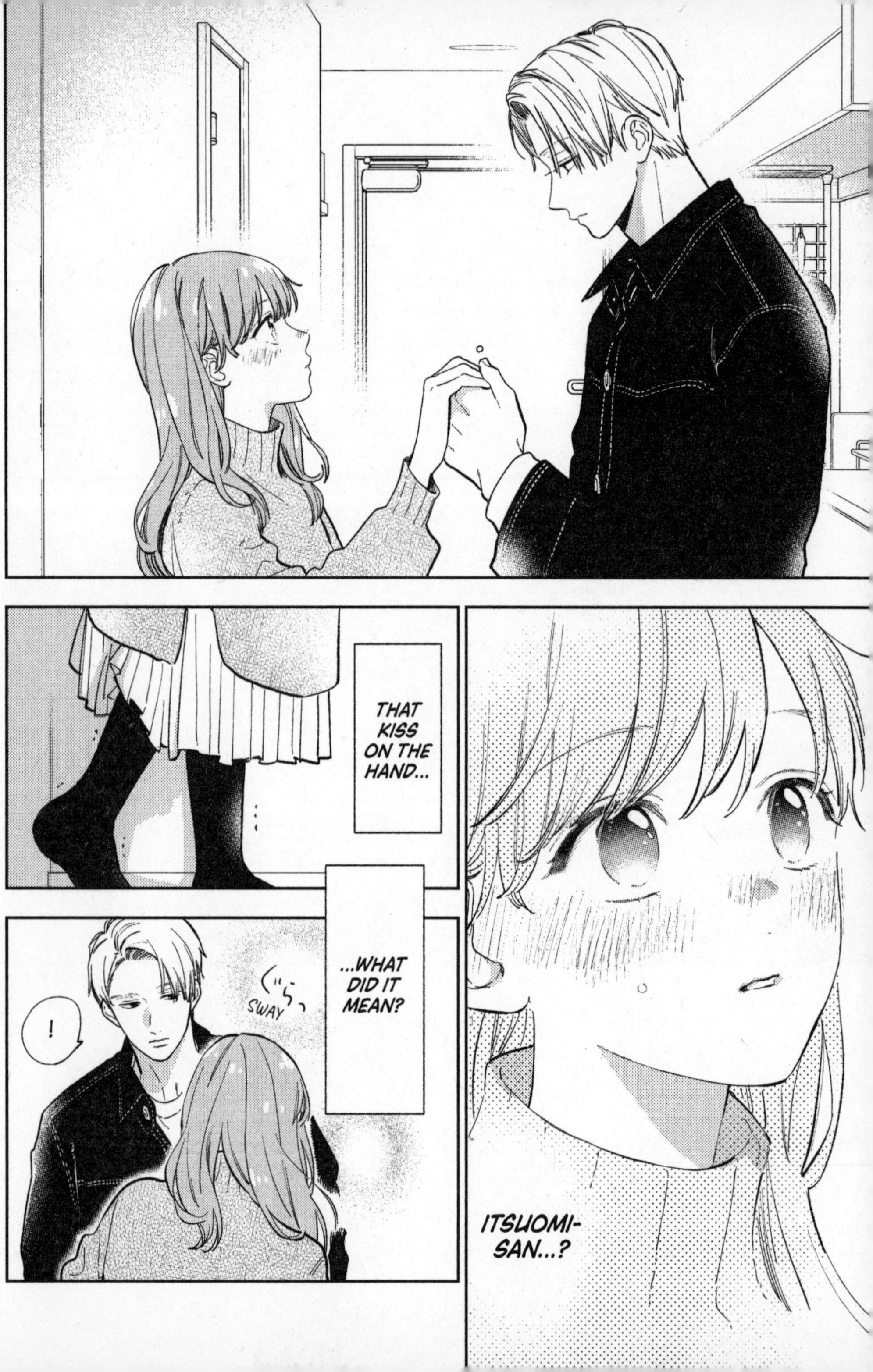
ITSUOMI-SAN...?
THAT KISS ON THE HAND...
...WHAT DID IT MEAN?
!
SWAY

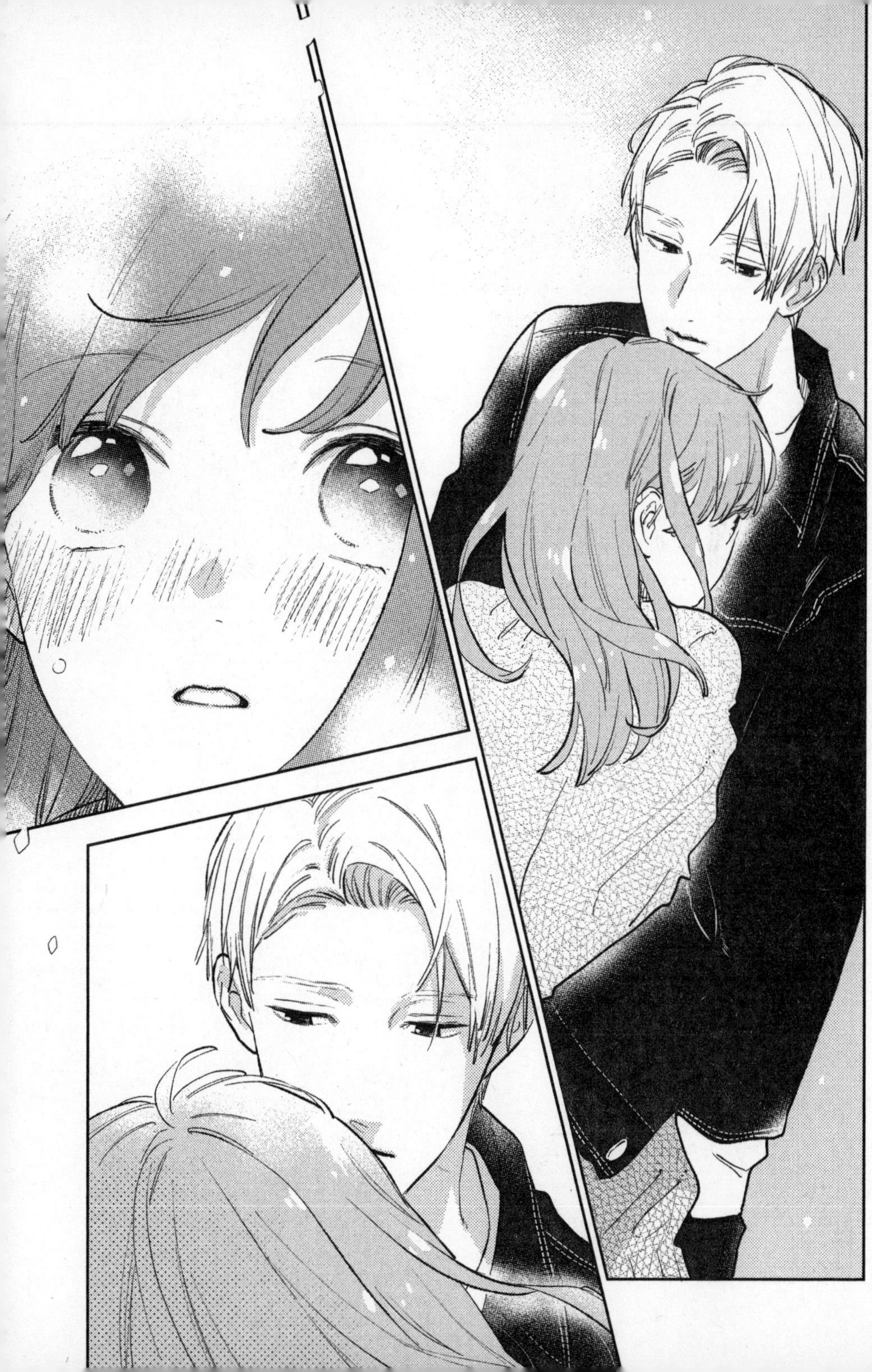

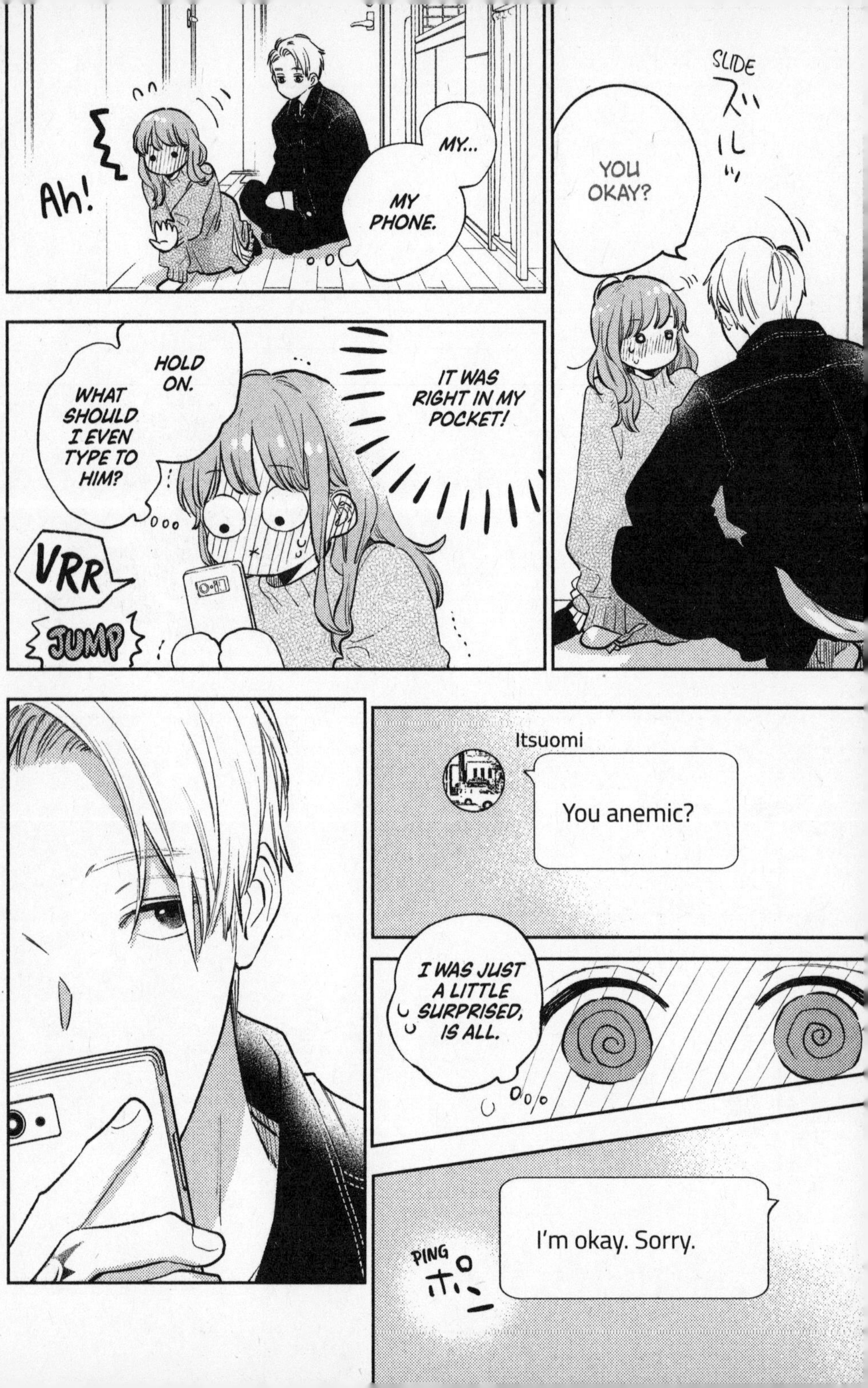
SLIDE
YOU OKAY?
MY... MY PHONE.
Ah!
IT WAS RIGHT IN MY POCKET!
HOLD ON. WHAT SHOULD I EVEN TYPE TO HIM?
VRR
JUMP
Itsuomi
You anemic?
I WAS JUST A LITTLE SURPRISED, IS ALL.
I'm okay. Sorry.
PING

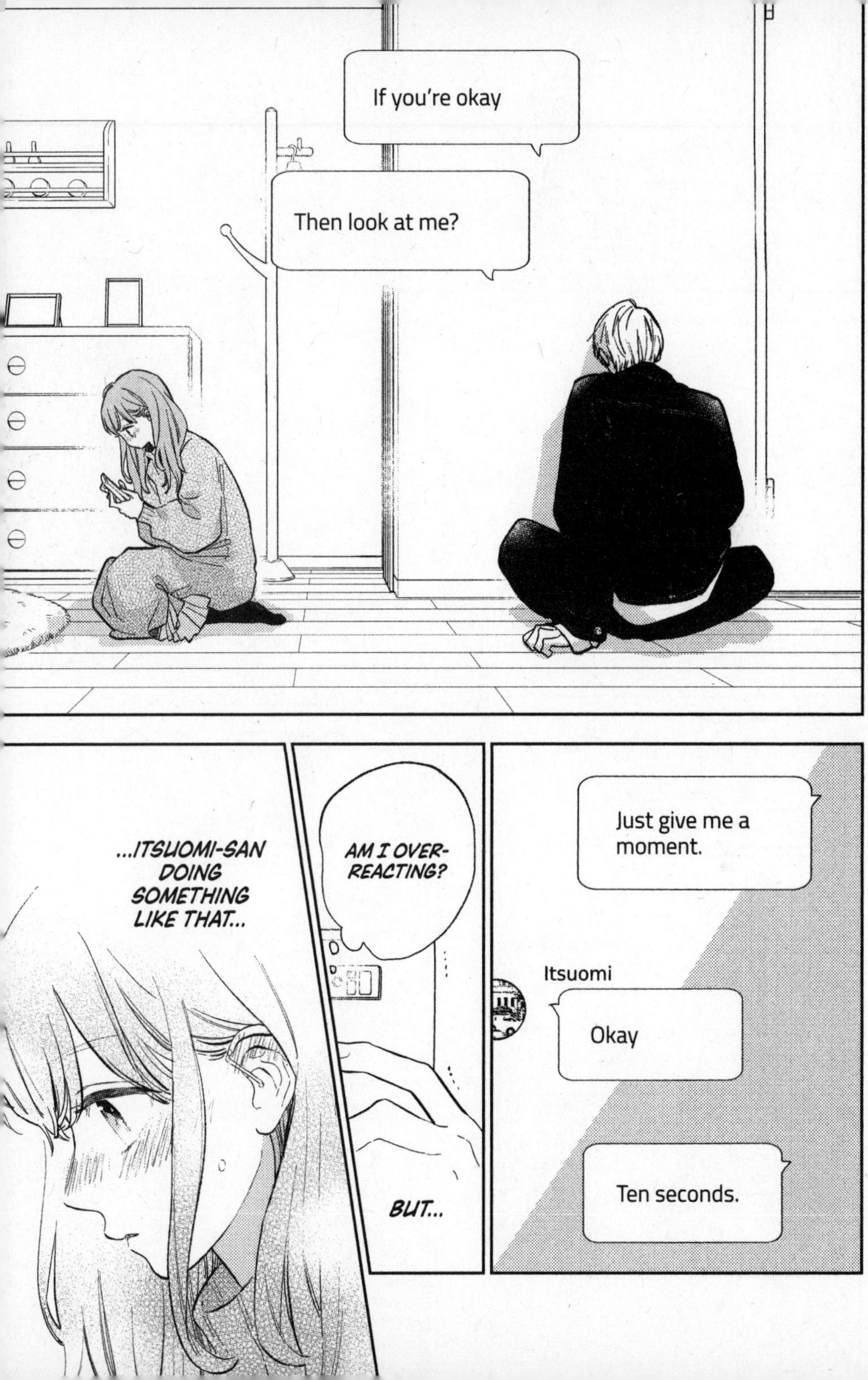
If you're okay
Then look at me?
Just give me a moment.
Itsuomi
Okay
Ten seconds.
AM I OVER-REACTING?
BUT...
...ITSUOMI-SAN DOING SOMETHING LIKE THAT...

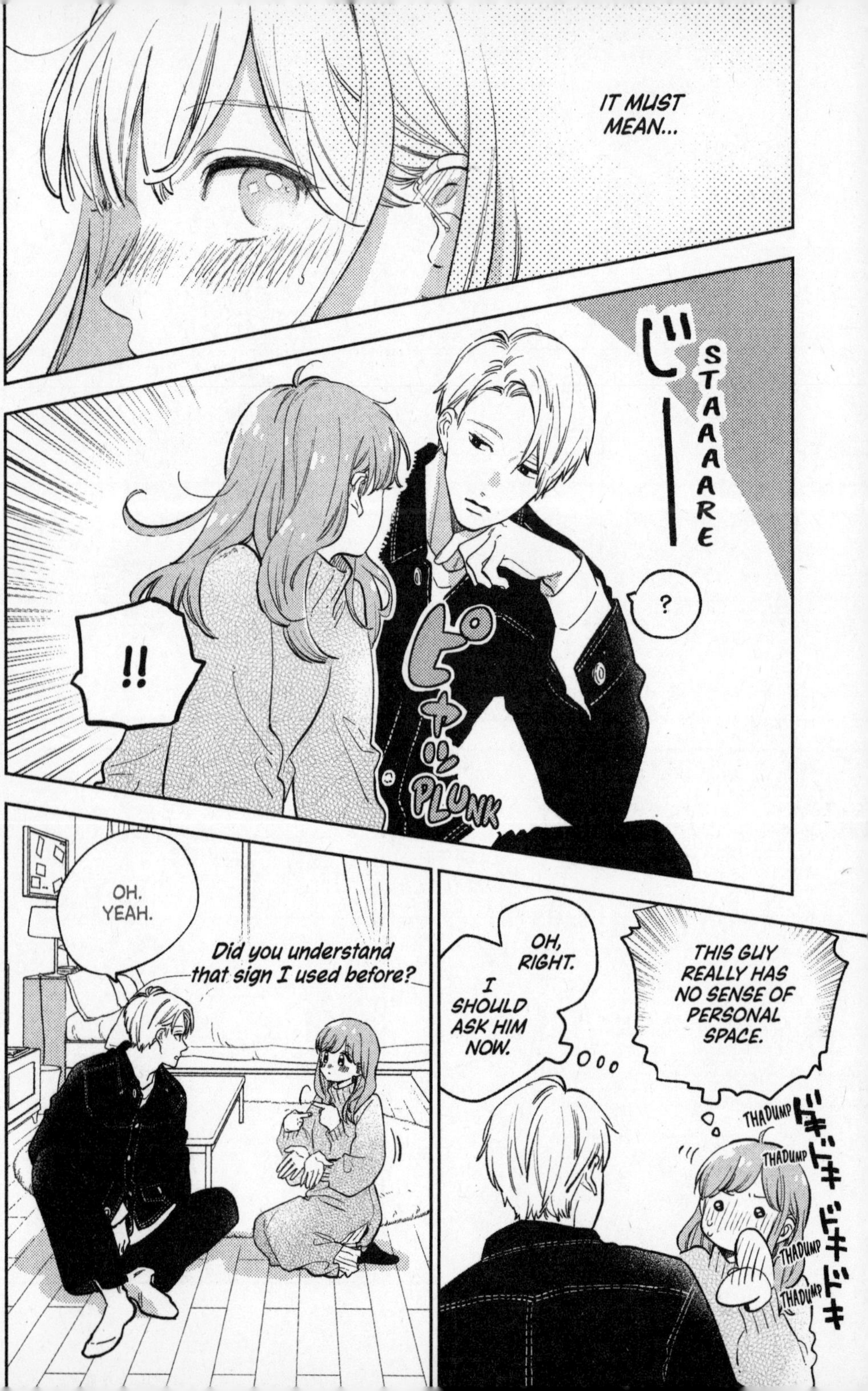
IT MUST MEAN...
じー
STAAAARE
?
!!
ピャッ
PLUNK
THIS GUY REALLY HAS NO SENSE OF PERSONAL SPACE.
OH, RIGHT. I SHOULD ASK HIM NOW.
ドキドキ
THADUMP
THADUMP
ドキドキ
THADUMP
THADUMP
Did you understand that sign I used before?
OH. YEAH.

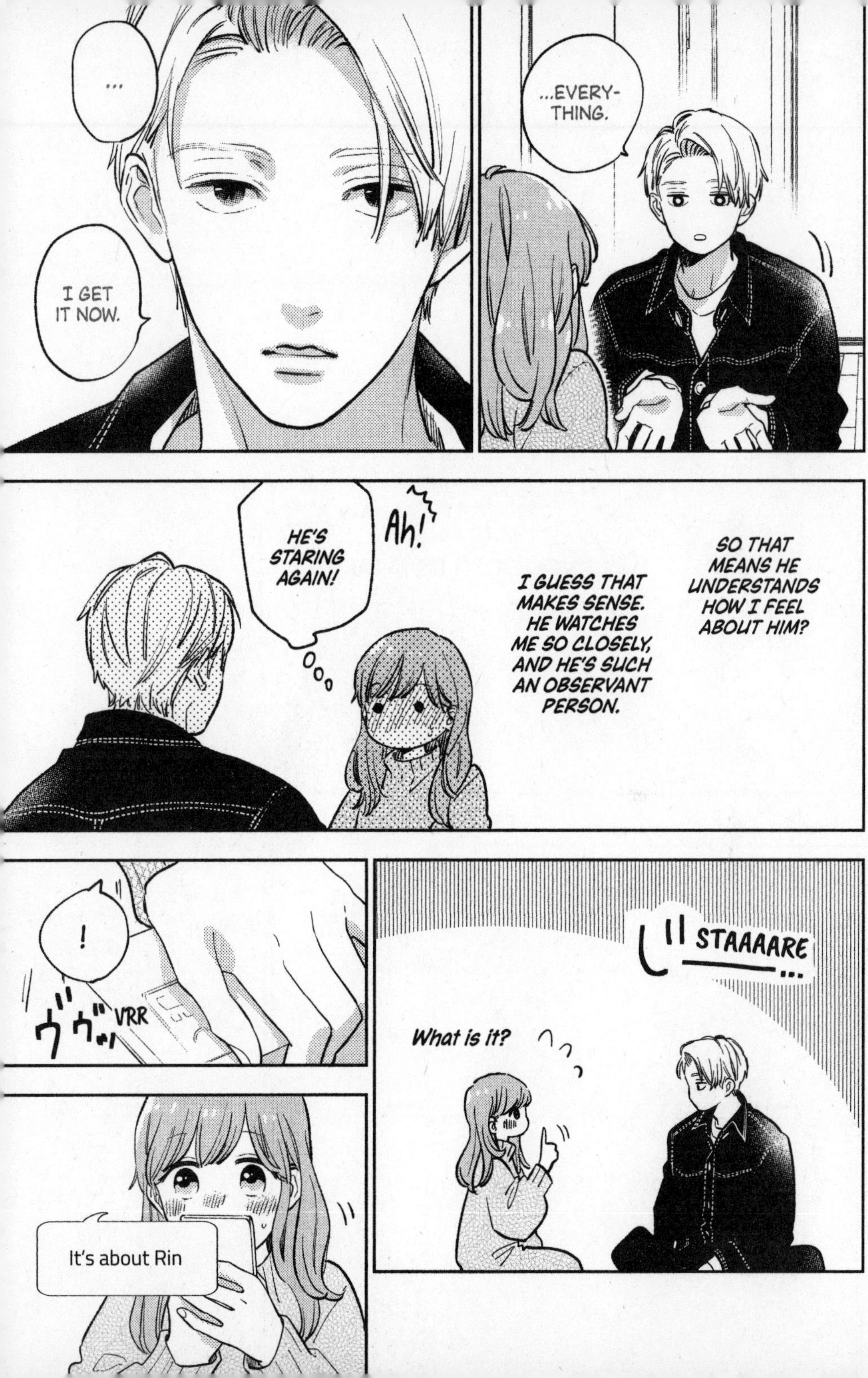
...EVERY-THING.
...
I GET IT NOW.
SO THAT MEANS HE UNDERSTANDS HOW I FEEL ABOUT HIM?
I GUESS THAT MAKES SENSE. HE WATCHES ME SO CLOSELY, AND HE'S SUCH AN OBSERVANT PERSON.
Ah!
HE'S STARING AGAIN!
STAAAARE...
What is it?
!
VRR
It's about Rin

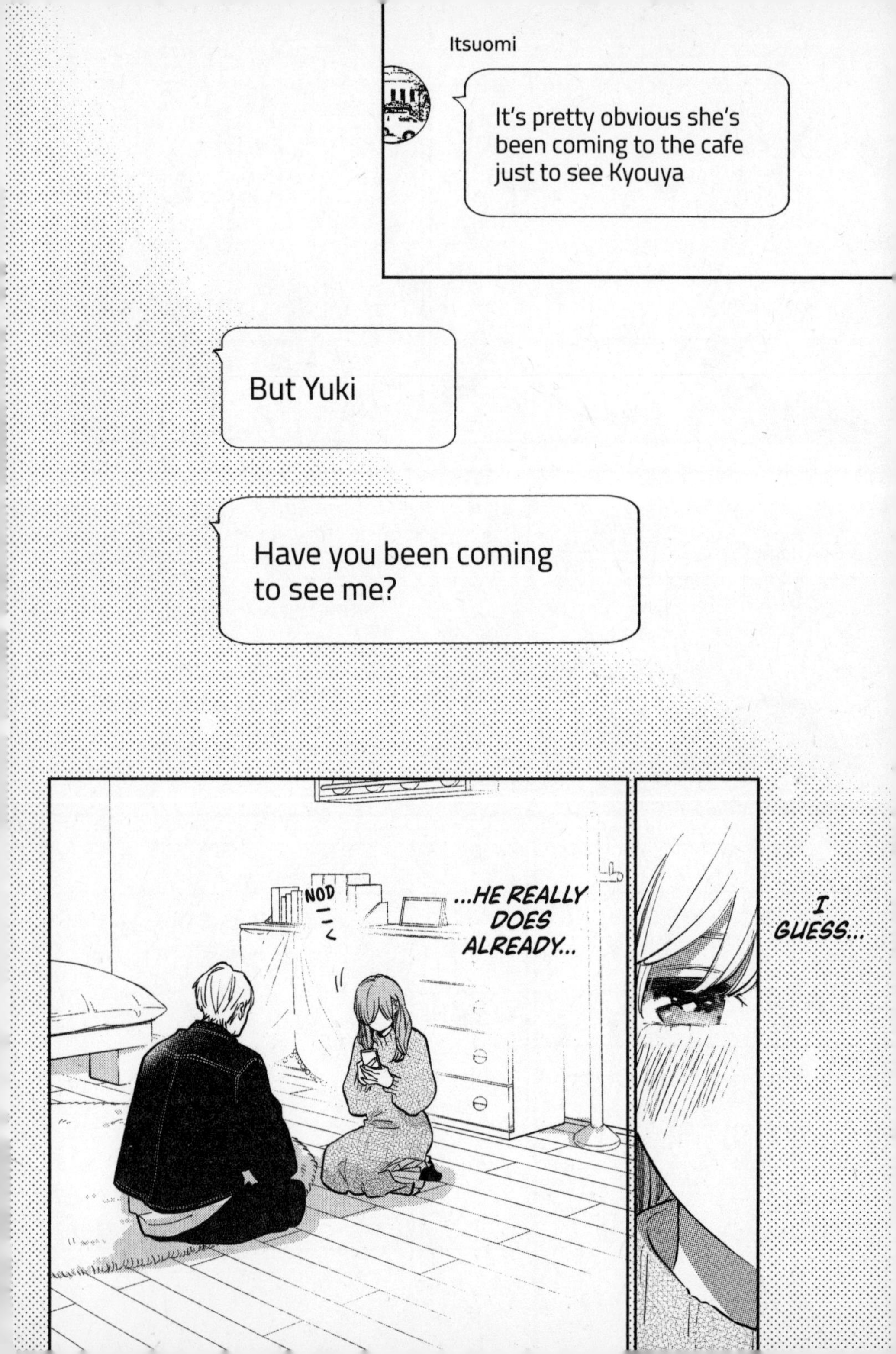

Itsuomi
It's pretty obvious she's been coming to the cafe just to see Kyouya
But Yuki
Have you been coming to see me?
I GUESS...
NOD
...HE REALLY DOES ALREADY...

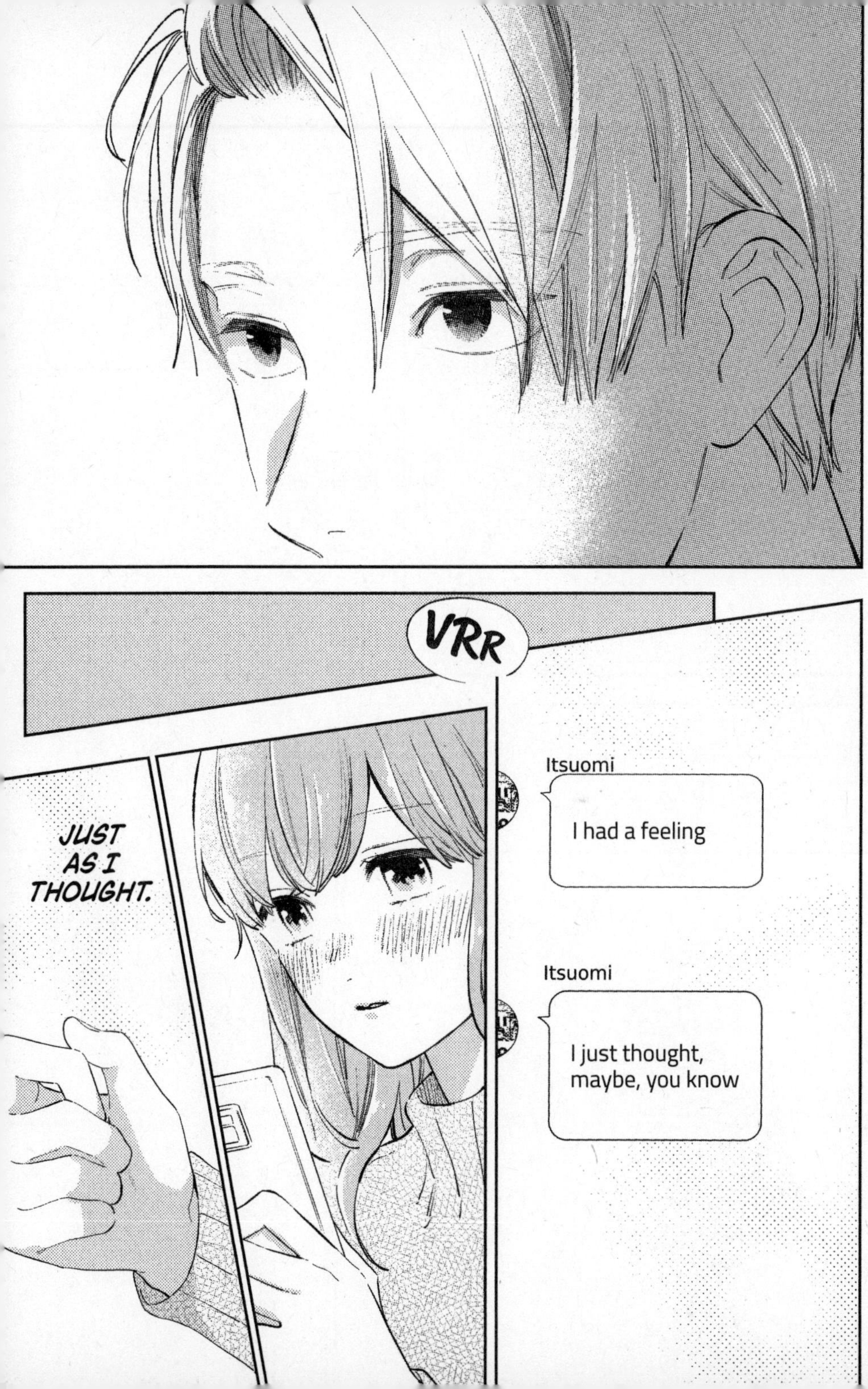
VRR
Itsuomi
I had a feeling
Itsuomi
I just thought, maybe, you know
JUST AS I THOUGHT.

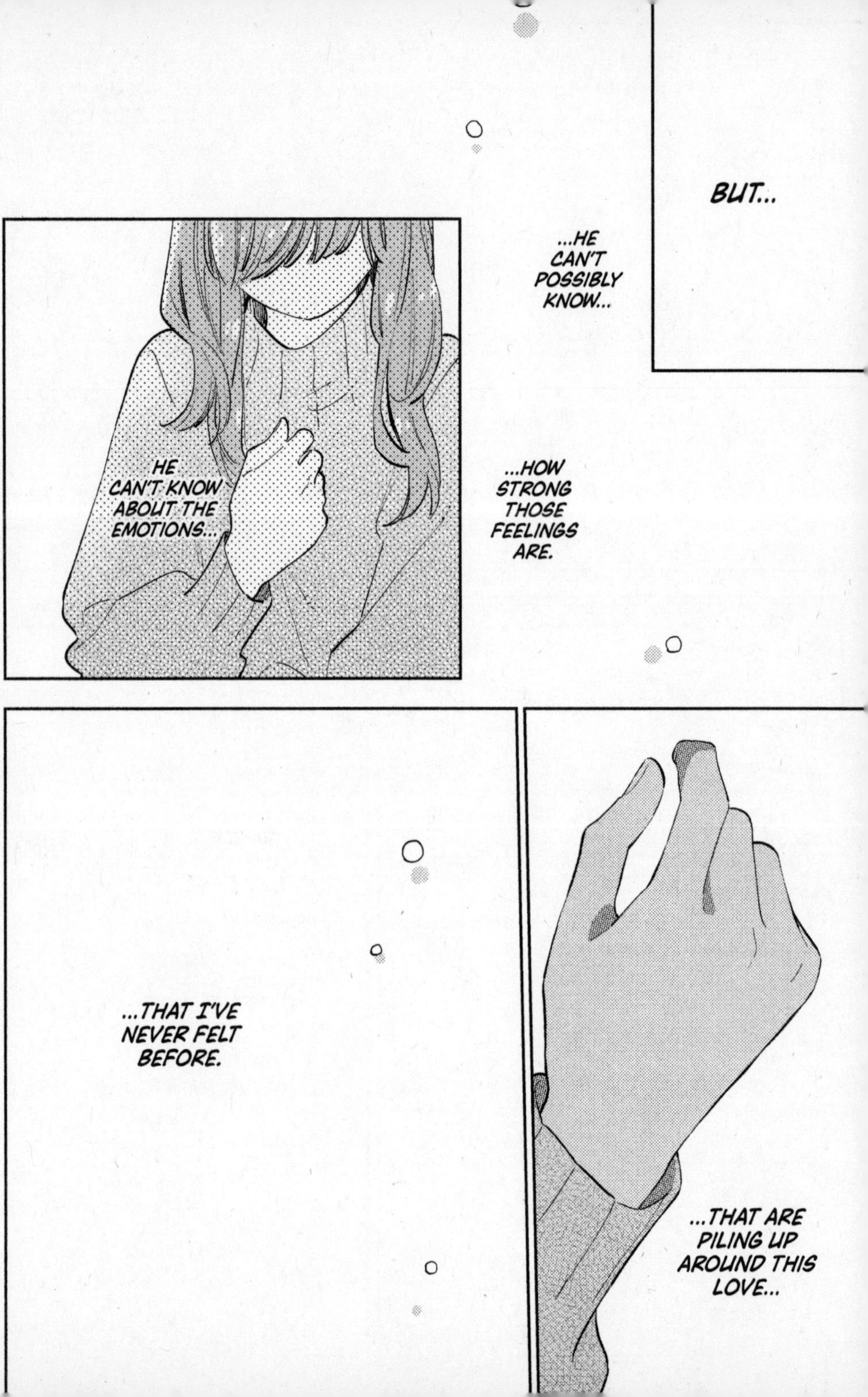
BUT...
...HE CAN'T POSSIBLY KNOW...
...HOW STRONG THOSE FEELINGS ARE.
HE CAN'T KNOW ABOUT THE EMOTIONS...
...THAT ARE PILING UP AROUND THIS LOVE...
...THAT I'VE NEVER FELT BEFORE.

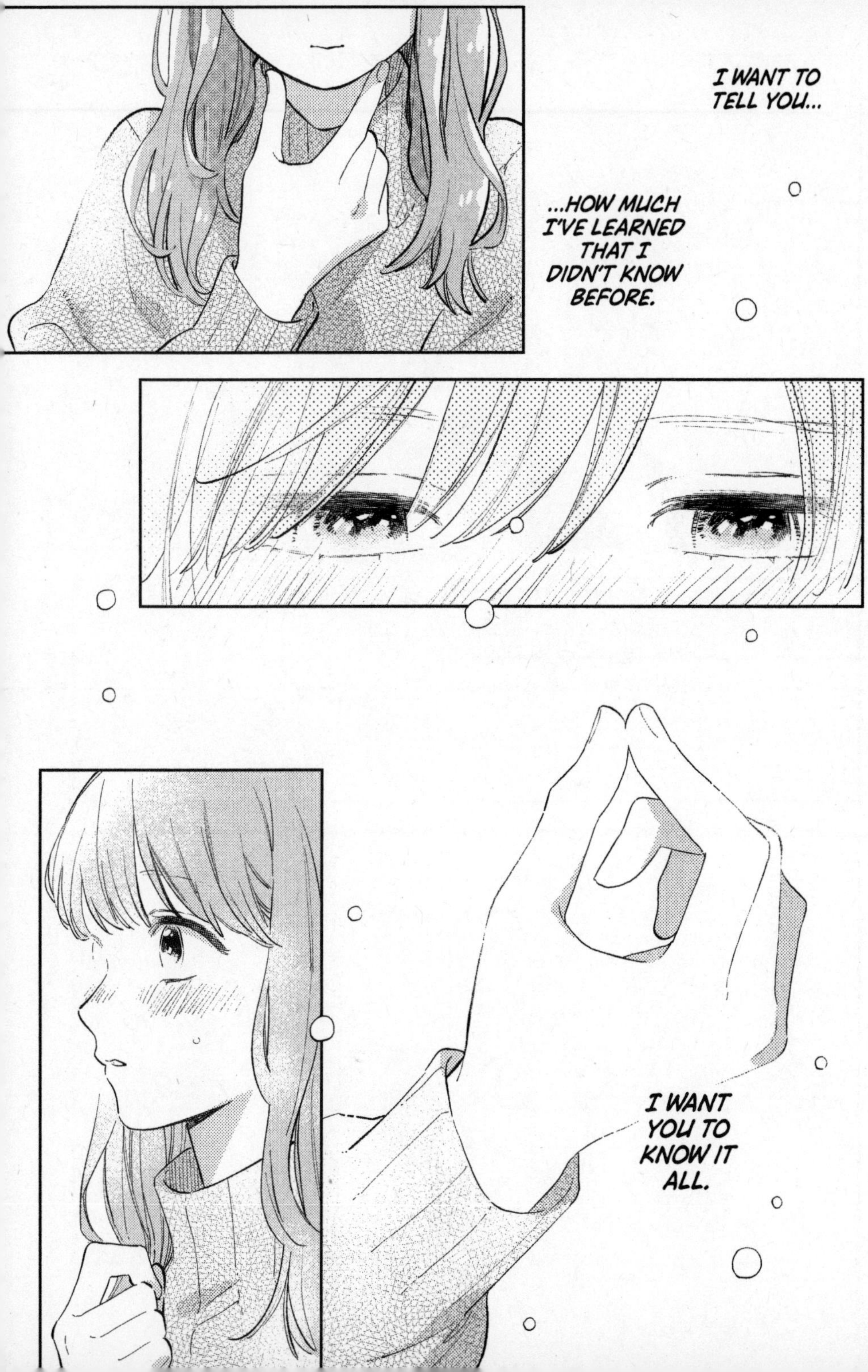
I WANT TO TELL YOU...
...HOW MUCH I'VE LEARNED THAT I DIDN'T KNOW BEFORE.
I WANT YOU TO KNOW IT ALL.

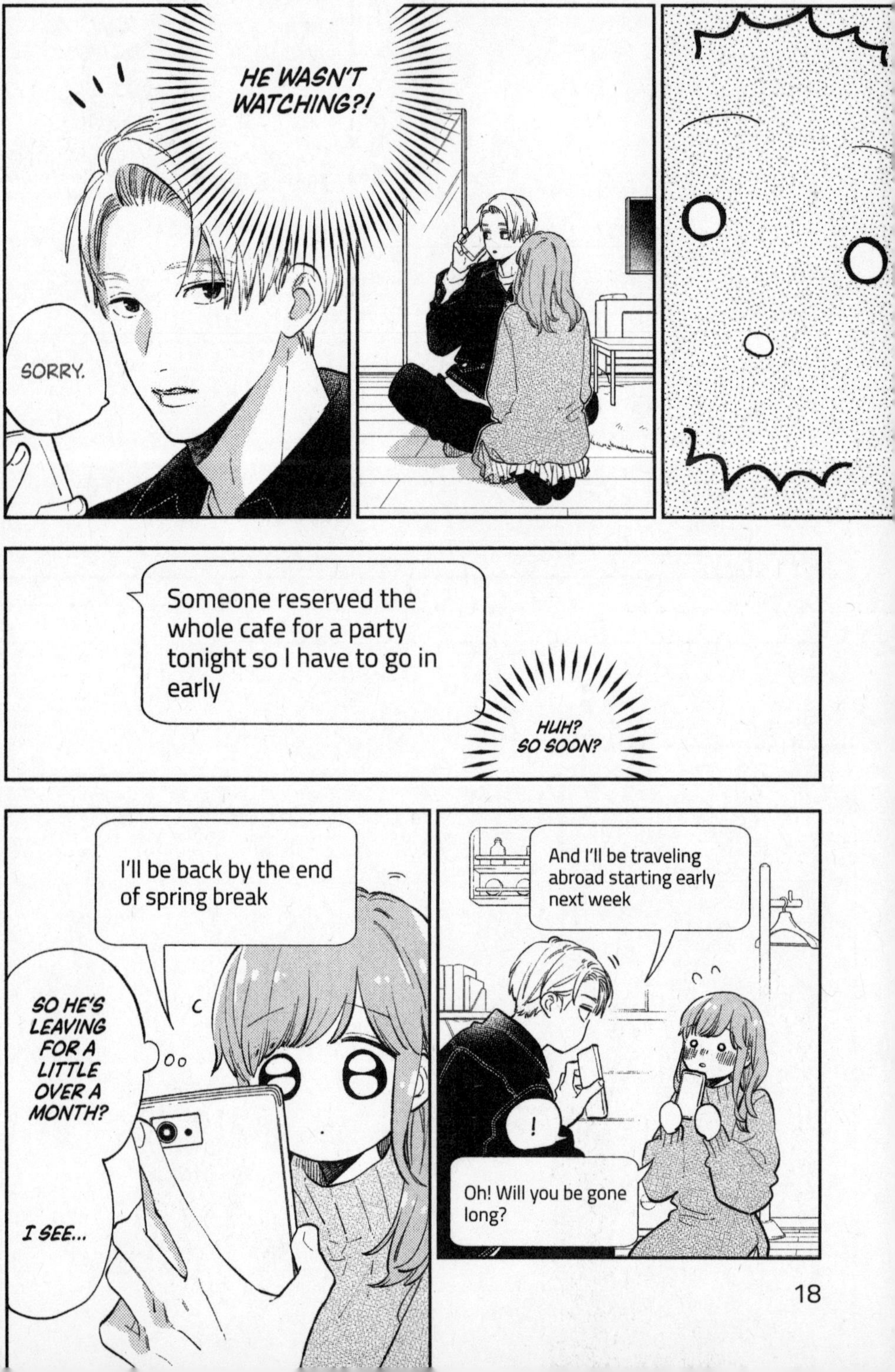
HE WASN'T WATCHING?!
SORRY.
Someone reserved the whole cafe for a party tonight so I have to go in early
HUH? SO SOON?
And I'll be traveling abroad starting early next week
Oh! Will you be gone long?
I'll be back by the end of spring break
SO HE'S LEAVING FOR A LITTLE OVER A MONTH?
I SEE...

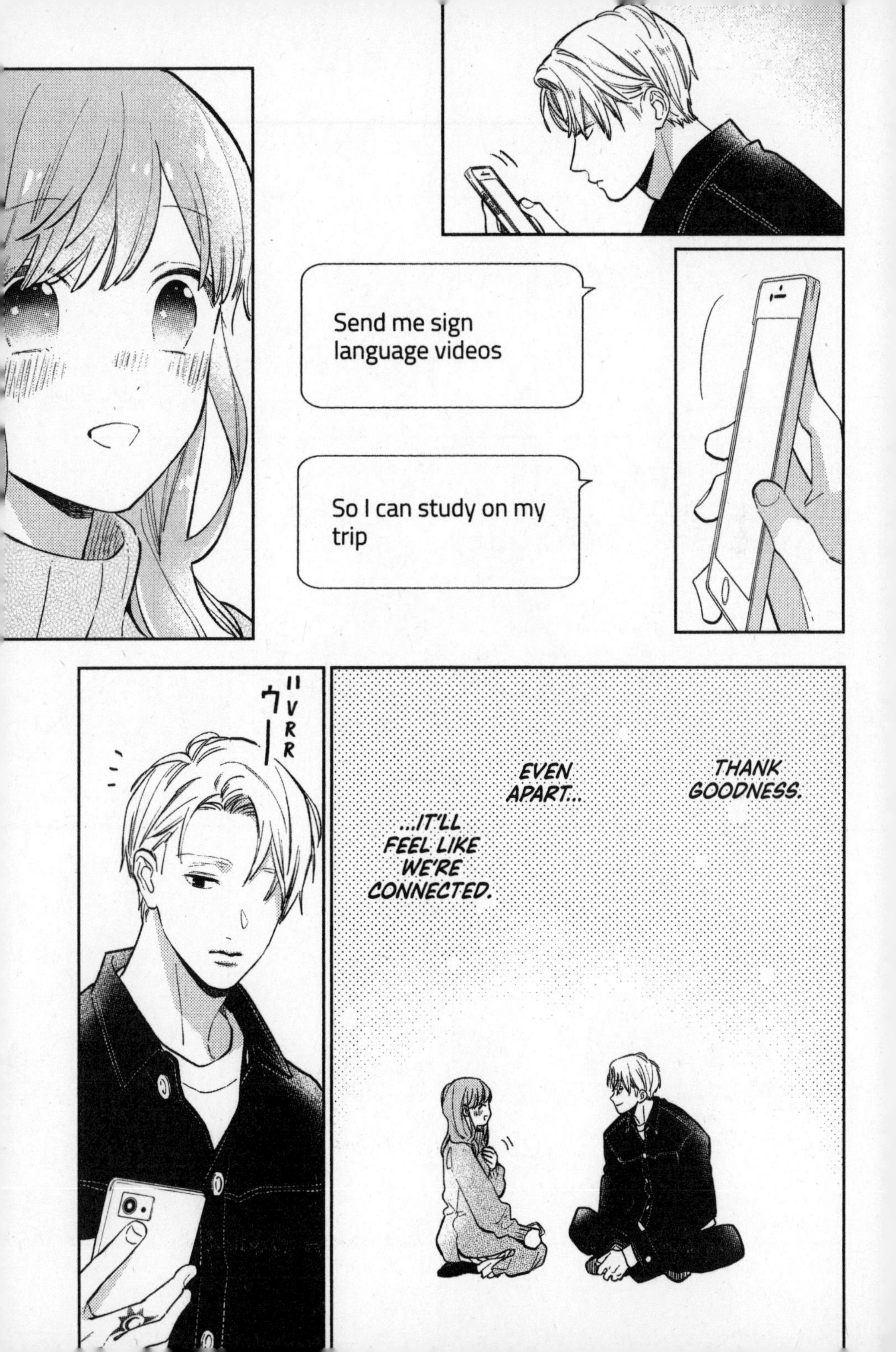

Send me sign language videos
So I can study on my trip
THANK GOODNESS.
EVEN APART...
...IT'LL FEEL LIKE WE'RE CONNECTED.
ヴー VRR

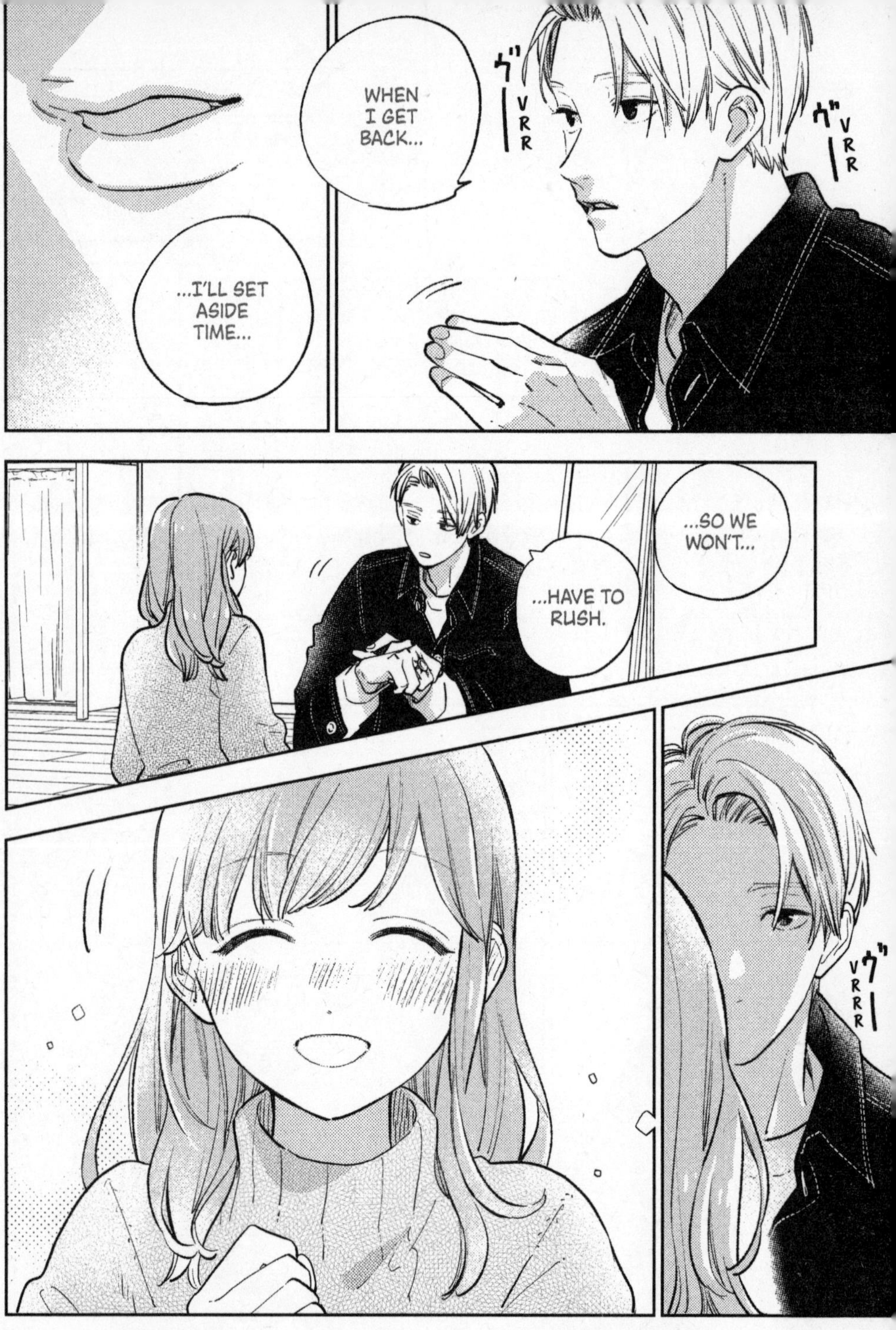
ヴ VRR
ヴ VRR
WHEN I GET BACK...
...I'LL SET ASIDE TIME...
...SO WE WON'T...
...HAVE TO RUSH.
ヴー VRRR

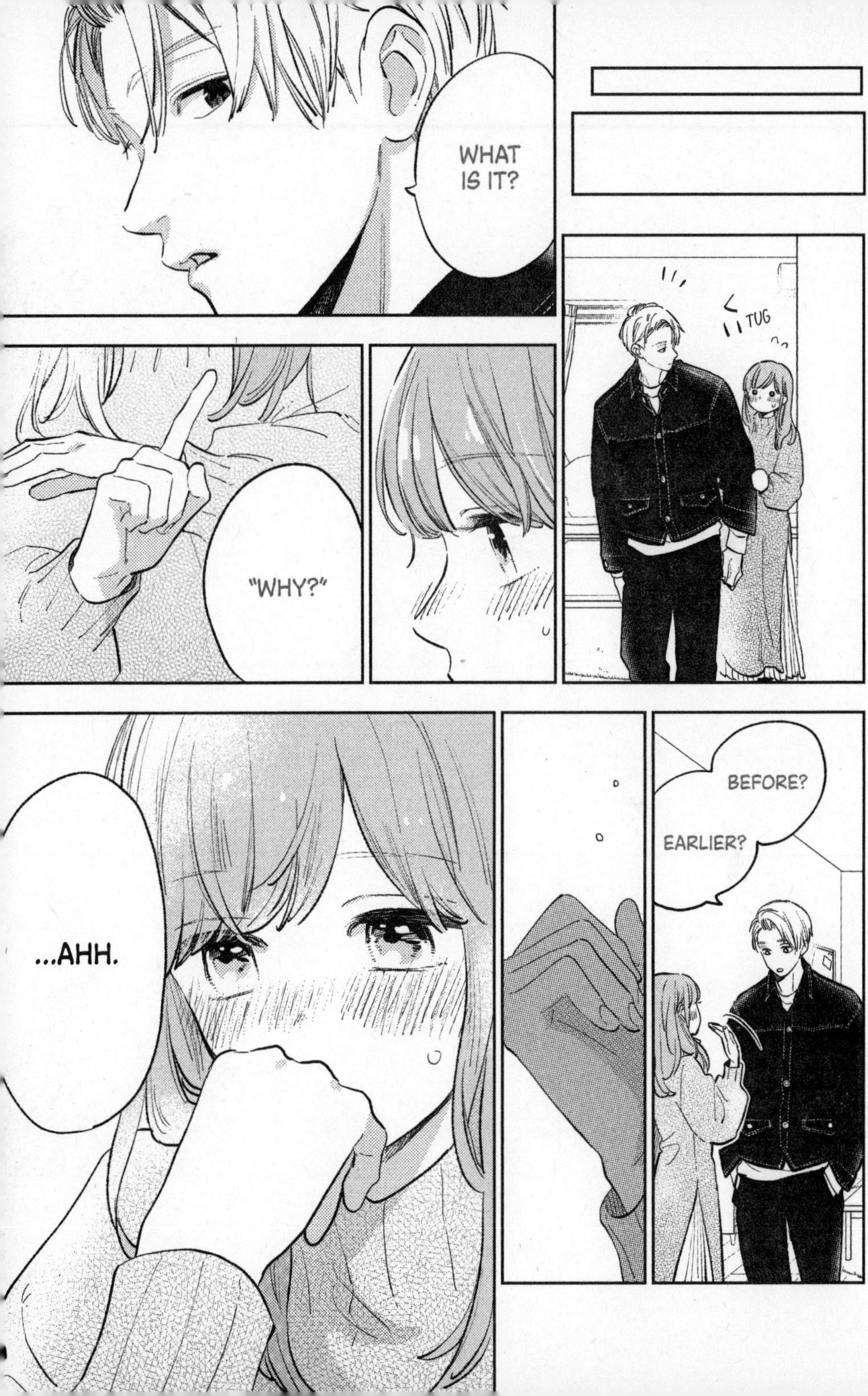
TUG
WHAT IS IT?
"WHY?"
BEFORE?
EARLIER?
...AHH.

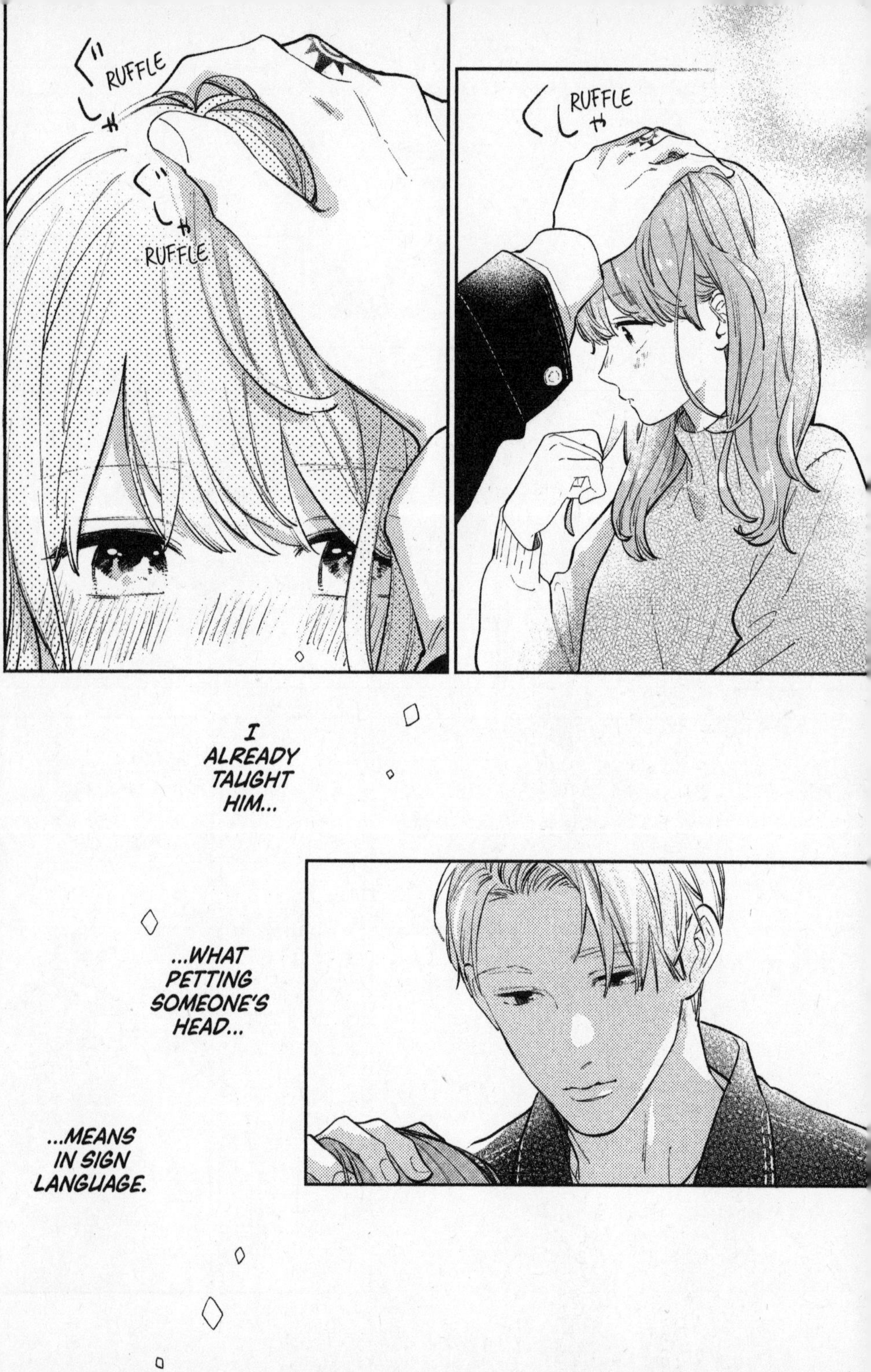
くしゃ
RUFFLE
ぐしゃ
RUFFLE
ぐしゃ
RUFFLE
I ALREADY TAUGHT HIM...
...WHAT PETTING SOMEONE'S HEAD...
...MEANS IN SIGN LANGUAGE.

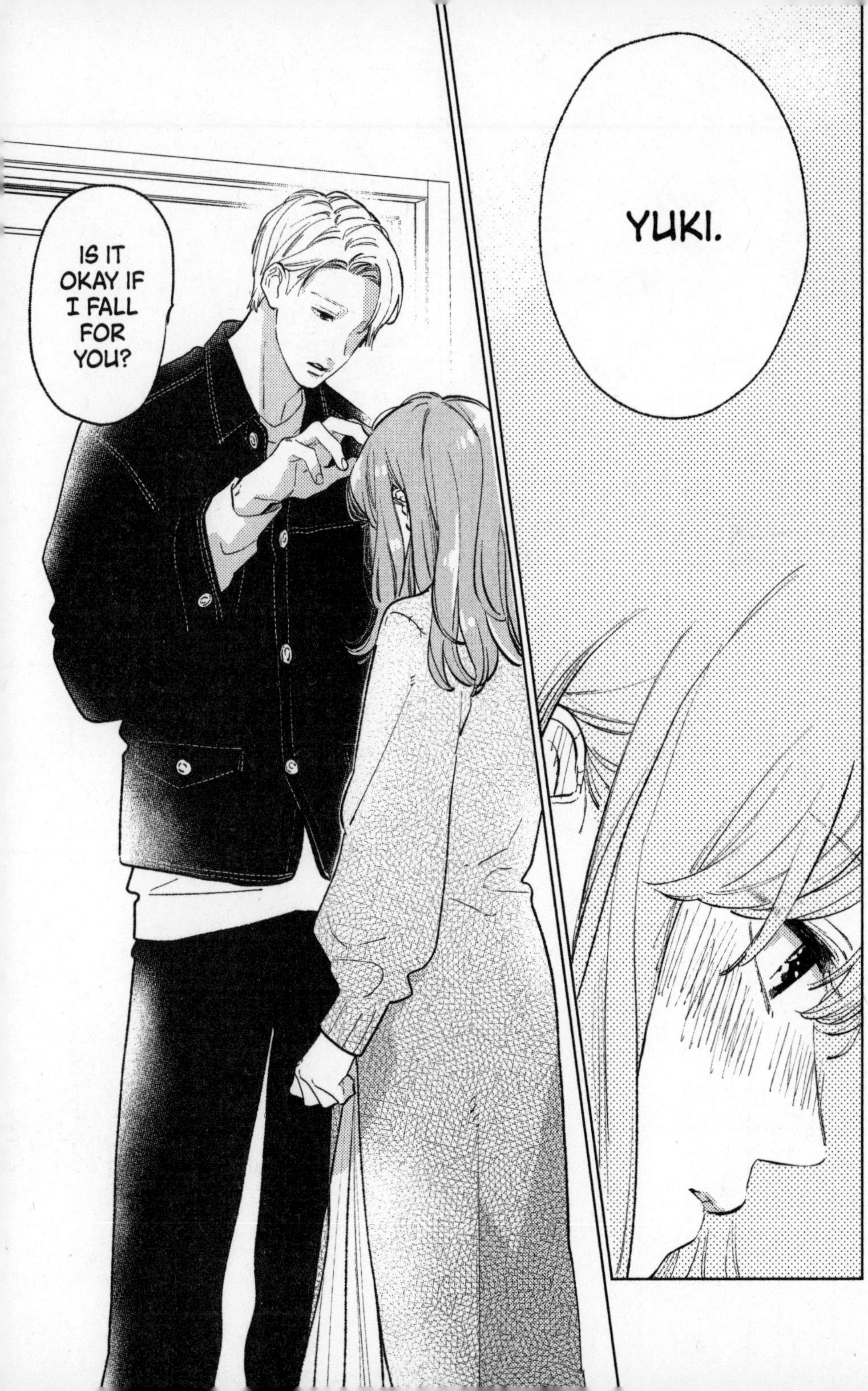
YUKI.
IS IT OKAY IF I FALL FOR YOU?

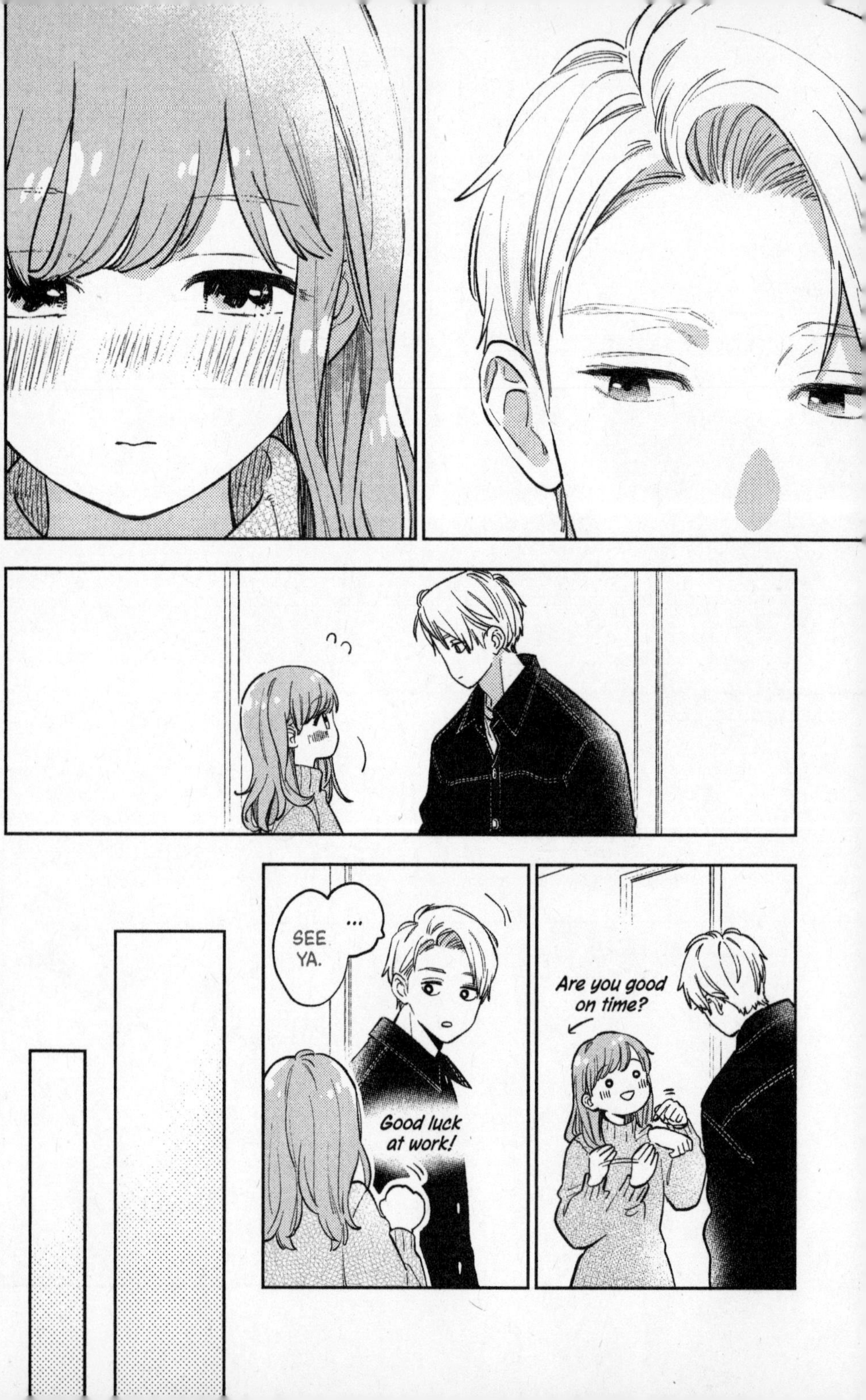
Are you good on time?
...
SEE YA.
Good luck at work!

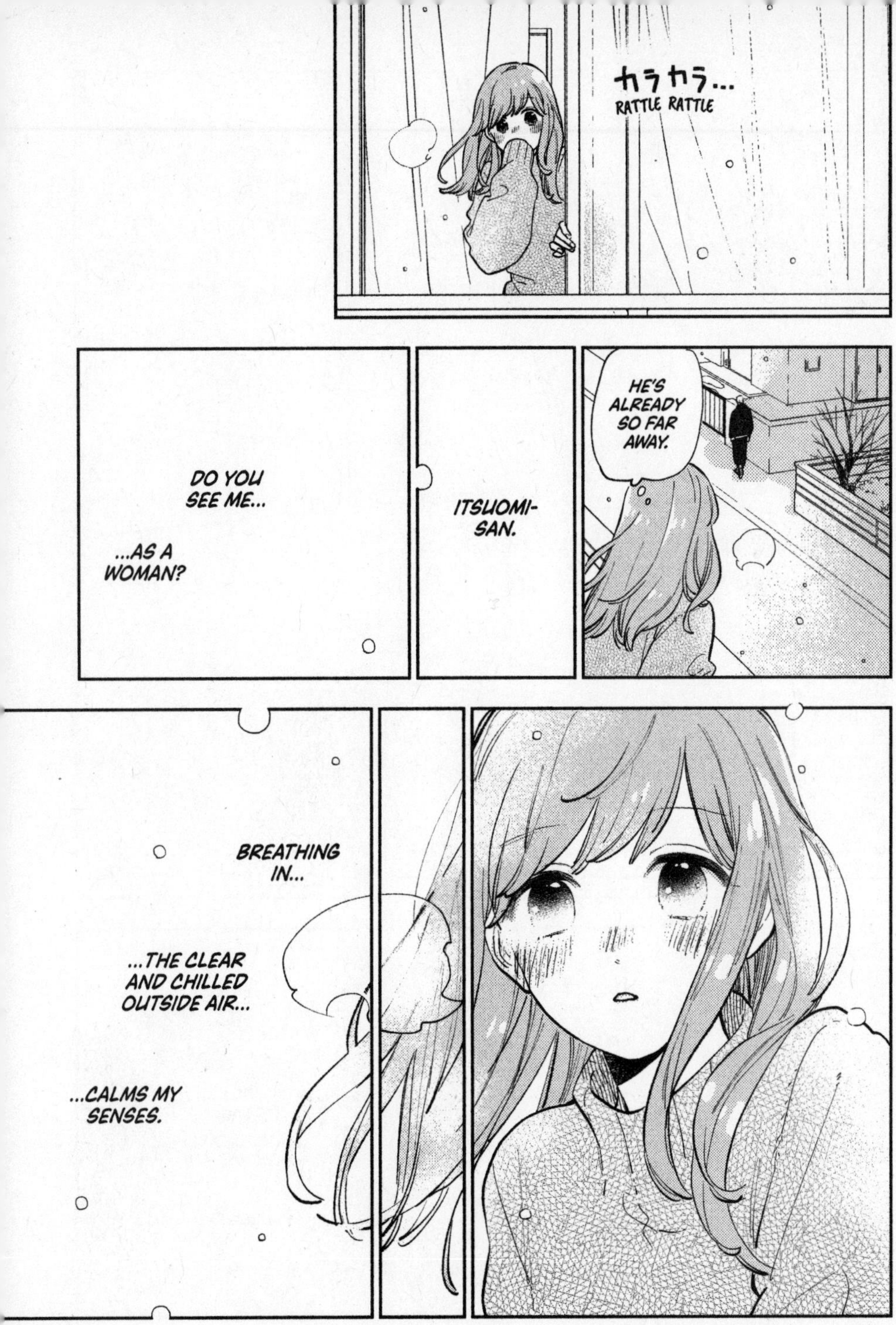
カラカラ…
RATTLE RATTLE
HE'S ALREADY SO FAR AWAY.
ITSUOMI-SAN.
DO YOU SEE ME...
...AS A WOMAN?
BREATHING IN...
...THE CLEAR AND CHILLED OUTSIDE AIR...
...CALMS MY SENSES.

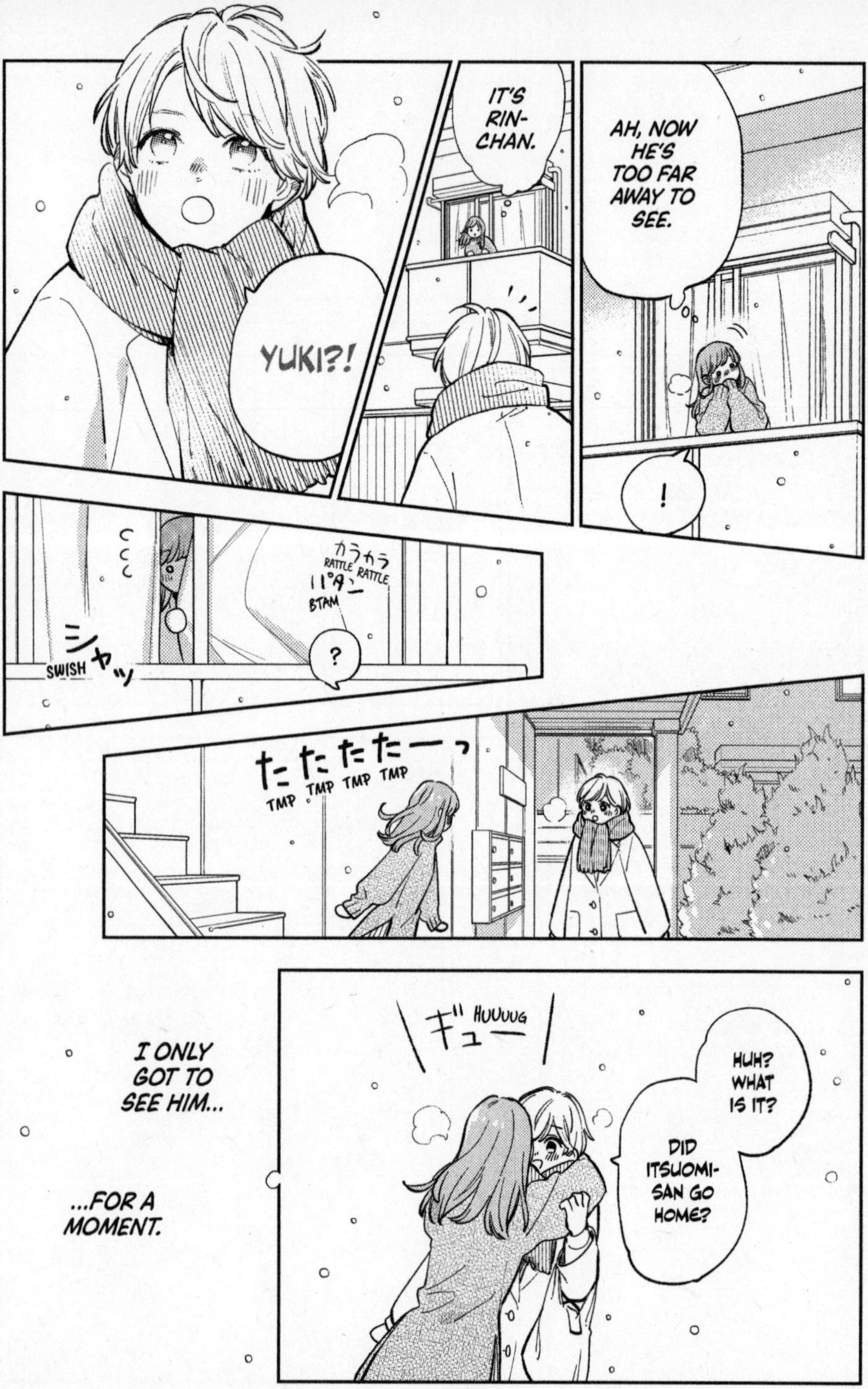

AH, NOW HE'S TOO FAR AWAY TO SEE.
!
IT'S RIN-CHAN.
YUKI?!
カラカラ RATTLE RATTLE
パタン BTAM
?
シャッ SWISH
たたたたーっ TMP TMP TMP TMP
ギュー HUUUUG
HUH? WHAT IS IT?
DID ITSUOMI-SAN GO HOME?
I ONLY GOT TO SEE HIM...
...FOR A MOMENT.

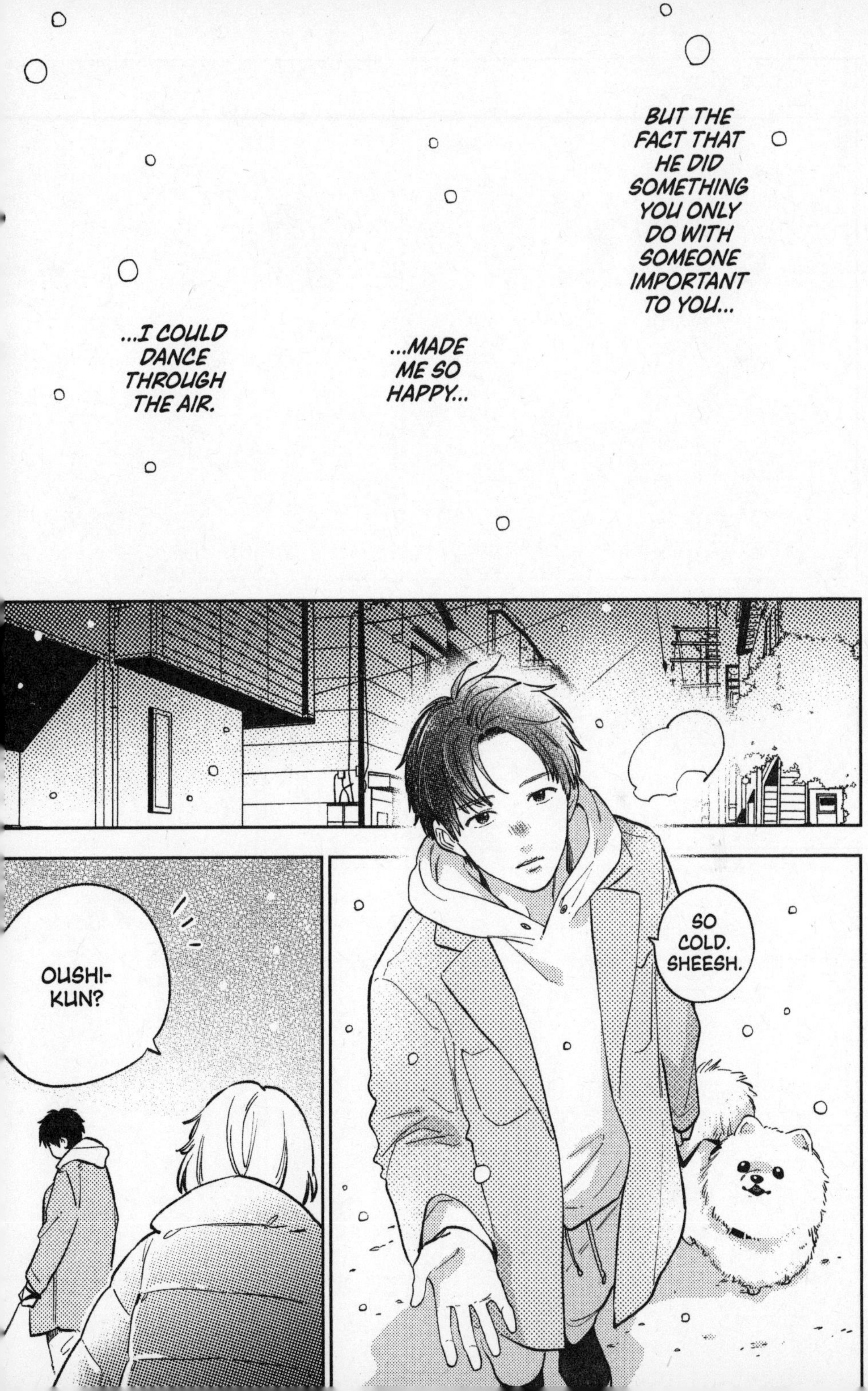
BUT THE FACT THAT HE DID SOMETHING YOU ONLY DO WITH SOMEONE IMPORTANT TO YOU...
...MADE ME SO HAPPY...
...I COULD DANCE THROUGH THE AIR.
SO COLD. SHEESH.
OUSHI-KUN?

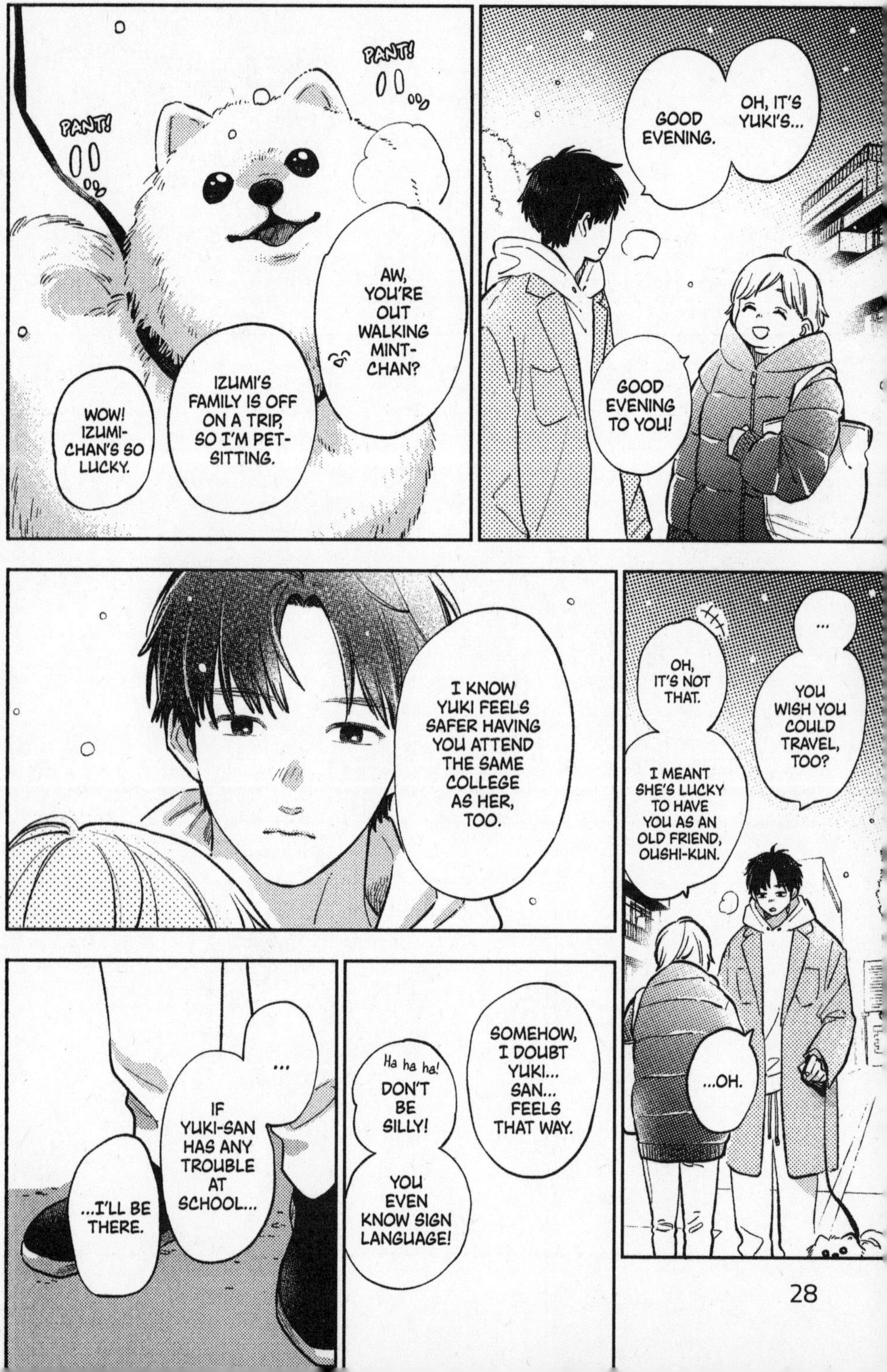
OH, IT'S YUKI'S...
GOOD EVENING.
GOOD EVENING TO YOU!
PANT!
PANT!
AW, YOU'RE OUT WALKING MINT-CHAN?
IZUMI'S FAMILY IS OFF ON A TRIP, SO I'M PET-SITTING.
WOW! IZUMI-CHAN'S SO LUCKY.
...
YOU WISH YOU COULD TRAVEL, TOO?
OH, IT'S NOT THAT.
I MEANT SHE'S LUCKY TO HAVE YOU AS AN OLD FRIEND, OUSHI-KUN.
...OH.
I KNOW YUKI FEELS SAFER HAVING YOU ATTEND THE SAME COLLEGE AS HER, TOO.
SOMEHOW, I DOUBT YUKI... SAN... FEELS THAT WAY.
Ha ha ha!
DON'T BE SILLY!
YOU EVEN KNOW SIGN LANGUAGE!
...
IF YUKI-SAN HAS ANY TROUBLE AT SCHOOL...
...I'LL BE THERE.

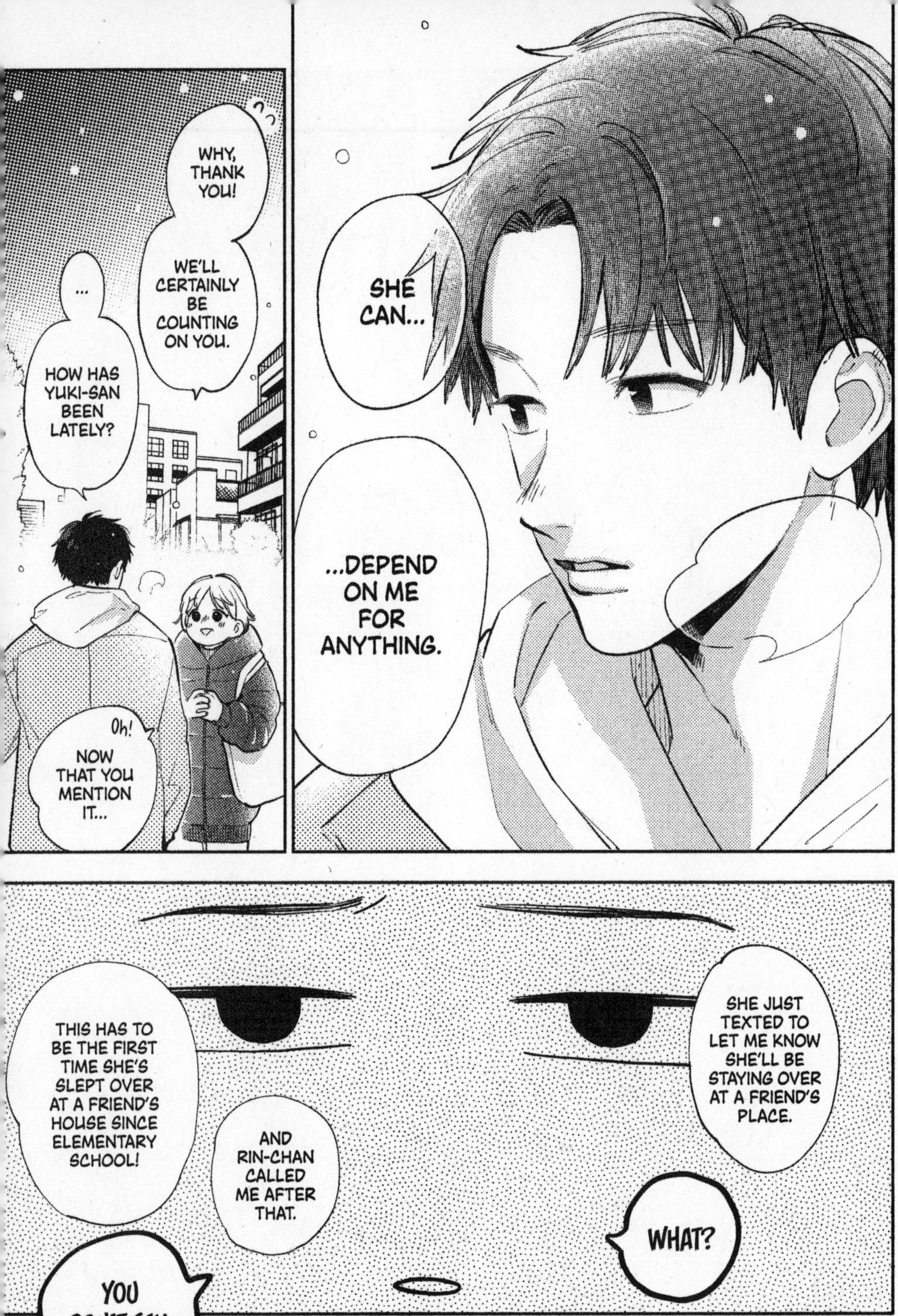
SHE CAN...
...DEPEND ON ME FOR ANYTHING.
WHY, THANK YOU!
WE'LL CERTAINLY BE COUNTING ON YOU.
...
HOW HAS YUKI-SAN BEEN LATELY?
Oh!
NOW THAT YOU MENTION IT...
SHE JUST TEXTED TO LET ME KNOW SHE'LL BE STAYING OVER AT A FRIEND'S PLACE.
THIS HAS TO BE THE FIRST TIME SHE'S SLEPT OVER AT A FRIEND'S HOUSE SINCE ELEMENTARY SCHOOL!
AND RIN-CHAN CALLED ME AFTER THAT.
WHAT?
YOU DON'T SAY.

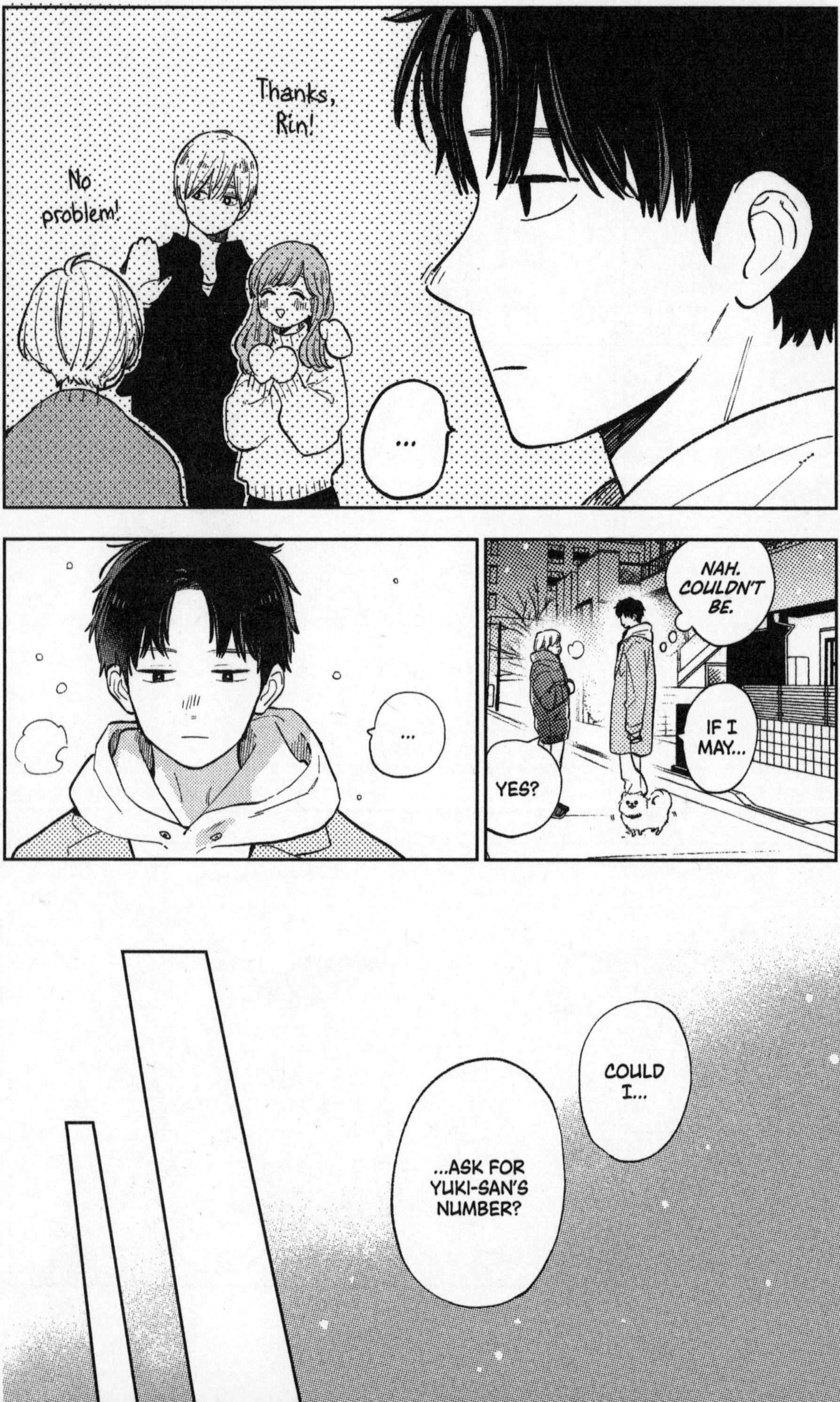
Thanks, Rin!
No problem!
...
NAH. COULDN'T BE.
IF I MAY...
YES?
...
COULD I...
...ASK FOR YUKI-SAN'S NUMBER?

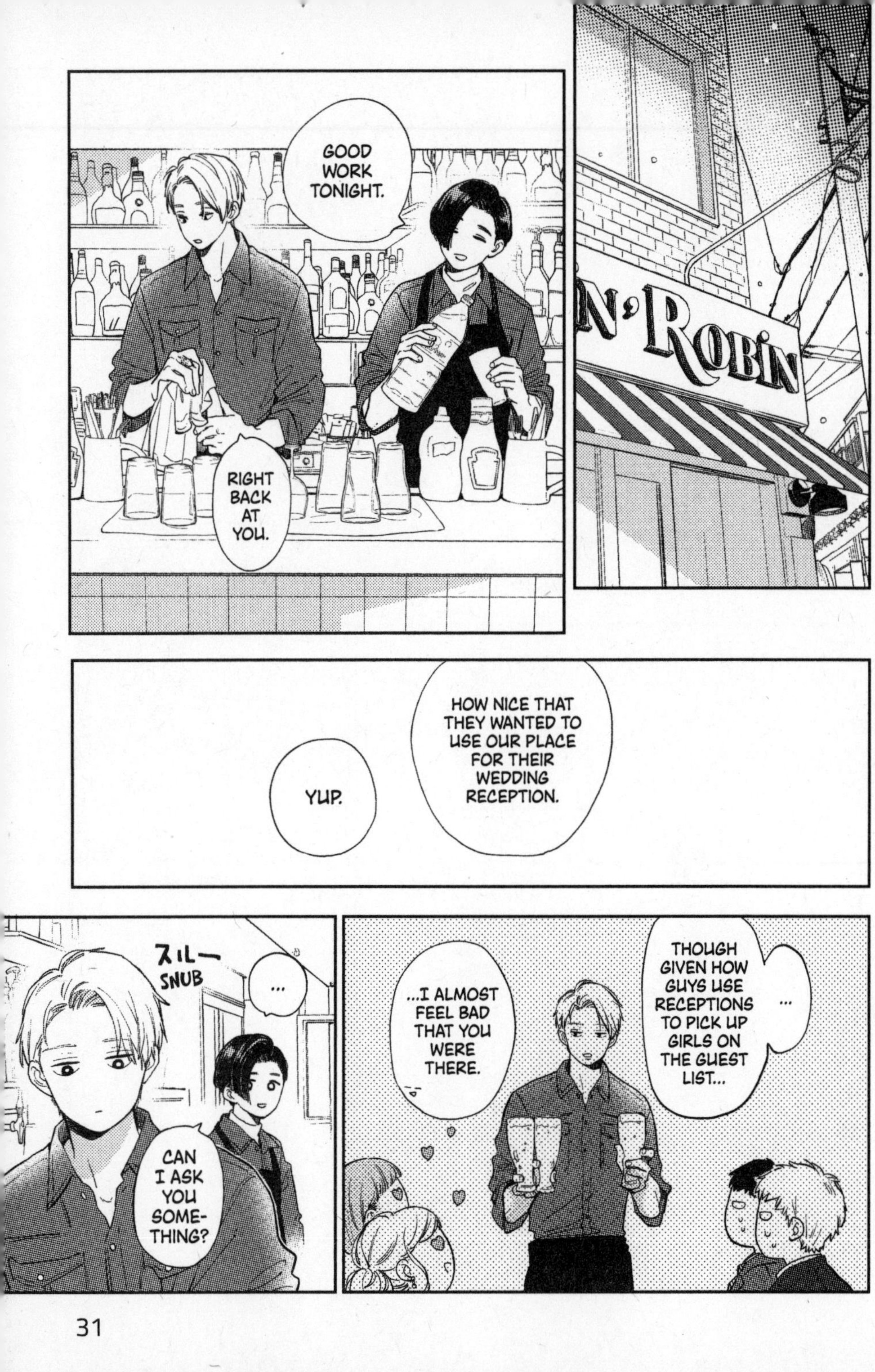
N·ROBIN
GOOD WORK TONIGHT.
RIGHT BACK AT YOU.
HOW NICE THAT THEY WANTED TO USE OUR PLACE FOR THEIR WEDDING RECEPTION.
YUP.
THOUGH GIVEN HOW GUYS USE RECEPTIONS TO PICK UP GIRLS ON THE GUEST LIST...
...
...I ALMOST FEEL BAD THAT YOU WERE THERE.
スルー
SNUB
...
CAN I ASK YOU SOME-THING?

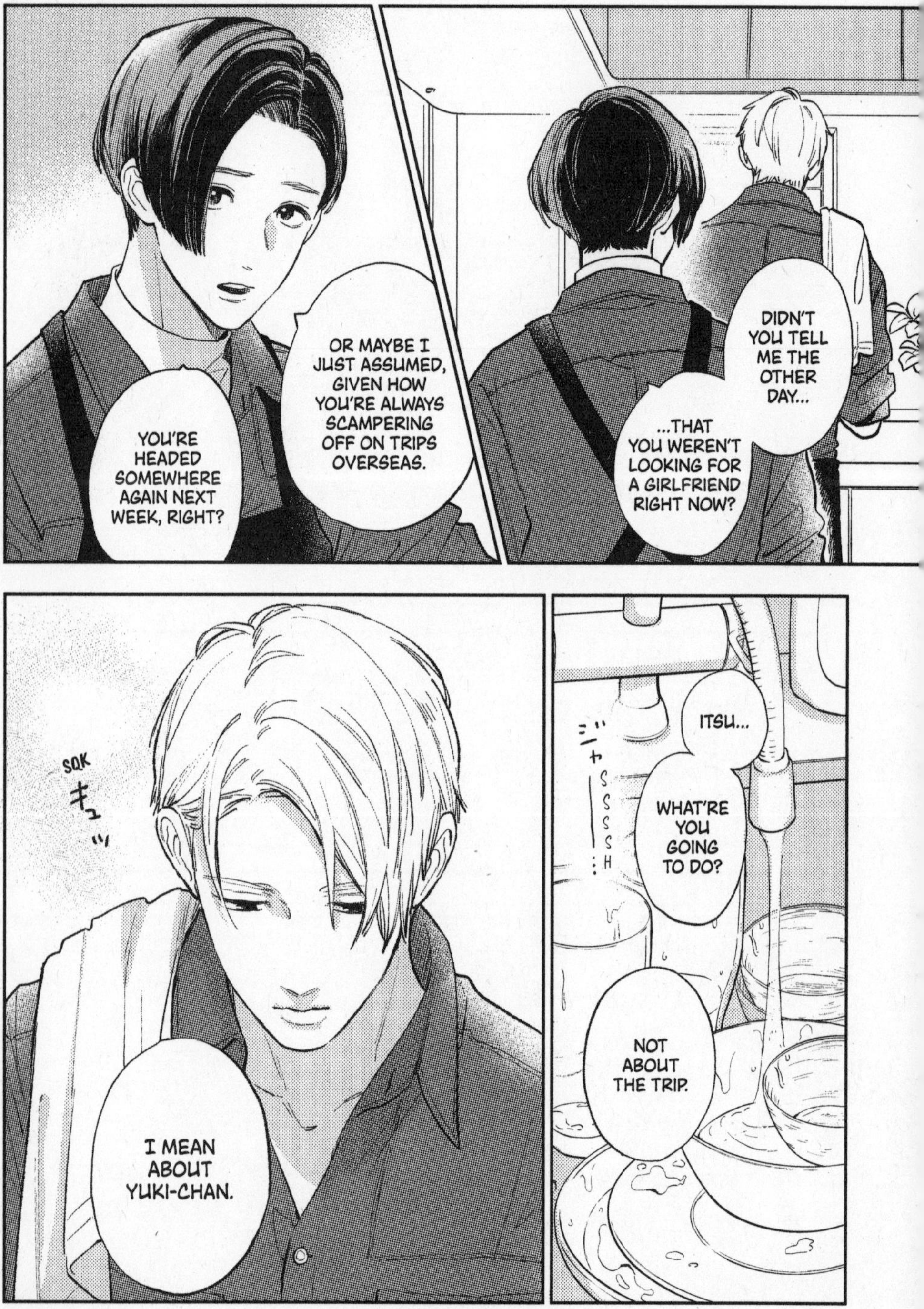
DIDN'T YOU TELL ME THE OTHER DAY...
...THAT YOU WEREN'T LOOKING FOR A GIRLFRIEND RIGHT NOW?
OR MAYBE I JUST ASSUMED, GIVEN HOW YOU'RE ALWAYS SCAMPERING OFF ON TRIPS OVERSEAS.
YOU'RE HEADED SOMEWHERE AGAIN NEXT WEEK, RIGHT?
ジャー
SSSSH...
ITSU...
WHAT'RE YOU GOING TO DO?
NOT ABOUT THE TRIP.
SQK
ギュッ
I MEAN ABOUT YUKI-CHAN.

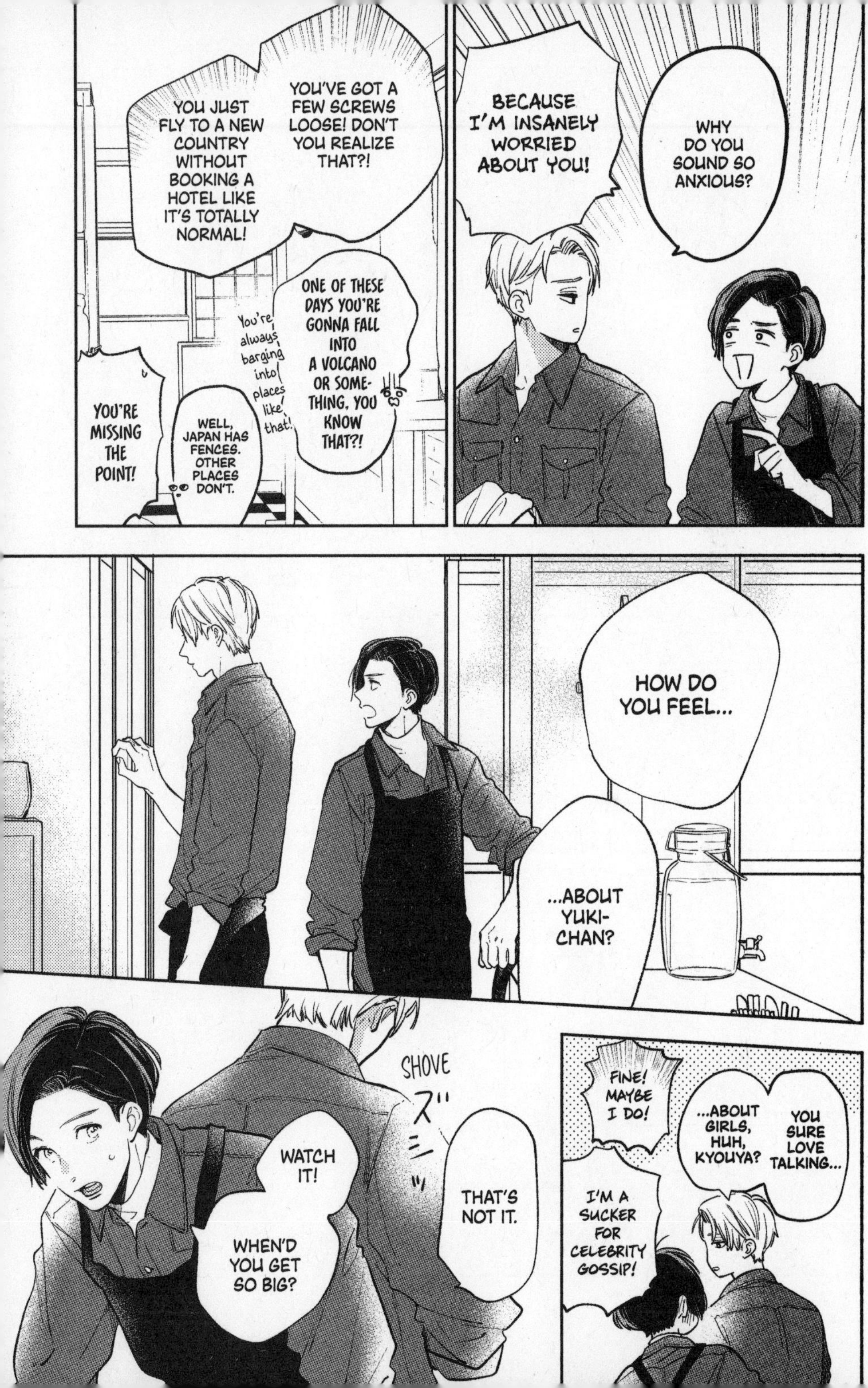
WHY DO YOU SOUND SO ANXIOUS?
BECAUSE I'M INSANELY WORRIED ABOUT YOU!
YOU'VE GOT A FEW SCREWS LOOSE! DON'T YOU REALIZE THAT?!
YOU JUST FLY TO A NEW COUNTRY WITHOUT BOOKING A HOTEL LIKE IT'S TOTALLY NORMAL!
ONE OF THESE DAYS YOU'RE GONNA FALL INTO A VOLCANO OR SOMETHING, YOU KNOW THAT?!
You're always barging into places like that!
WELL, JAPAN HAS FENCES. OTHER PLACES DON'T.
YOU'RE MISSING THE POINT!
HOW DO YOU FEEL...
...ABOUT YUKI-CHAN?
YOU SURE LOVE TALKING...
...ABOUT GIRLS, HUH, KYOUYA?
FINE! MAYBE I DO!
I'M A SUCKER FOR CELEBRITY GOSSIP!
THAT'S NOT IT.
SHOVE
WATCH IT!
WHEN'D YOU GET SO BIG?

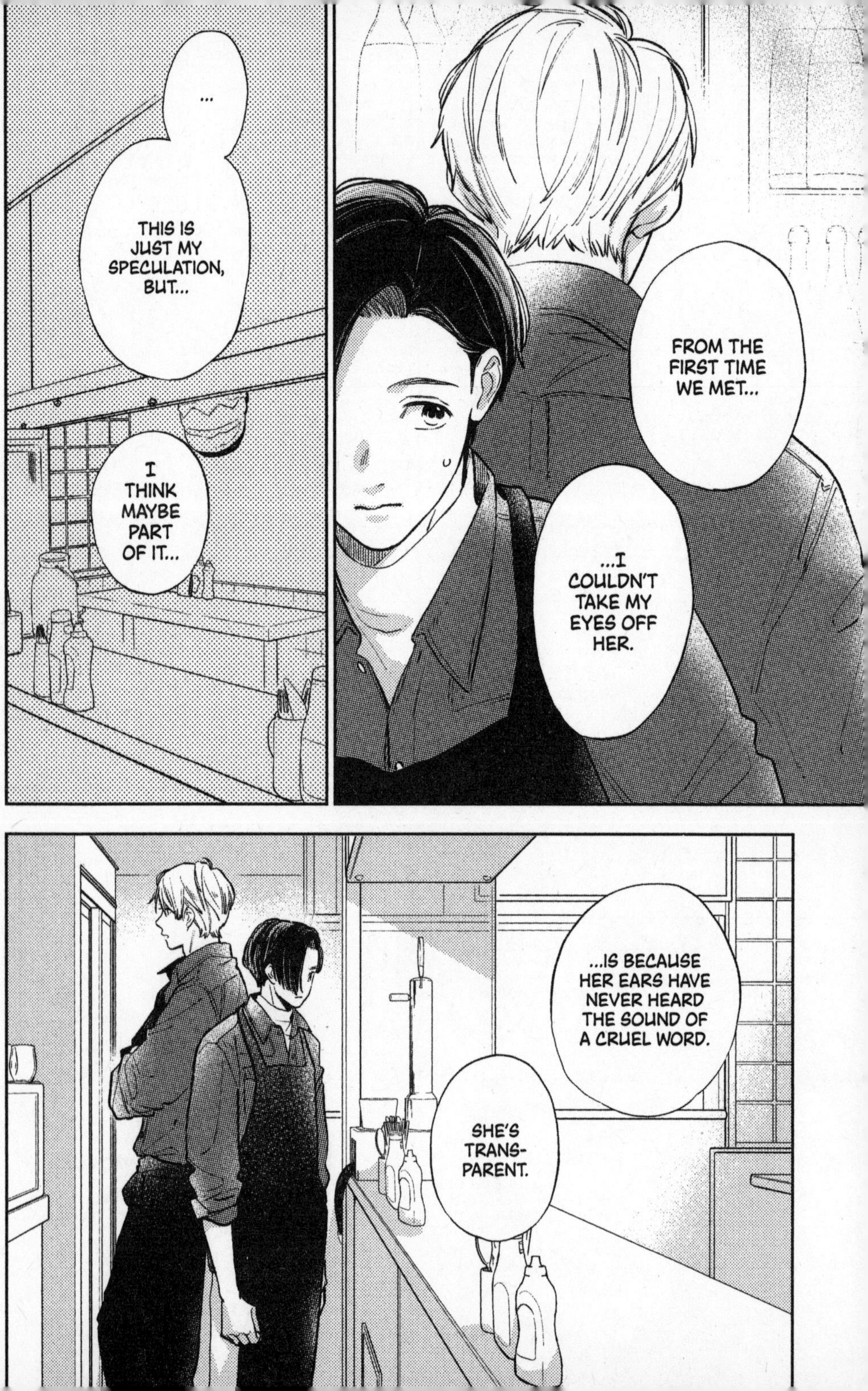
FROM THE FIRST TIME WE MET...
...I COULDN'T TAKE MY EYES OFF HER.
...
THIS IS JUST MY SPECULATION, BUT...
I THINK MAYBE PART OF IT...
...IS BECAUSE HER EARS HAVE NEVER HEARD THE SOUND OF A CRUEL WORD.
SHE'S TRANS-PARENT.

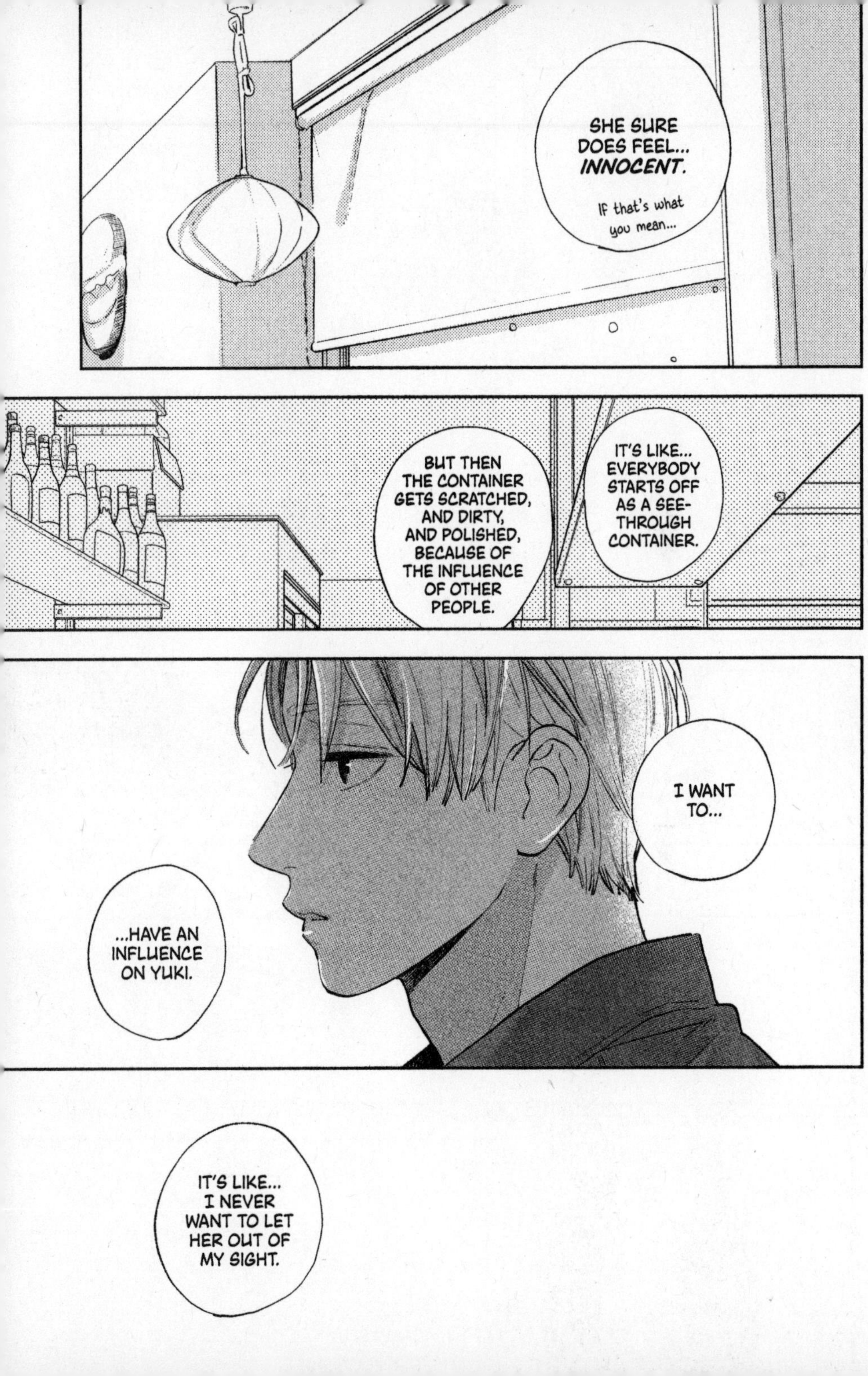
SHE SURE DOES FEEL... INNOCENT.
If that's what you mean...
IT'S LIKE... EVERYBODY STARTS OFF AS A SEE-THROUGH CONTAINER.
BUT THEN THE CONTAINER GETS SCRATCHED, AND DIRTY, AND POLISHED, BECAUSE OF THE INFLUENCE OF OTHER PEOPLE.
I WANT TO...
...HAVE AN INFLUENCE ON YUKI.
IT'S LIKE... I NEVER WANT TO LET HER OUT OF MY SIGHT.

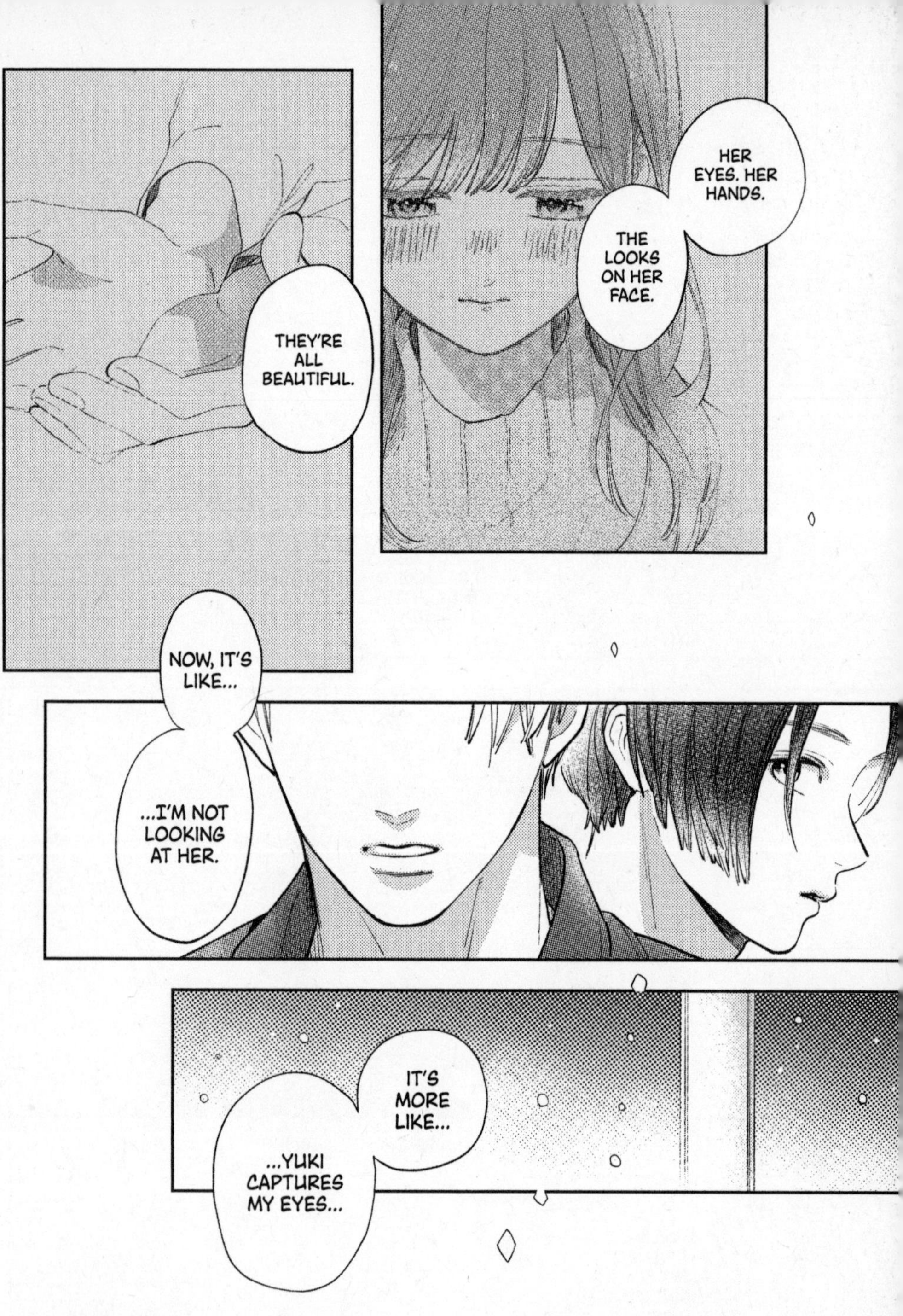
HER EYES. HER HANDS.
THE LOOKS ON HER FACE.
THEY'RE ALL BEAUTIFUL.
NOW, IT'S LIKE...
...I'M NOT LOOKING AT HER.
IT'S MORE LIKE...
...YUKI CAPTURES MY EYES...

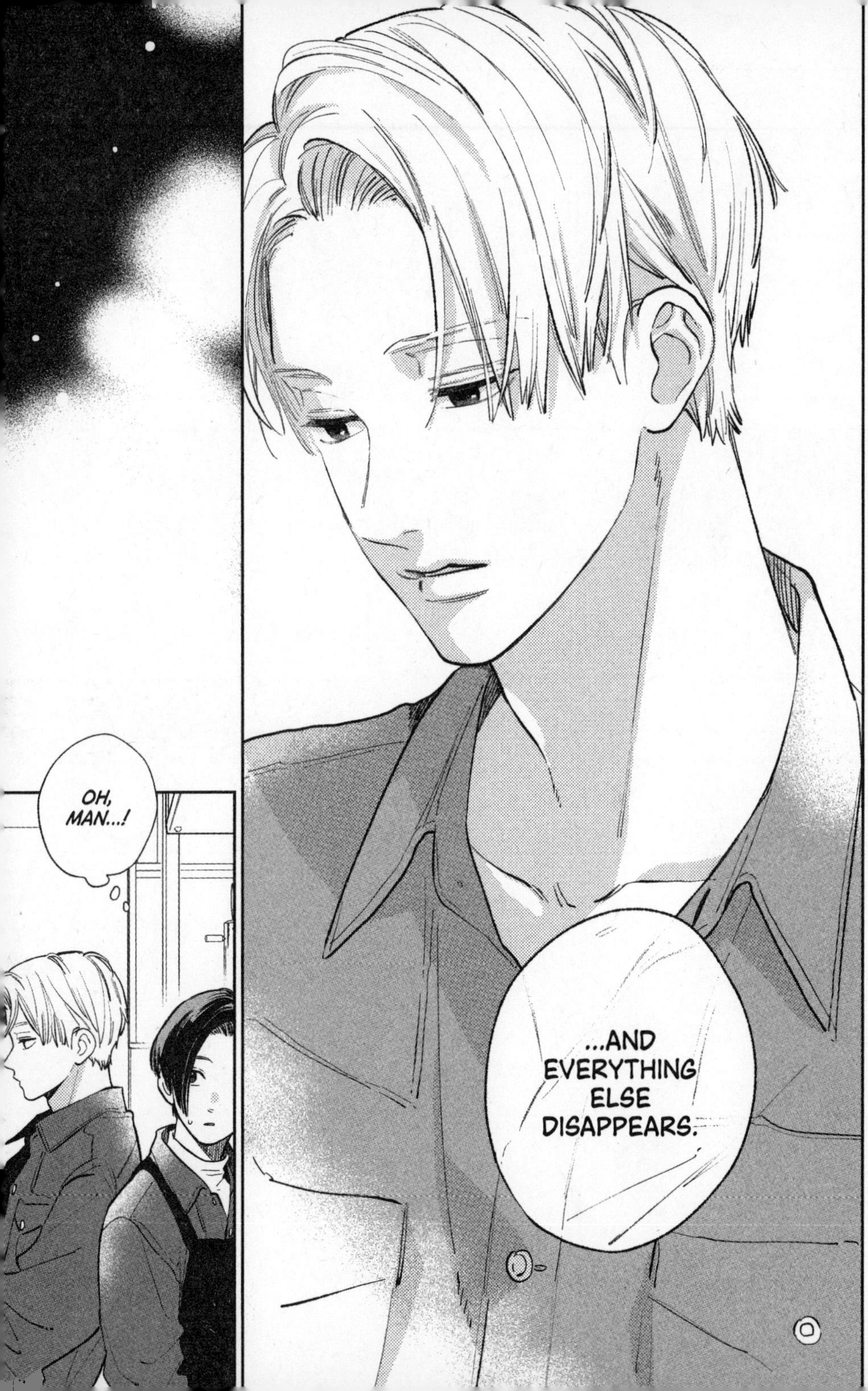
...AND EVERYTHING ELSE DISAPPEARS.
OH, MAN...!

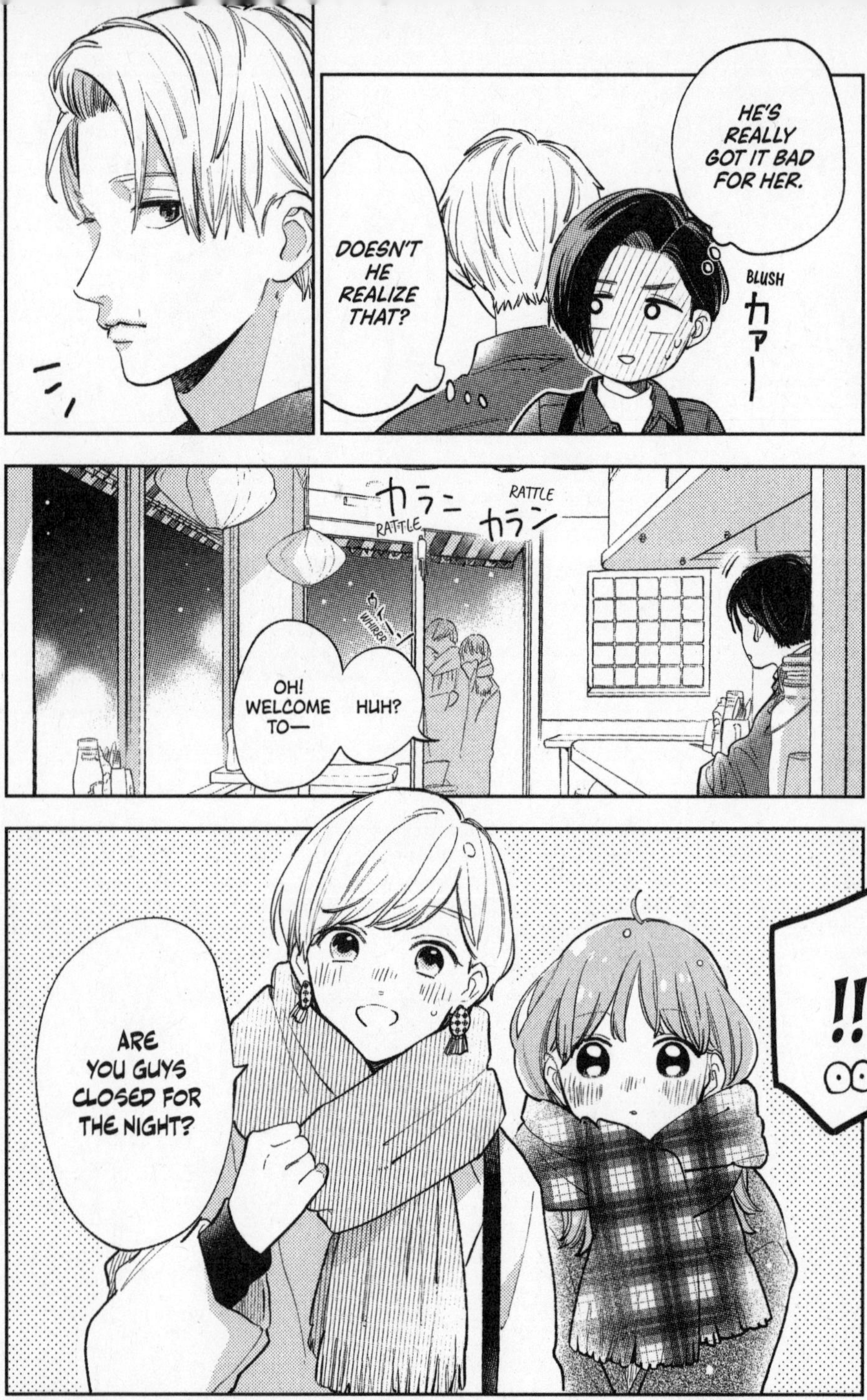
HE'S REALLY GOT IT BAD FOR HER.
BLUSH
カァー
DOESN'T HE REALIZE THAT?
RATTLE
カラン
RATTLE
カラン
WHIRRR
OH! WELCOME TO— HUH?
!!
ARE YOU GUYS CLOSED FOR THE NIGHT?

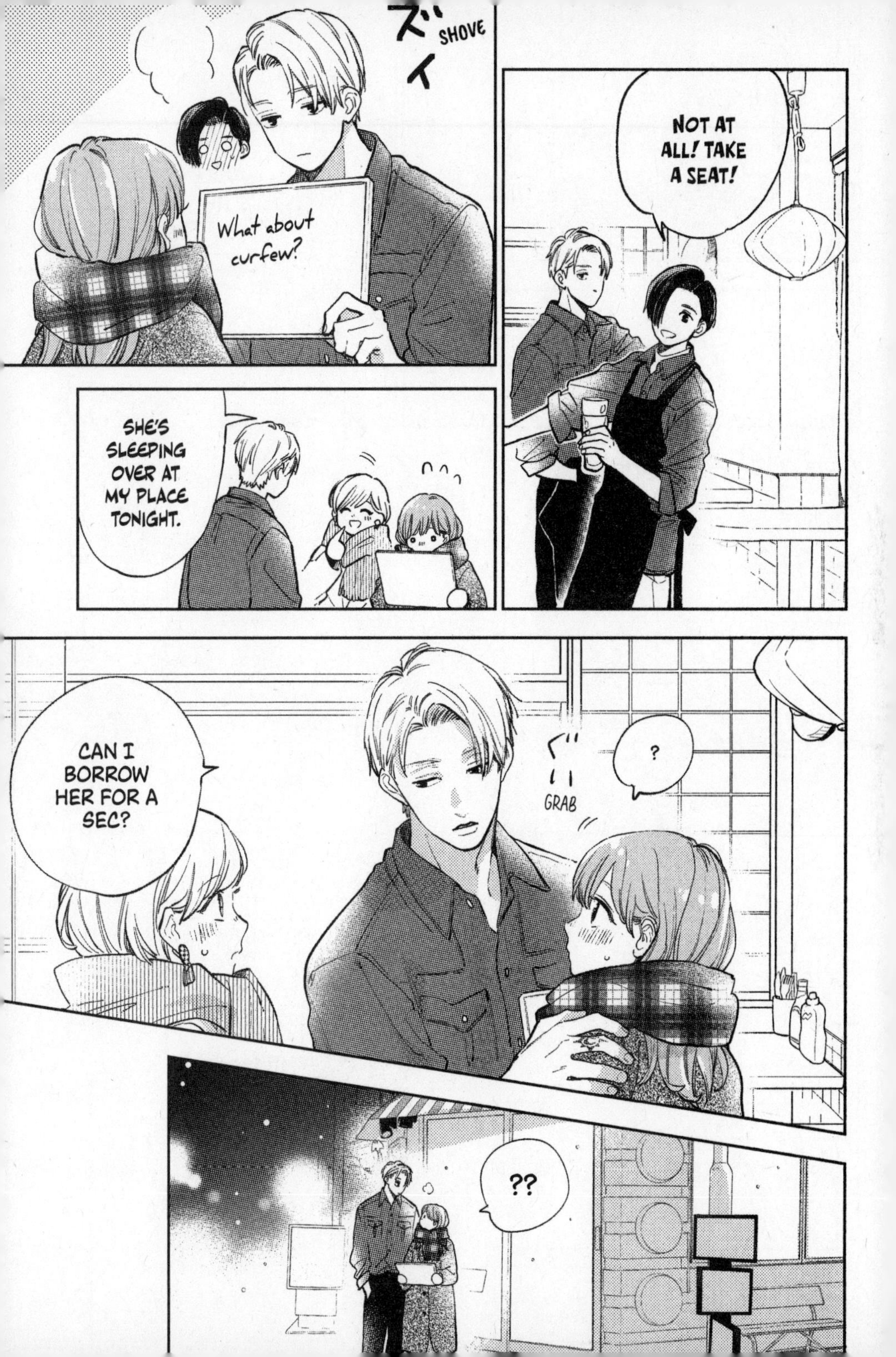
NOT AT ALL! TAKE A SEAT!
ズイ
SHOVE
What about curfew?
SHE'S SLEEPING OVER AT MY PLACE TONIGHT.
?
GRAB
CAN I BORROW HER FOR A SEC?
??

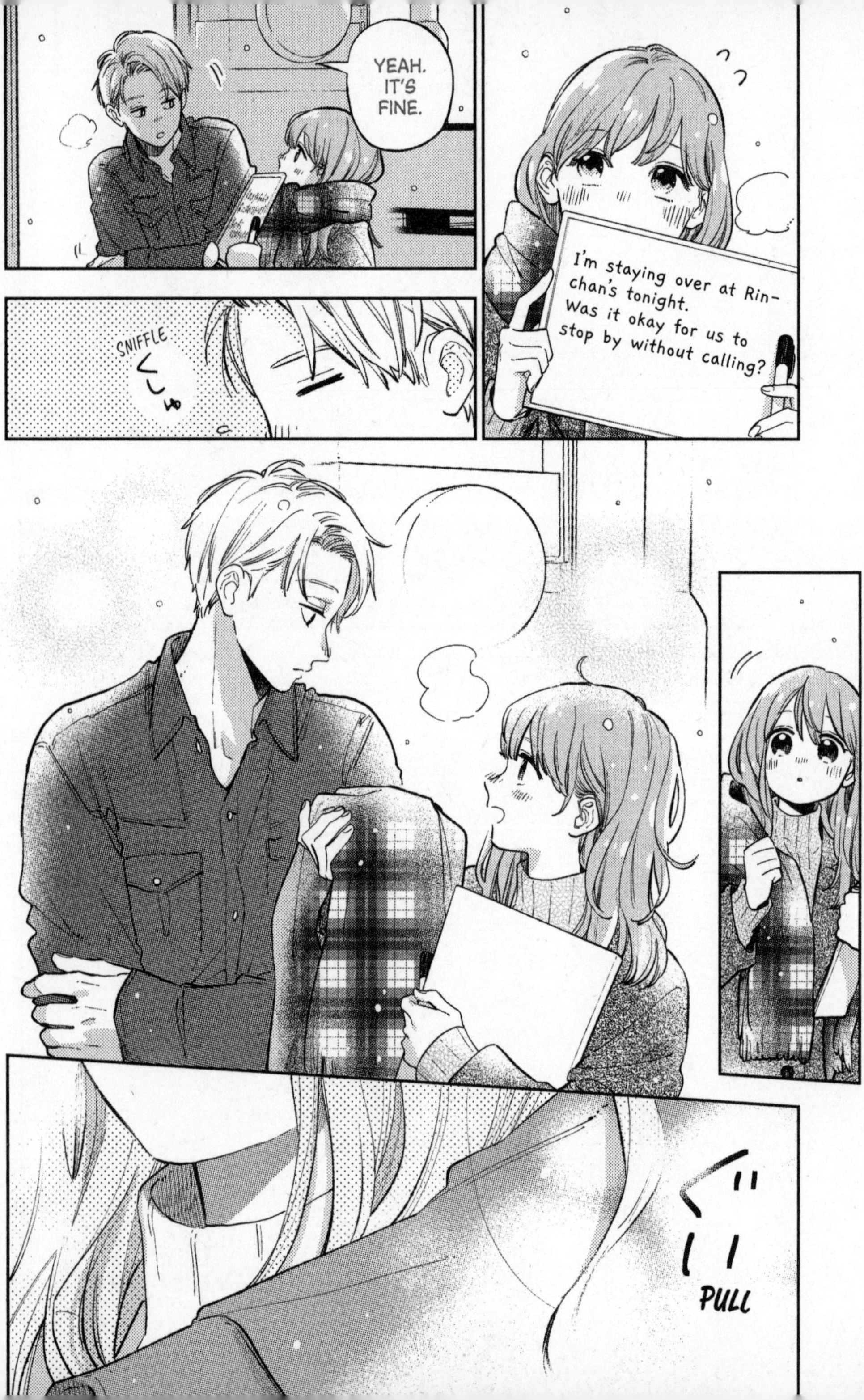
I'm staying over at Rin-chan's tonight. Was it okay for us to stop by without calling?
YEAH. IT'S FINE.
SNIFFLE
くしゅ
PULL

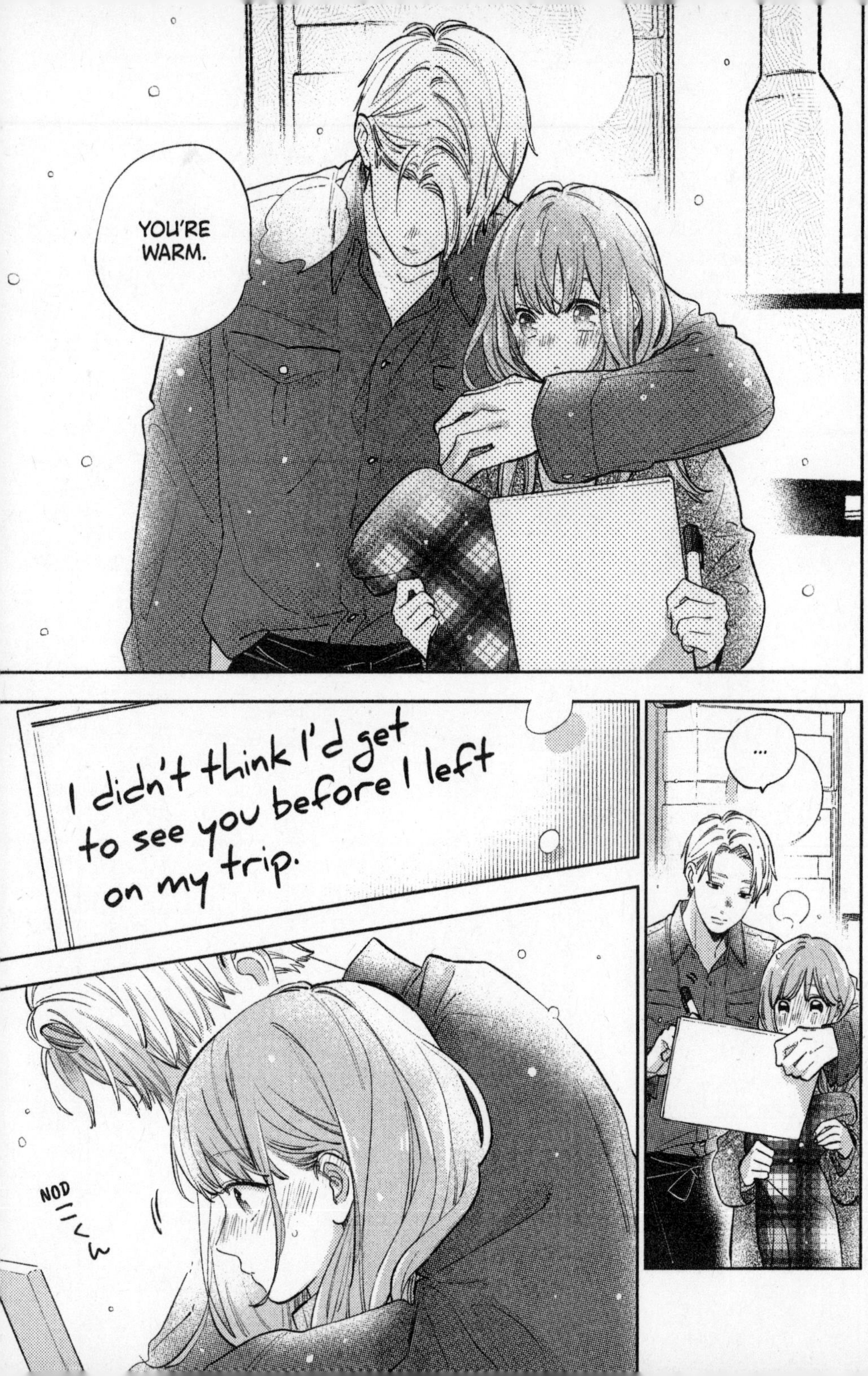
YOU'RE WARM.
...
I didn't think I'd get to see you before I left on my trip.
NOD

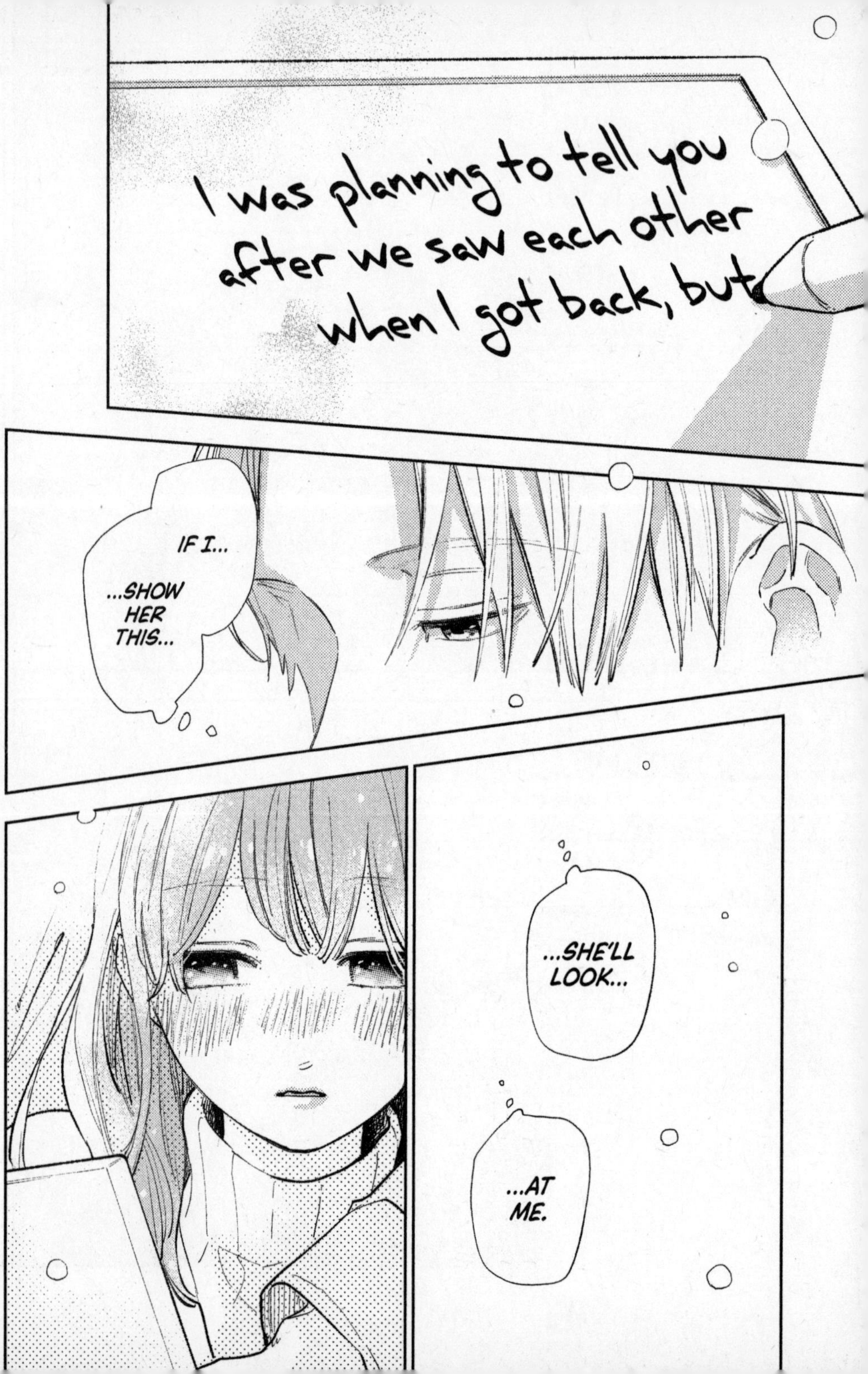
I was planning to tell you after we saw each other when I got back, but
IF I...
...SHOW HER THIS...
...SHE'LL LOOK...
...AT ME.

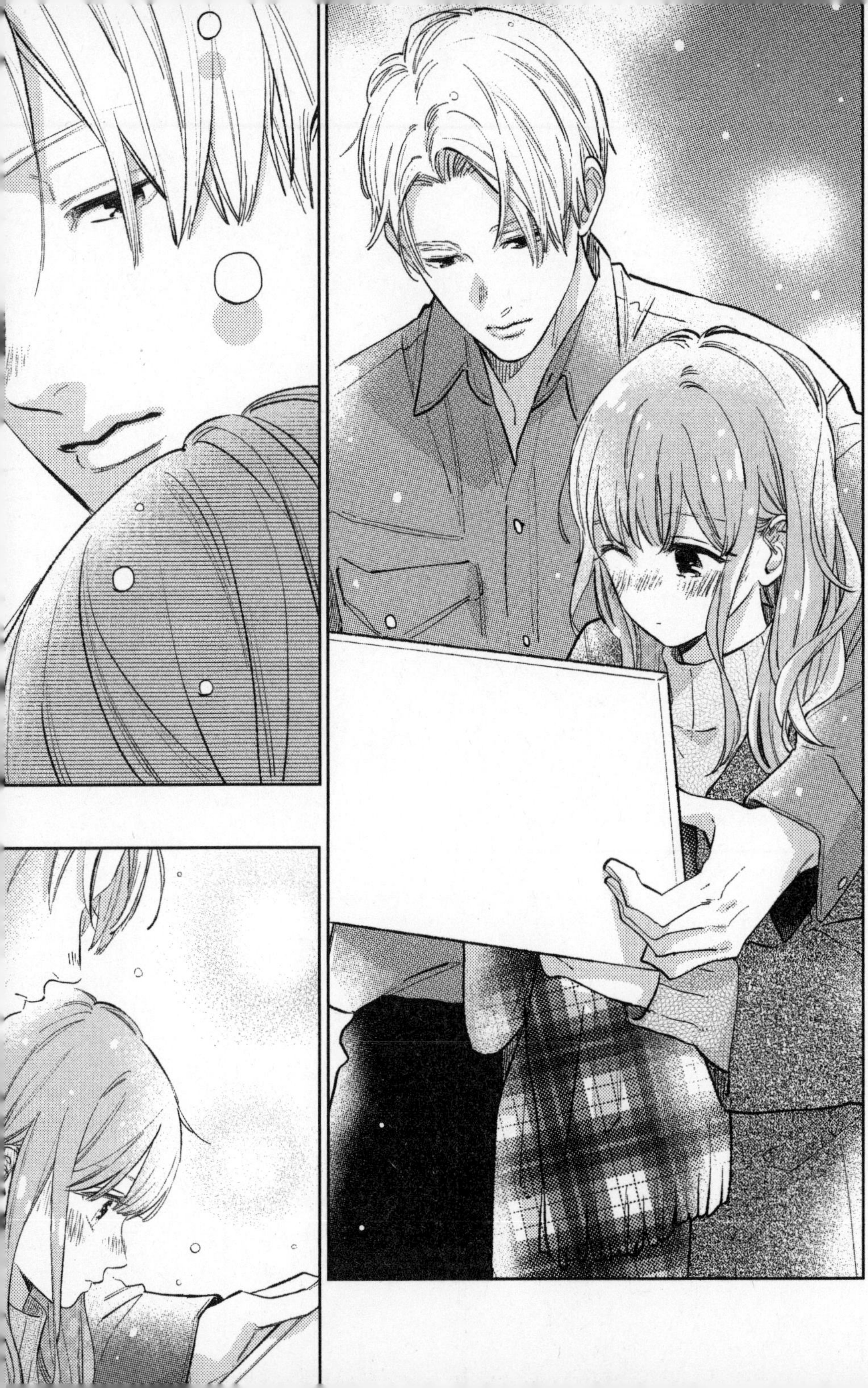

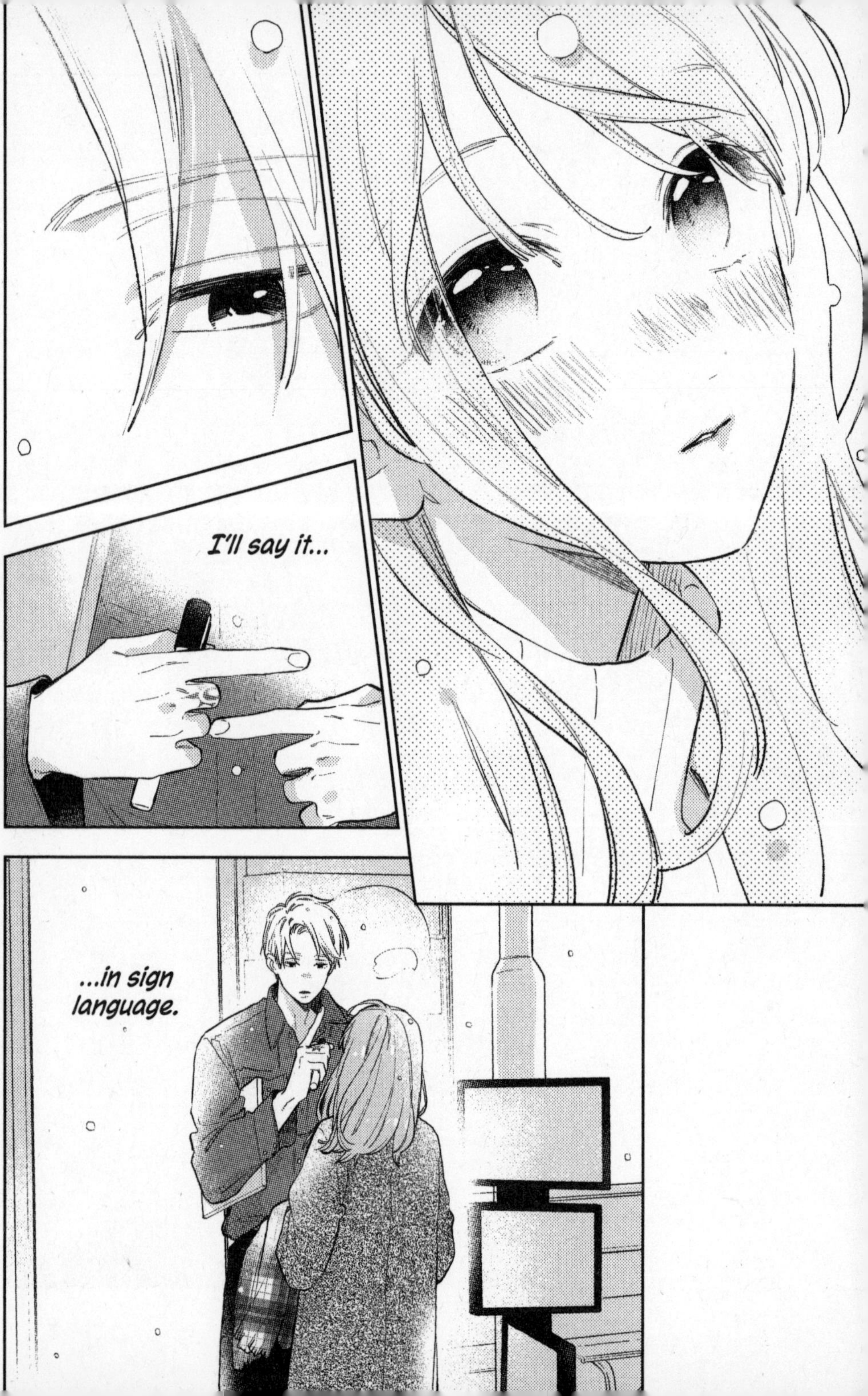
I'll say it...
...in sign language.

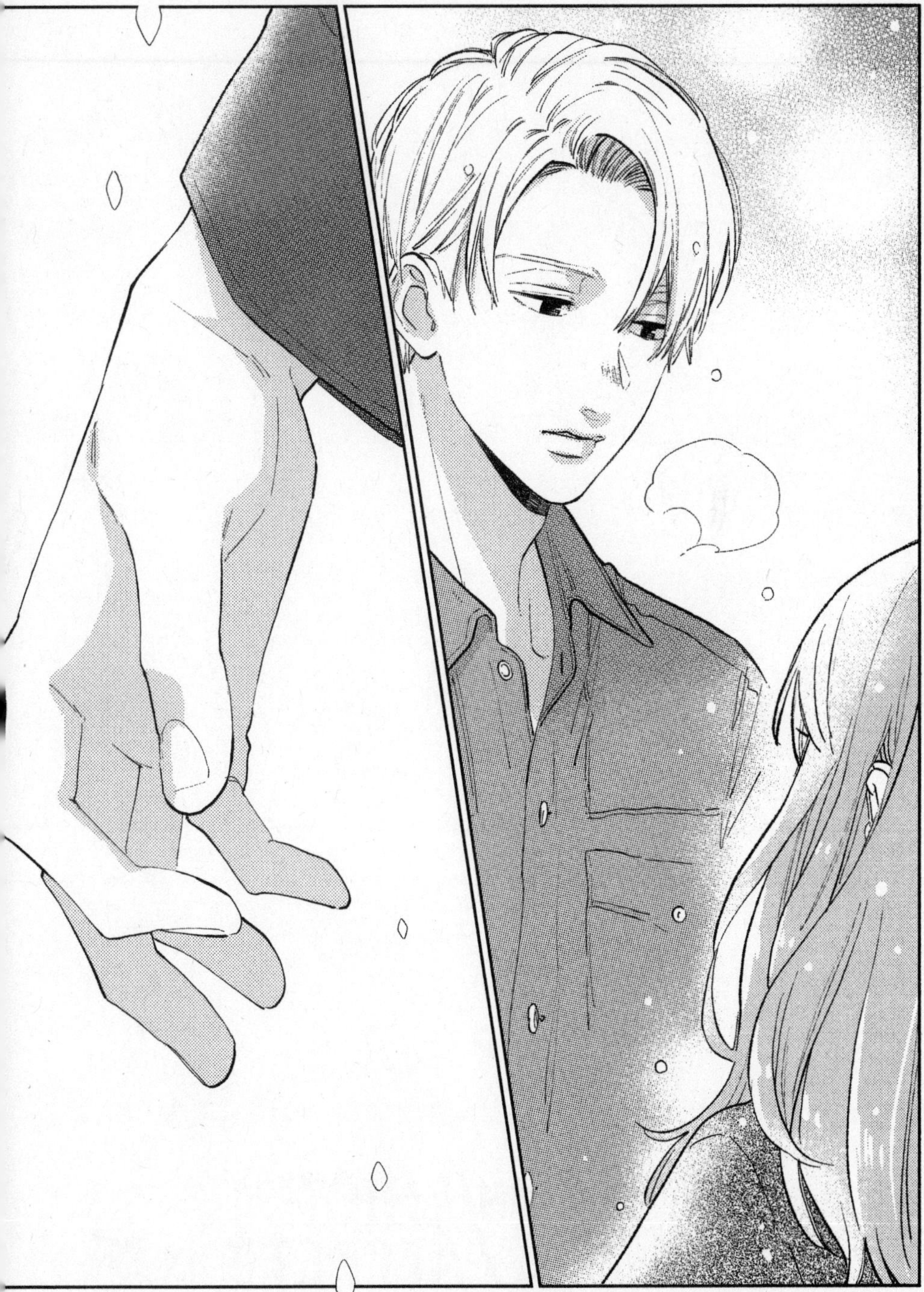

A SIGN OF AFFECTION

Sign.10

FEBRUARY 21ST

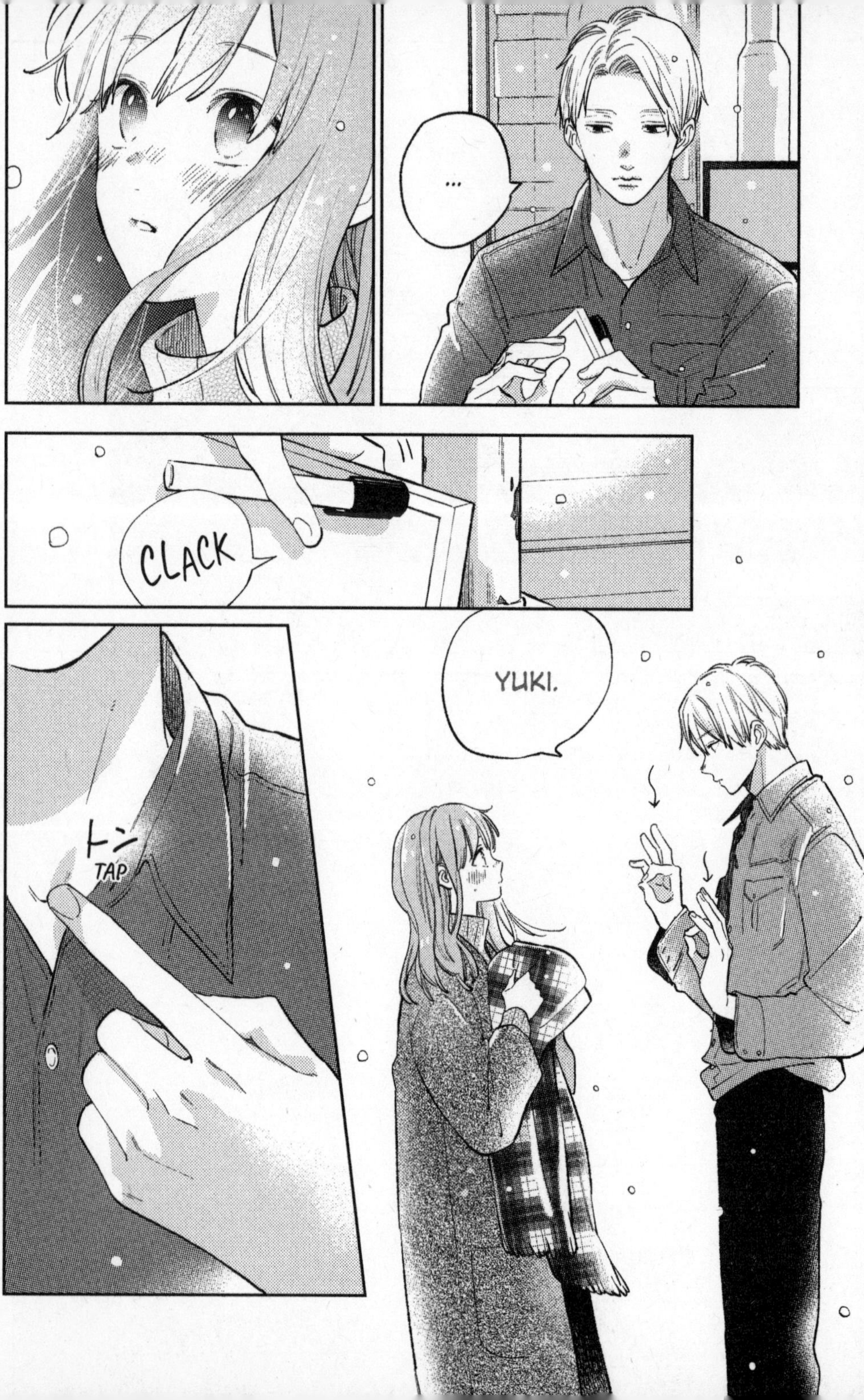
...
CLACK
YUKI.
トン
TAP

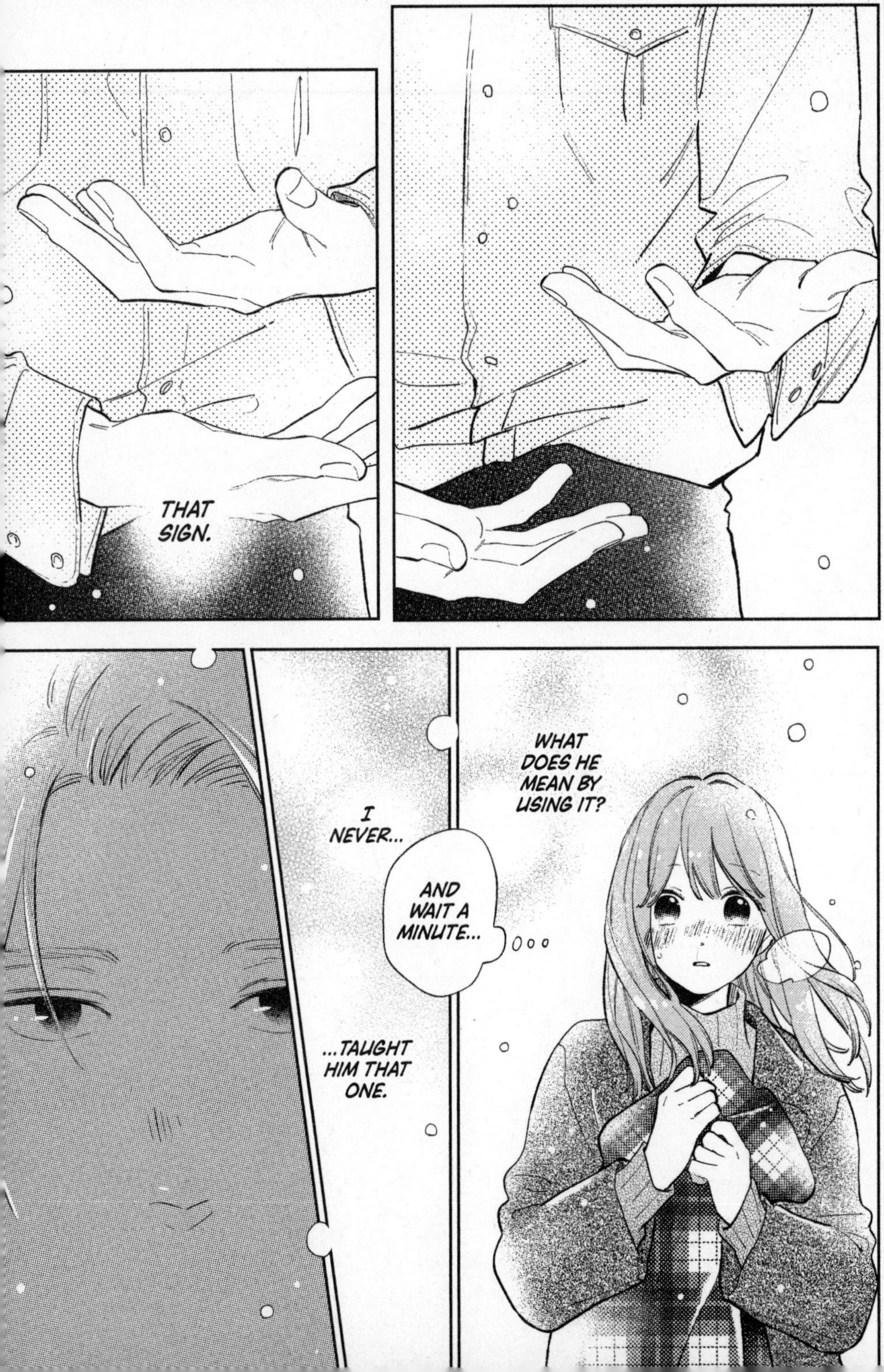
THAT SIGN.
WHAT DOES HE MEAN BY USING IT?
AND WAIT A MINUTE...
I NEVER...
...TAUGHT HIM THAT ONE.

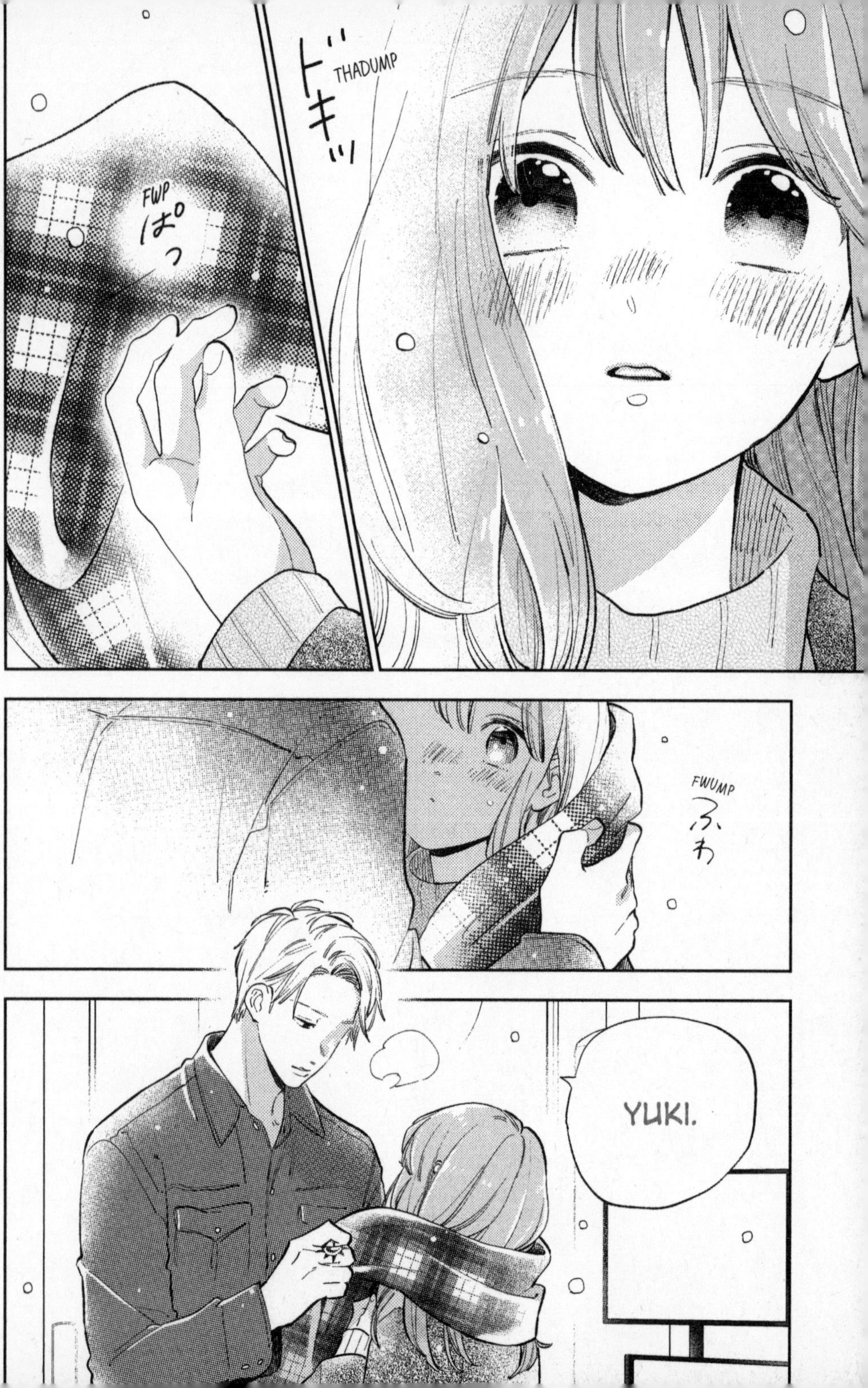
THADUMP
ドキッ
FWP
ぱっ
FWUMP
ふわ
YUKI.

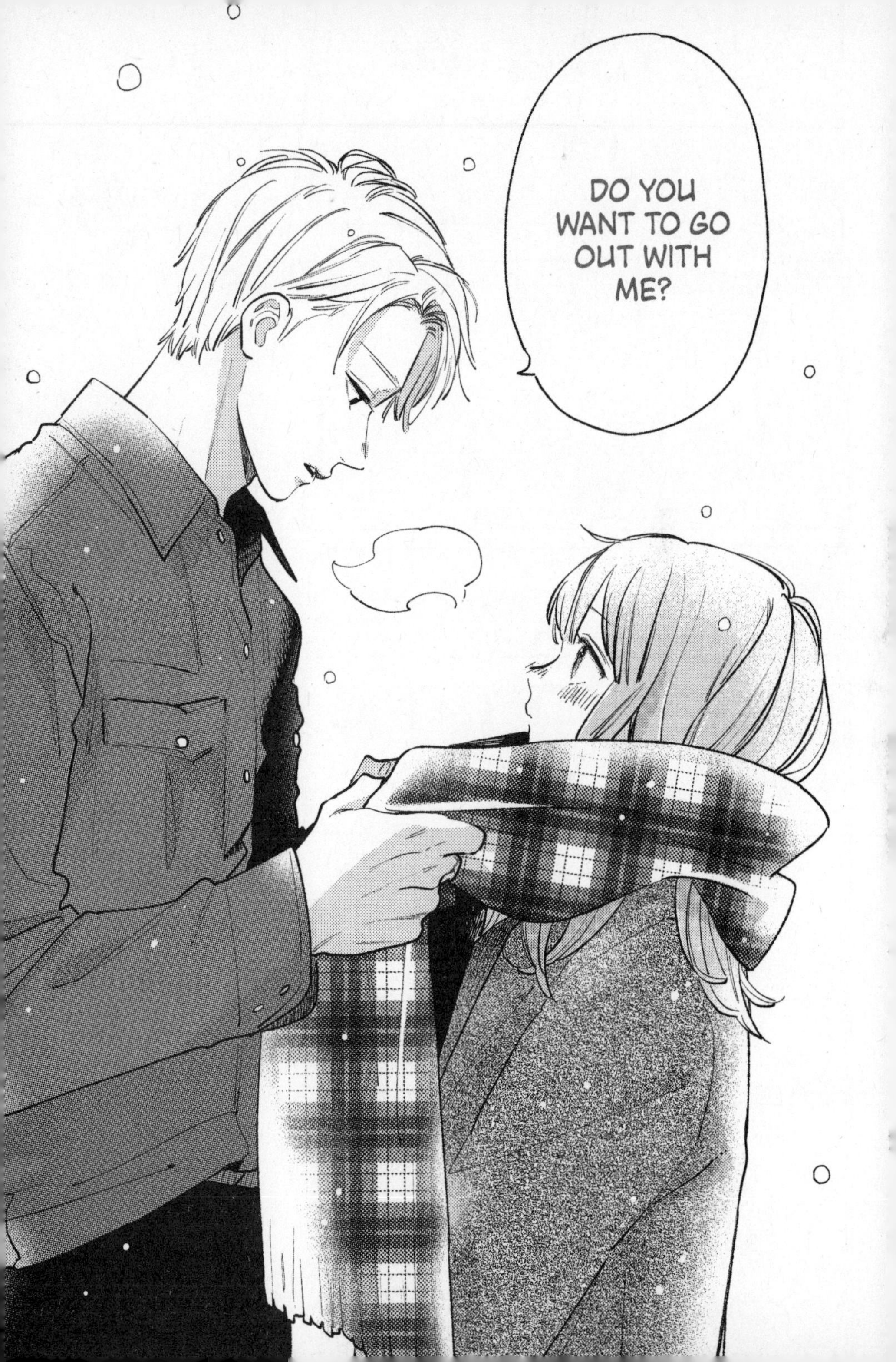
DO YOU WANT TO GO OUT WITH ME?

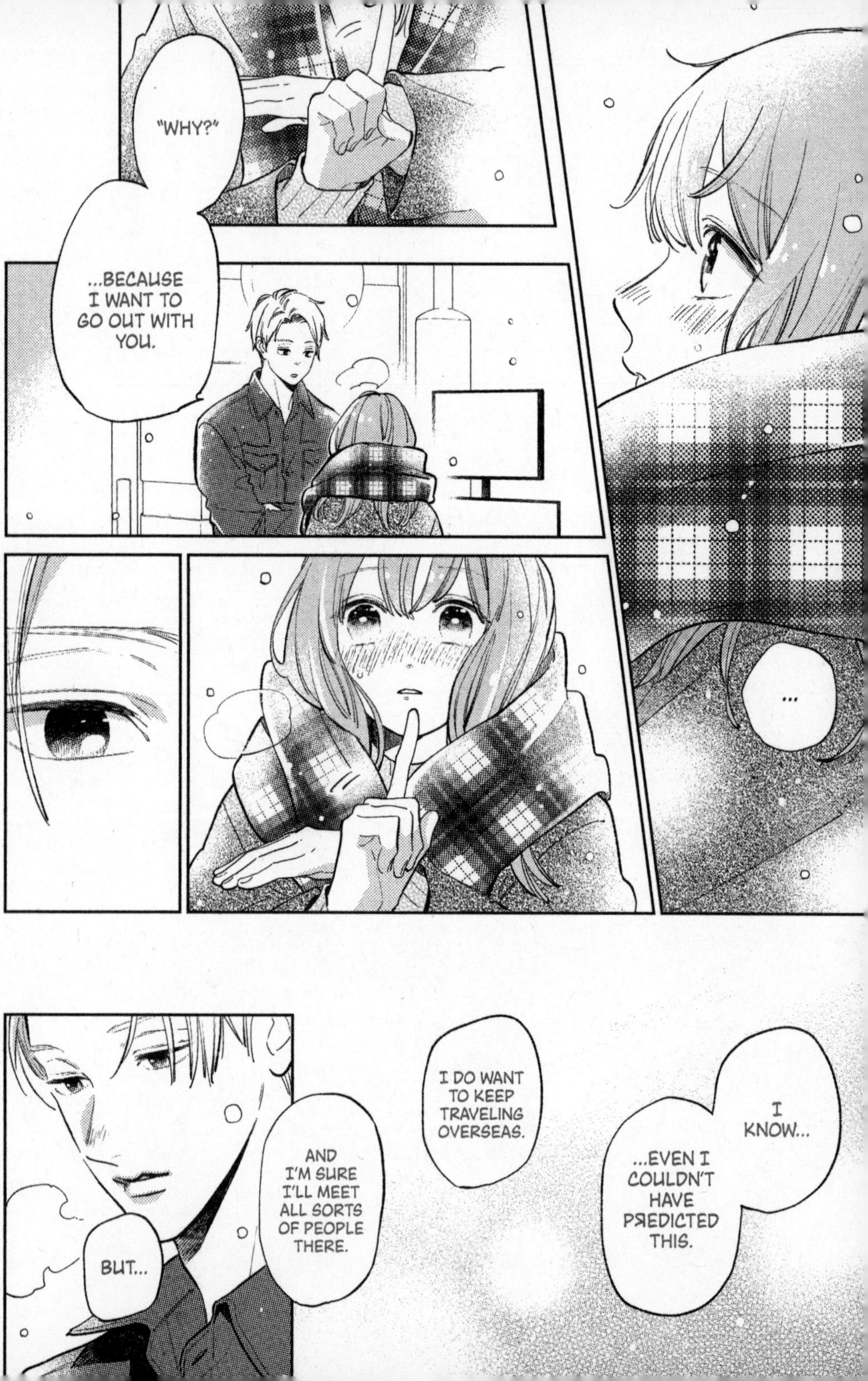
...
"WHY?"
...BECAUSE I WANT TO GO OUT WITH YOU.
I KNOW...
...EVEN I COULDN'T HAVE PREDICTED THIS.
I DO WANT TO KEEP TRAVELING OVERSEAS.
AND I'M SURE I'LL MEET ALL SORTS OF PEOPLE THERE.
BUT...

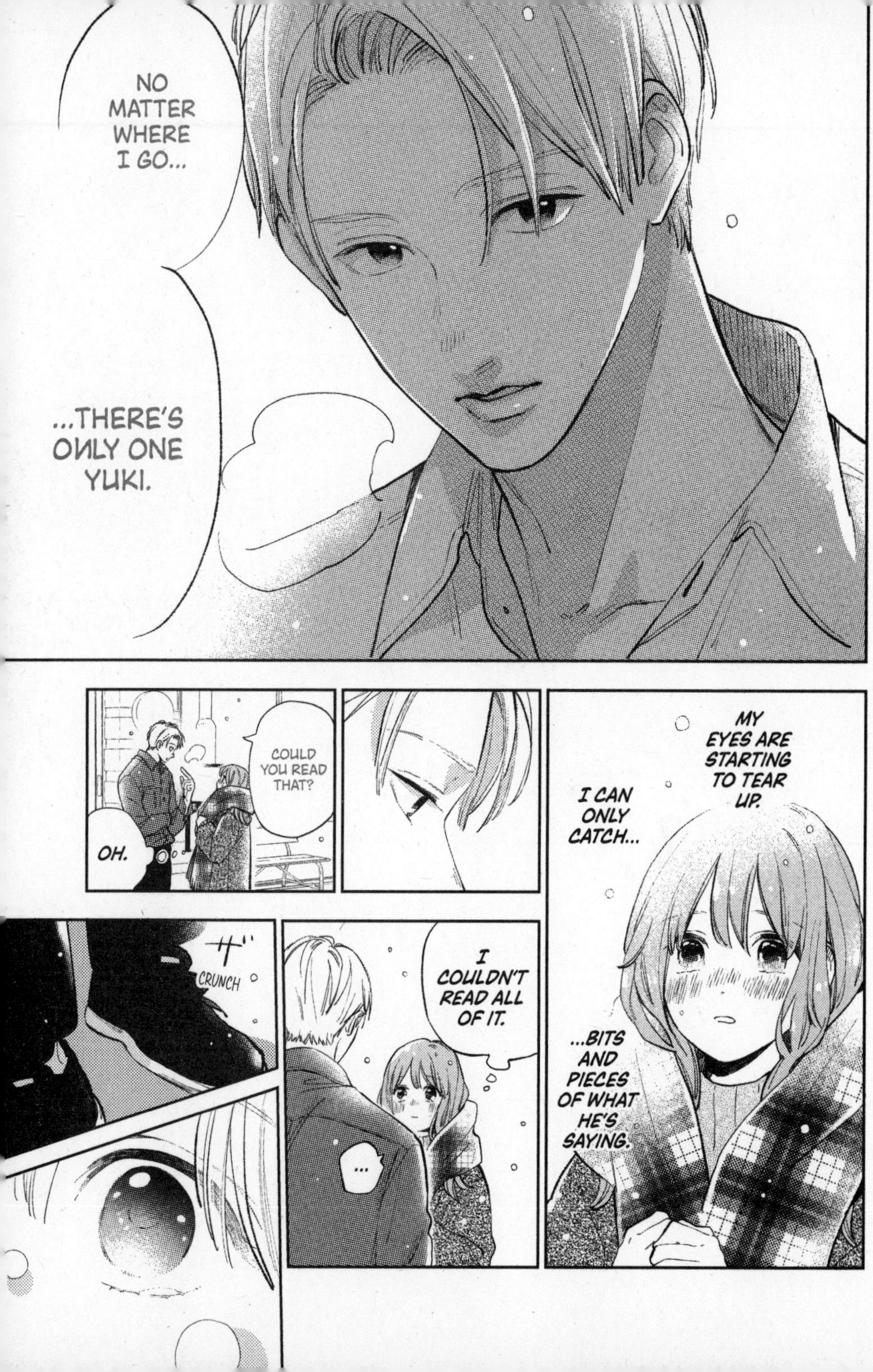
NO MATTER WHERE I GO...
...THERE'S ONLY ONE YUKI.
MY EYES ARE STARTING TO TEAR UP.
I CAN ONLY CATCH...
...BITS AND PIECES OF WHAT HE'S SAYING.
COULD YOU READ THAT?
OH.
I COULDN'T READ ALL OF IT.
...
サ"
CRUNCH

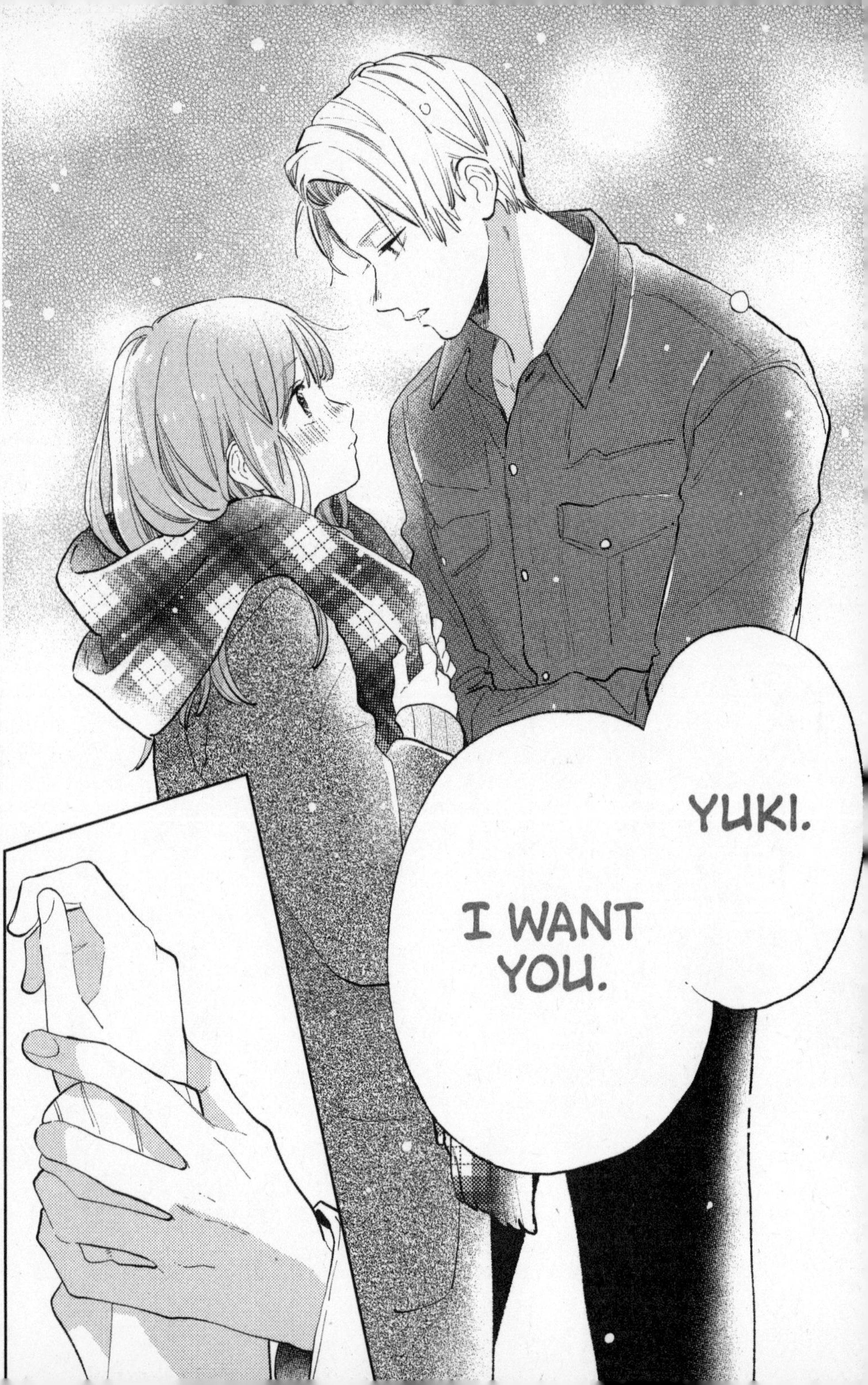
YUKI.
I WANT YOU.

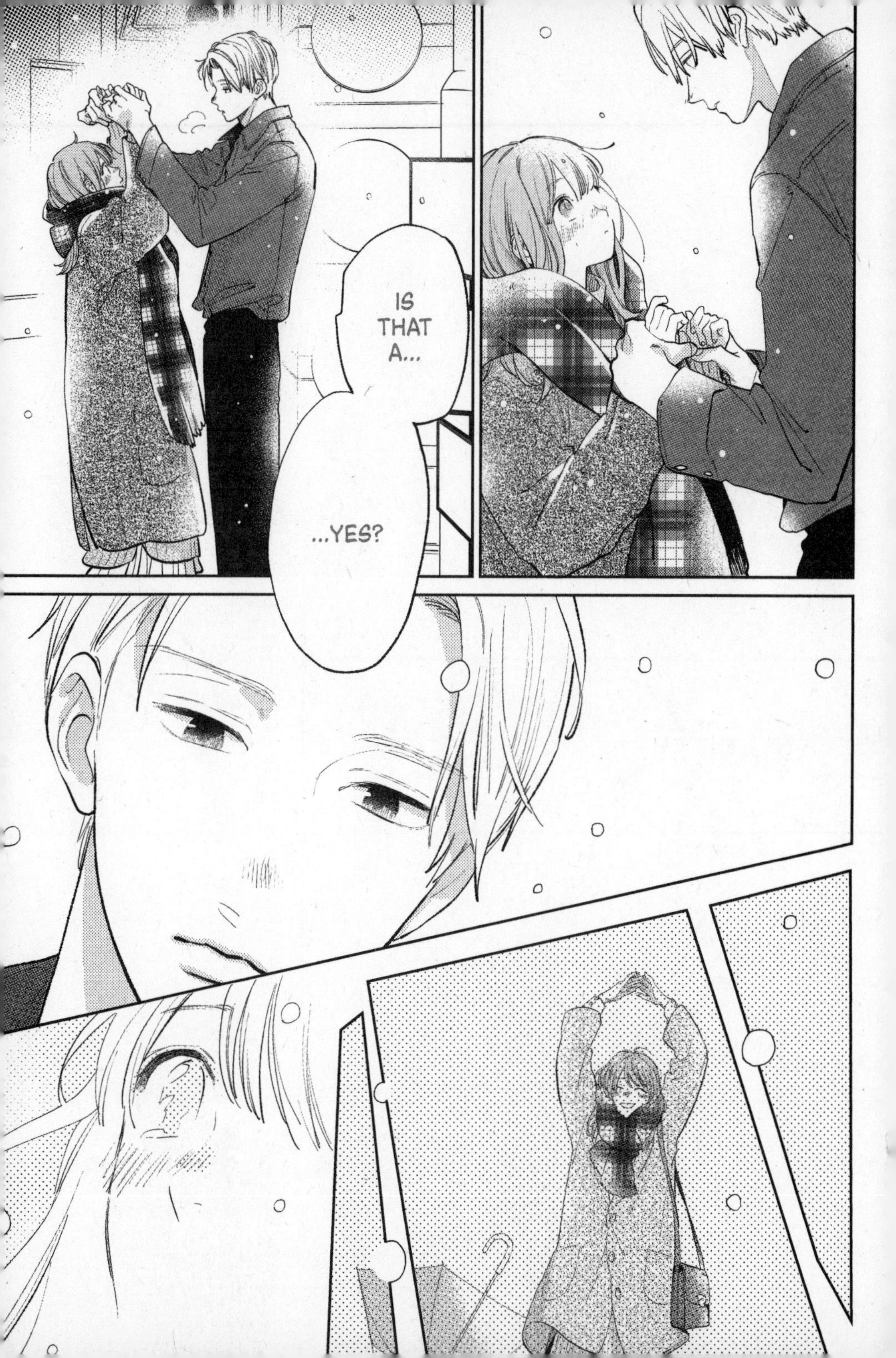
IS THAT A...
...YES?

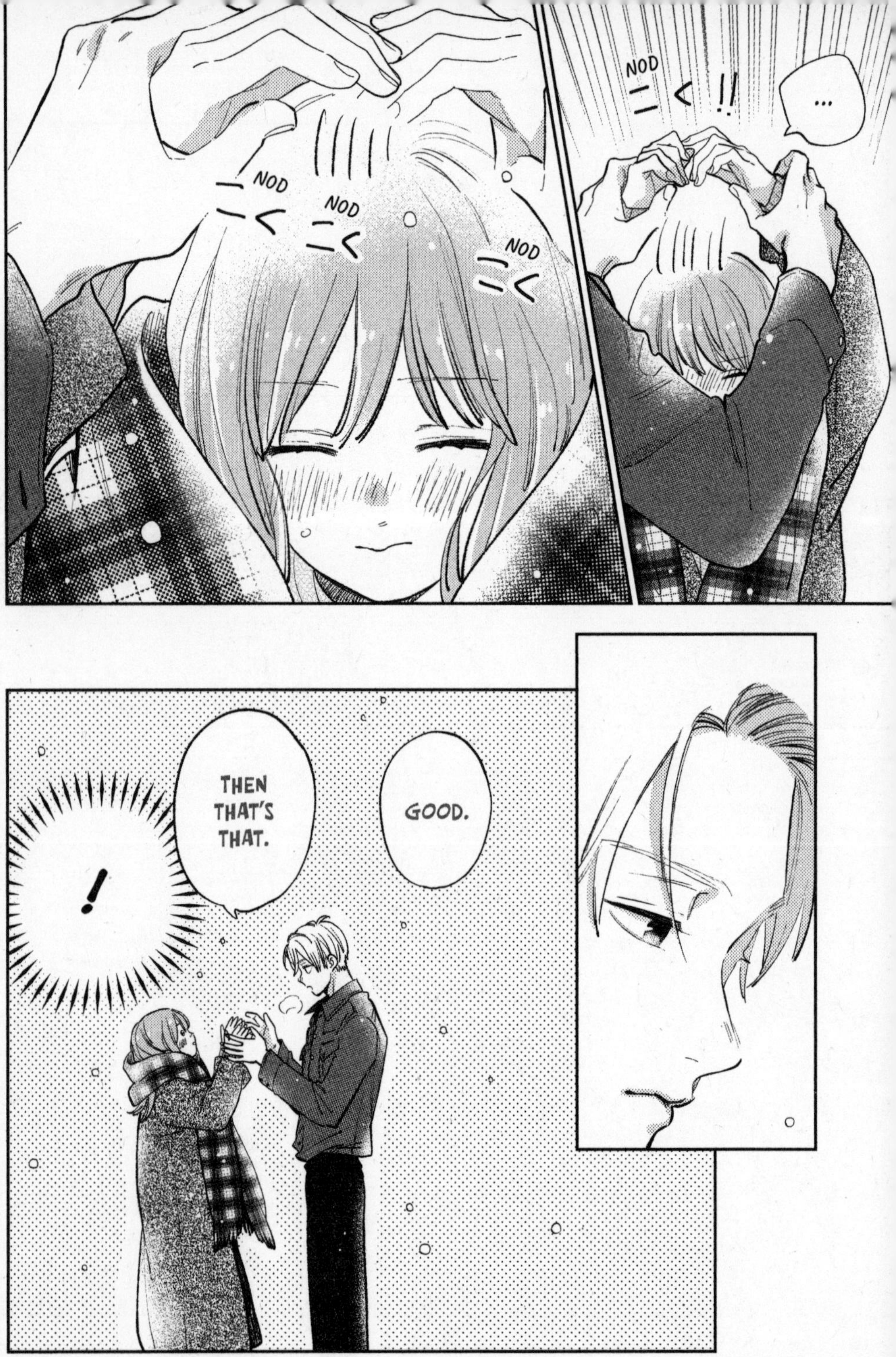
NOD
...
NOD
NOD
NOD
GOOD.
THEN THAT'S THAT.
!

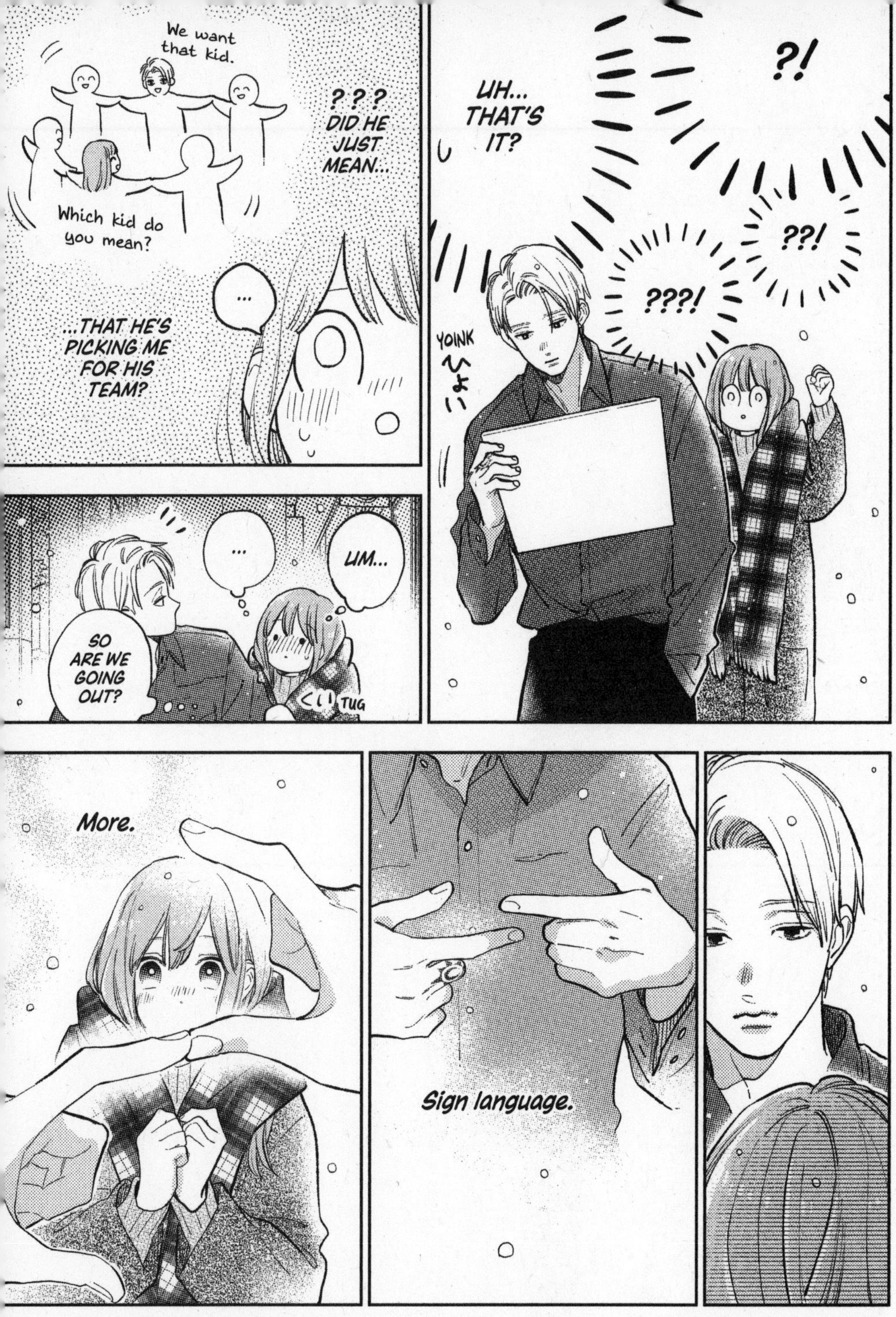
UH... THAT'S IT?
?!
??!
???!
YOINK
ひょい
??? DID HE JUST MEAN...
We want that kid.
Which kid do you mean?
...
...THAT HE'S PICKING ME FOR HIS TEAM?
UM...
...
SO ARE WE GOING OUT?
くい
TUG
Sign language.
More.

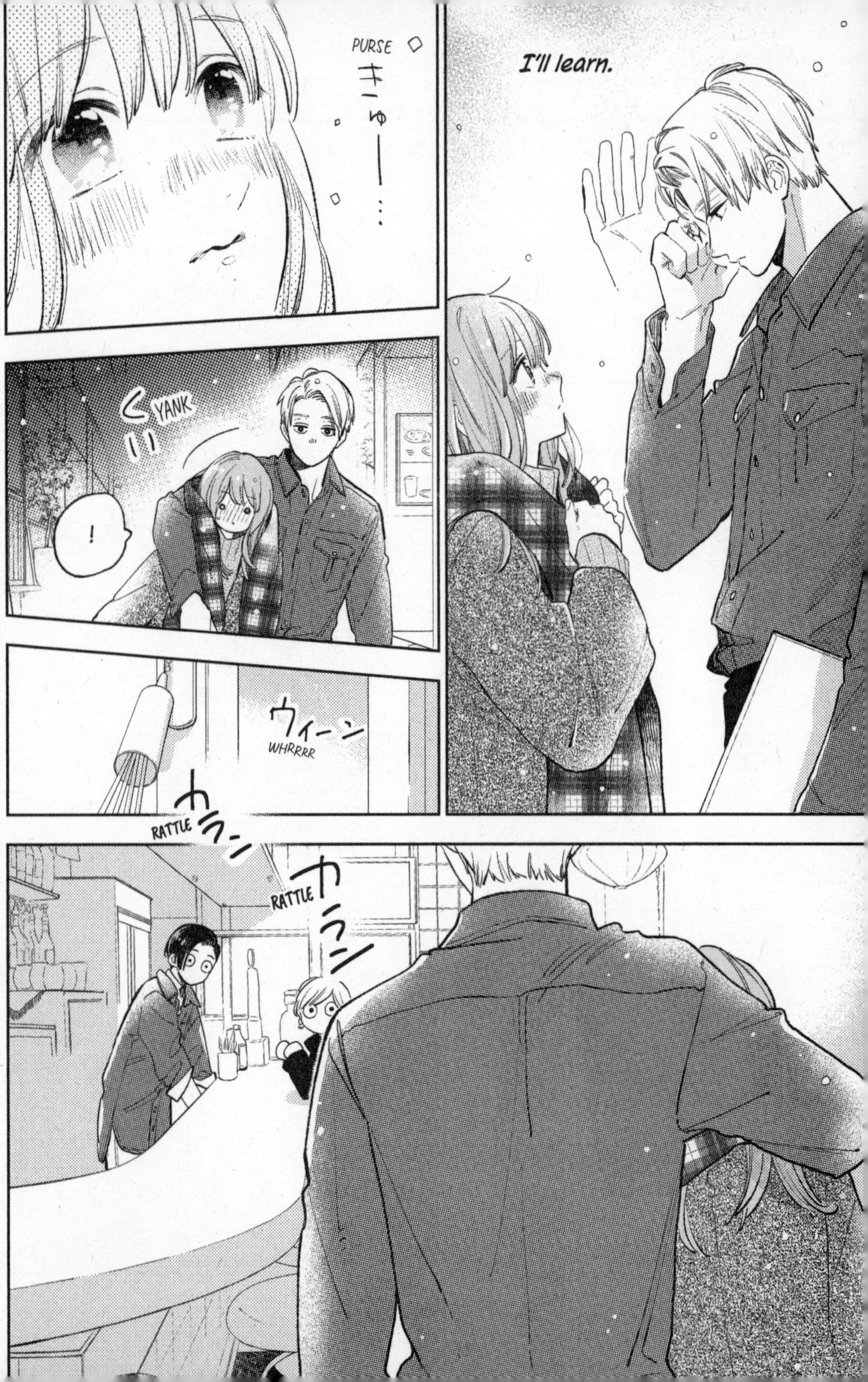
I'll learn.
PURSE
きゅー…
YANK
く
!
ウィーン
WHRRRR
RATTLE
カラン
RATTLE
カラン

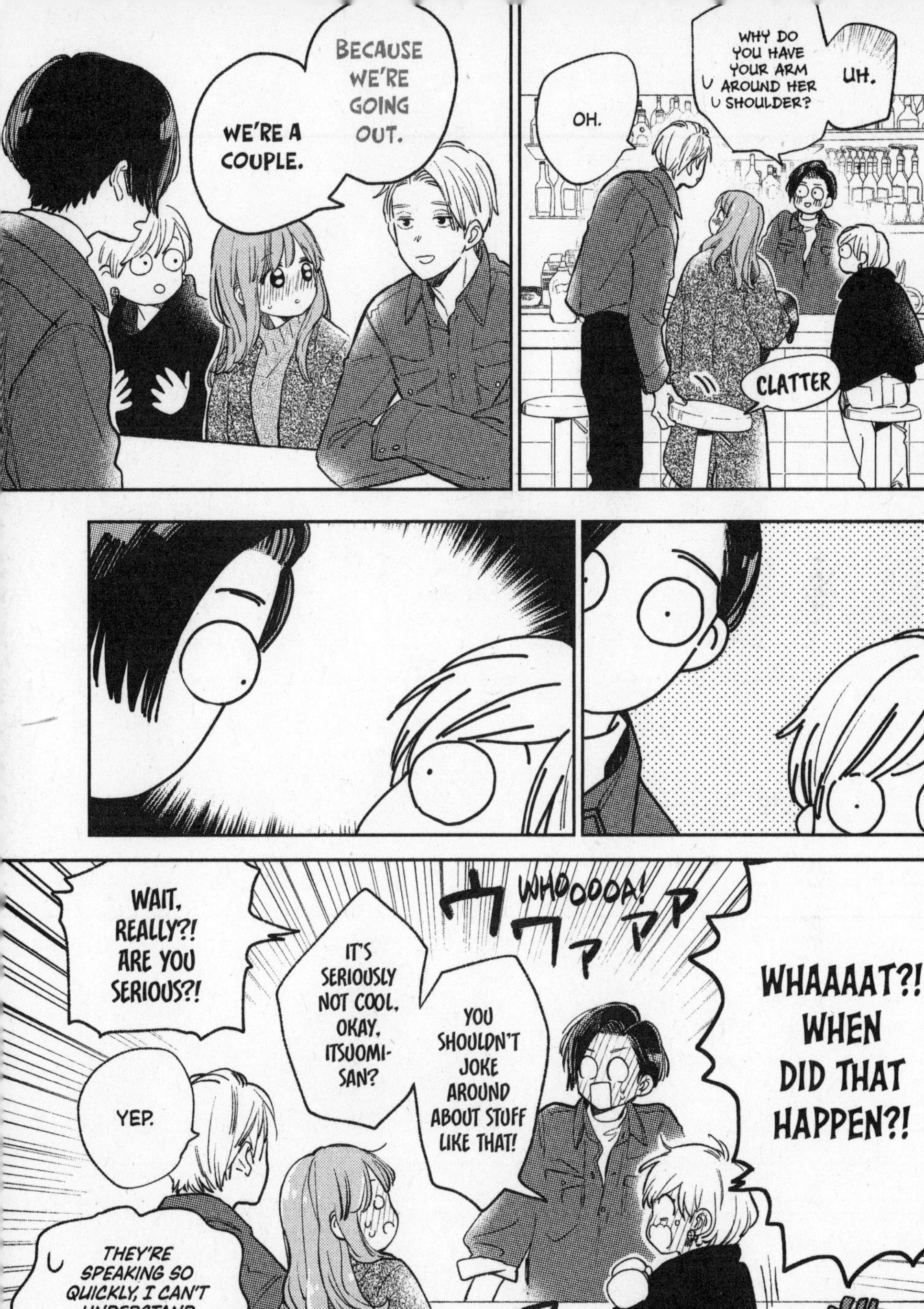
WHY DO YOU HAVE YOUR ARM AROUND HER SHOULDER?
UH.
OH.
CLATTER
BECAUSE WE'RE GOING OUT.
WE'RE A COUPLE.
WHAAAAT?! WHEN DID THAT HAPPEN?!
WHOOOOA! ウワァァア
YOU SHOULDN'T JOKE AROUND ABOUT STUFF LIKE THAT!
IT'S SERIOUSLY NOT COOL, OKAY, ITSUOMI-SAN?
WAIT, REALLY?! ARE YOU SERIOUS?!
YEP.
ガタタ CLATTER
AAAH! アァ
THEY'RE SPEAKING SO QUICKLY, I CAN'T UNDERSTAND WHAT THEY'RE SAYING!

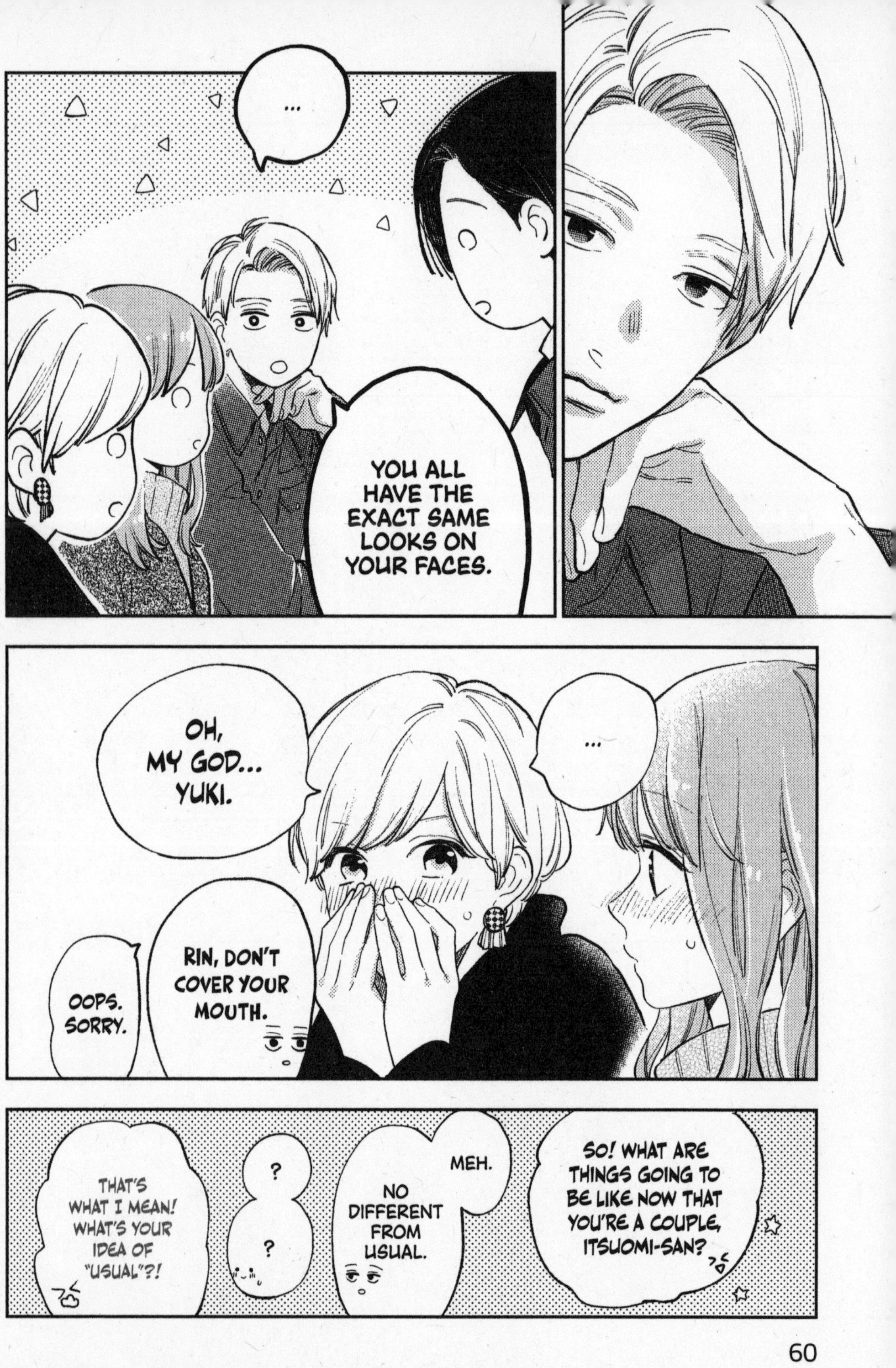
...
YOU ALL HAVE THE EXACT SAME LOOKS ON YOUR FACES.
...
OH, MY GOD... YUKI.
RIN, DON'T COVER YOUR MOUTH.
OOPS. SORRY.
SO! WHAT ARE THINGS GOING TO BE LIKE NOW THAT YOU'RE A COUPLE, ITSUOMI-SAN?
MEH.
NO DIFFERENT FROM USUAL.
?
?
THAT'S WHAT I MEAN! WHAT'S YOUR IDEA OF "USUAL"?!

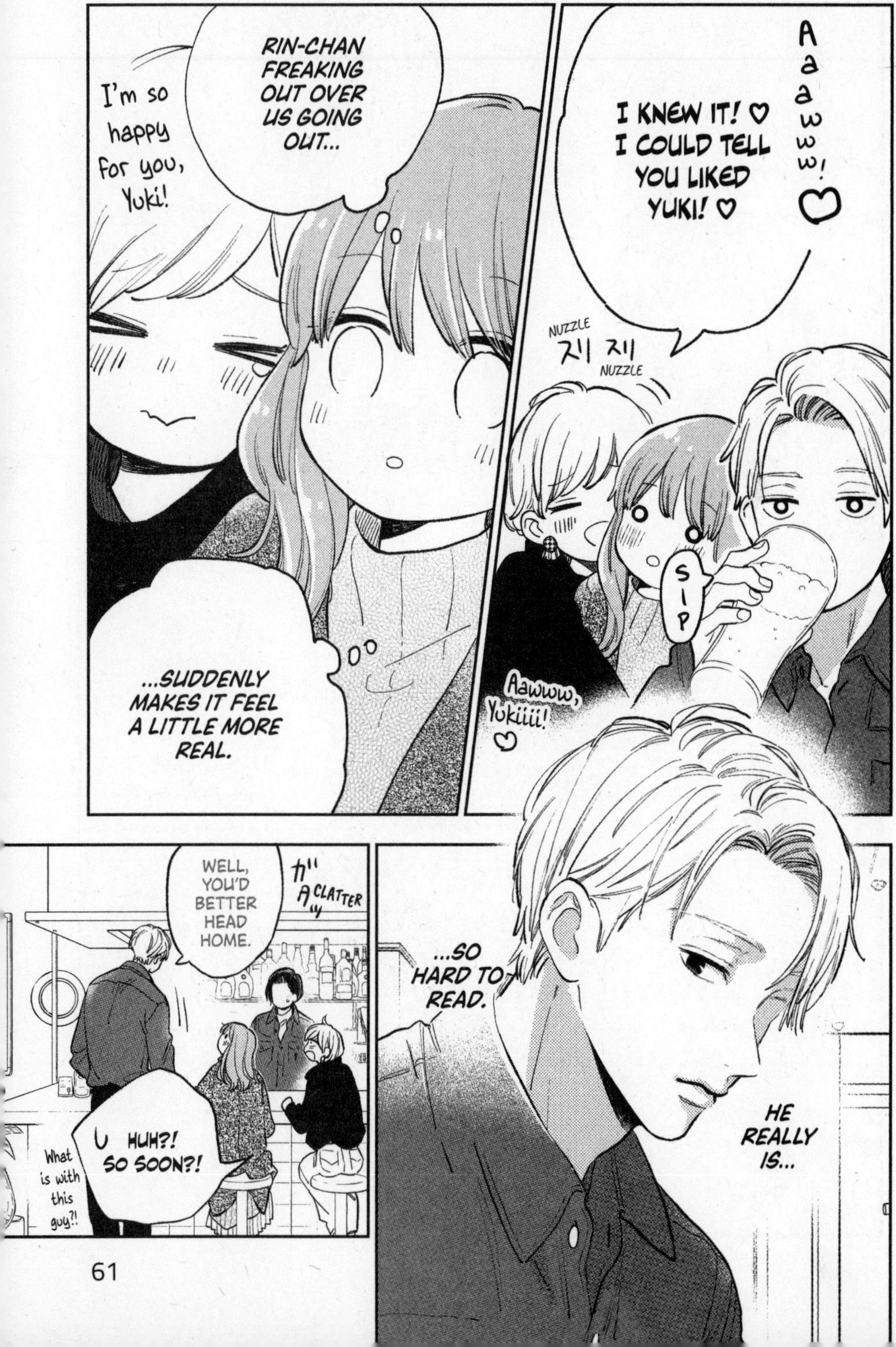
Aawww! ♡
I KNEW IT! ♡ I COULD TELL YOU LIKED YUKI! ♡
NUZZLE NUZZLE
SIP
Aawww, Yukiii! ♡
RIN-CHAN FREAKING OUT OVER US GOING OUT...
I'm so happy for you, Yuki!
...SUDDENLY MAKES IT FEEL A LITTLE MORE REAL.
...SO HARD TO READ.
HE REALLY IS...
CLATTER
WELL, YOU'D BETTER HEAD HOME.
HUH?! SO SOON?!
What is with this guy?!

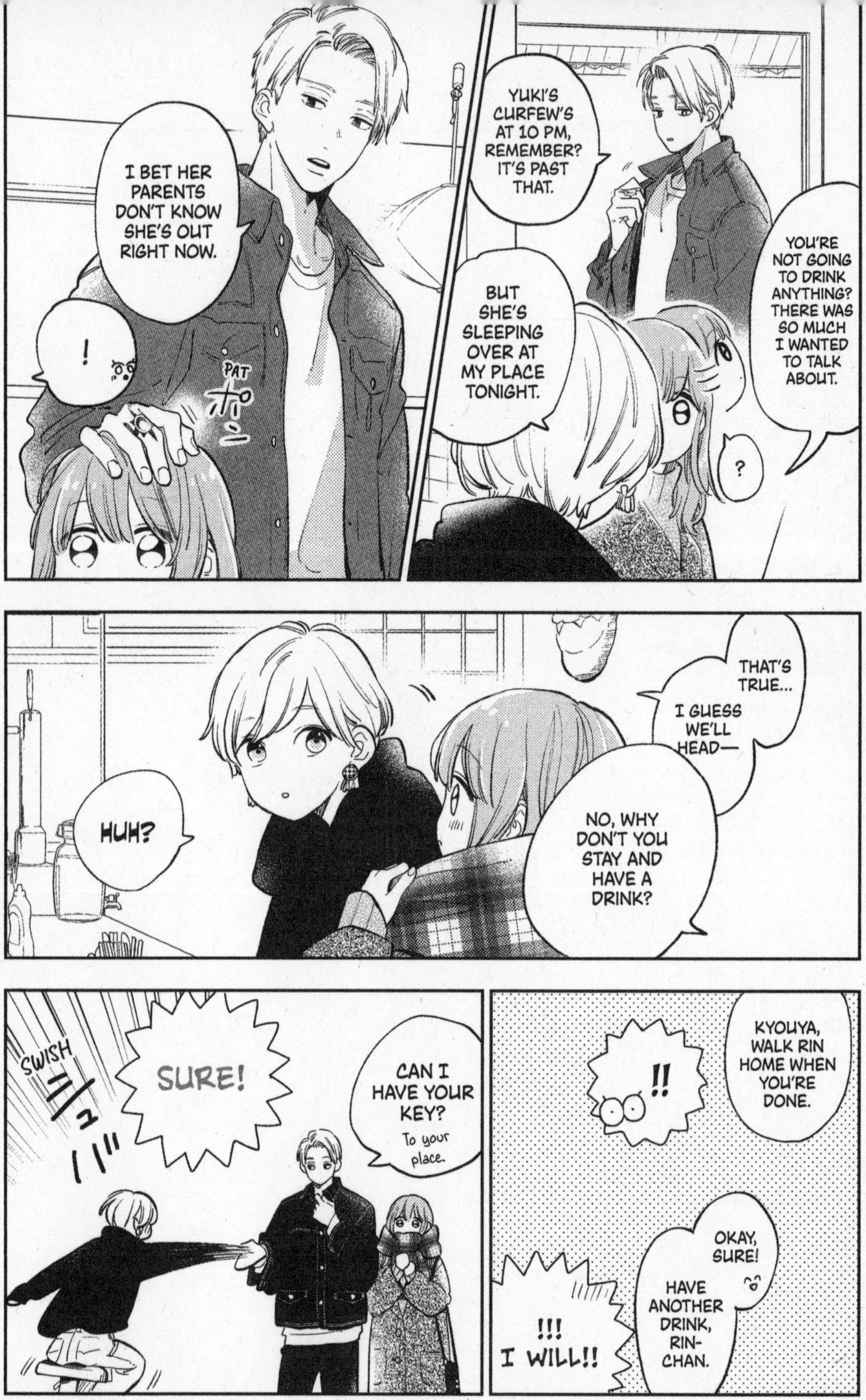
YUKI'S CURFEW'S AT 10 PM, REMEMBER? IT'S PAST THAT.
YOU'RE NOT GOING TO DRINK ANYTHING? THERE WAS SO MUCH I WANTED TO TALK ABOUT.
BUT SHE'S SLEEPING OVER AT MY PLACE TONIGHT.
?
I BET HER PARENTS DON'T KNOW SHE'S OUT RIGHT NOW.
!
PAT
THAT'S TRUE...
I GUESS WE'LL HEAD—
NO, WHY DON'T YOU STAY AND HAVE A DRINK?
HUH?
KYOUYA, WALK RIN HOME WHEN YOU'RE DONE.
!!
OKAY, SURE!
HAVE ANOTHER DRINK, RIN-CHAN.
!!!
I WILL!!
CAN I HAVE YOUR KEY?
To your place.
SURE!
SWISH

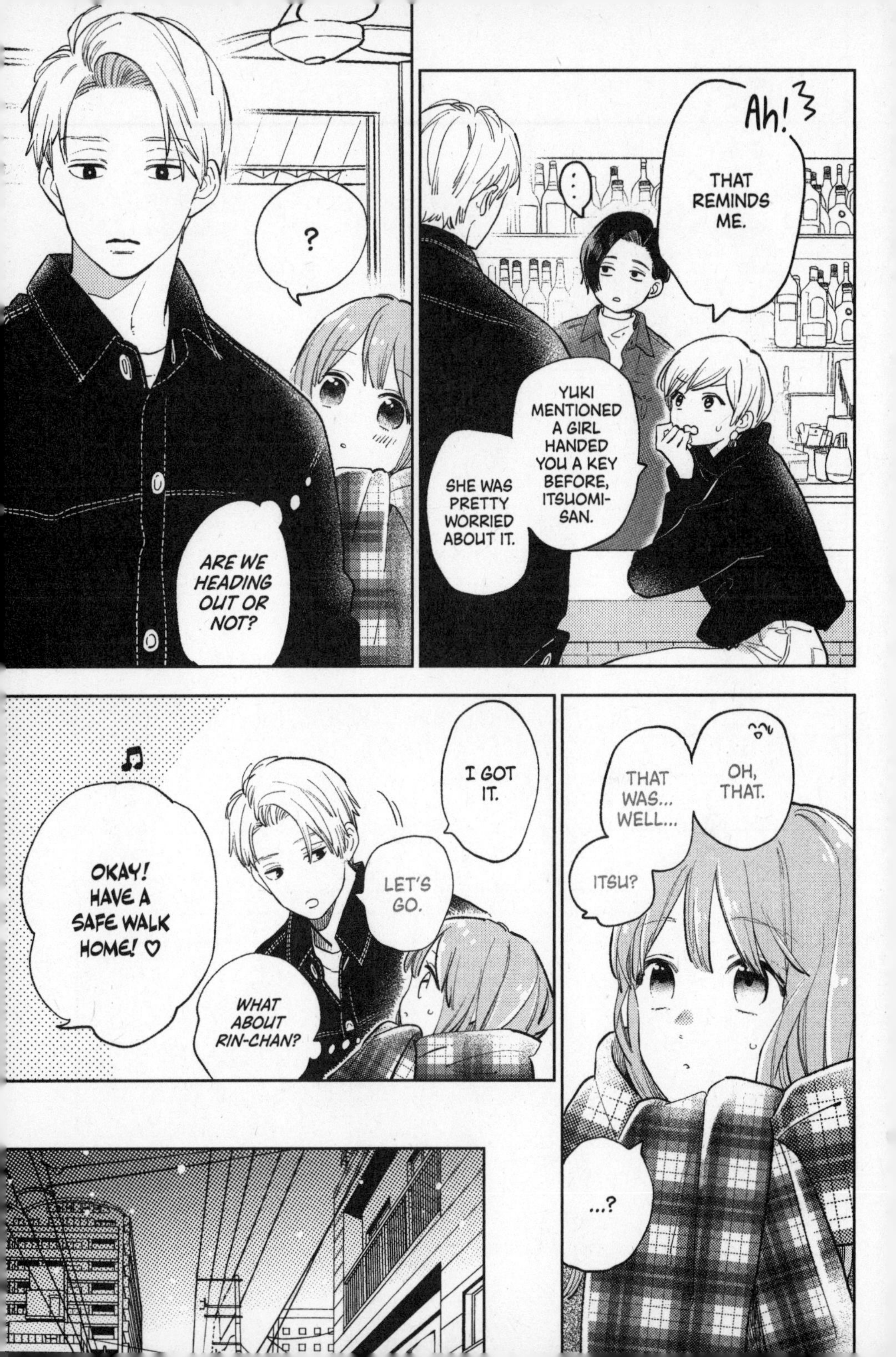
Ah!
THAT REMINDS ME.
...
YUKI MENTIONED A GIRL HANDED YOU A KEY BEFORE, ITSUOMI-SAN.
SHE WAS PRETTY WORRIED ABOUT IT.
?
ARE WE HEADING OUT OR NOT?
OH, THAT.
THAT WAS... WELL...
ITSU?
...?
I GOT IT.
LET'S GO.
OKAY! HAVE A SAFE WALK HOME! ♡
WHAT ABOUT RIN-CHAN?

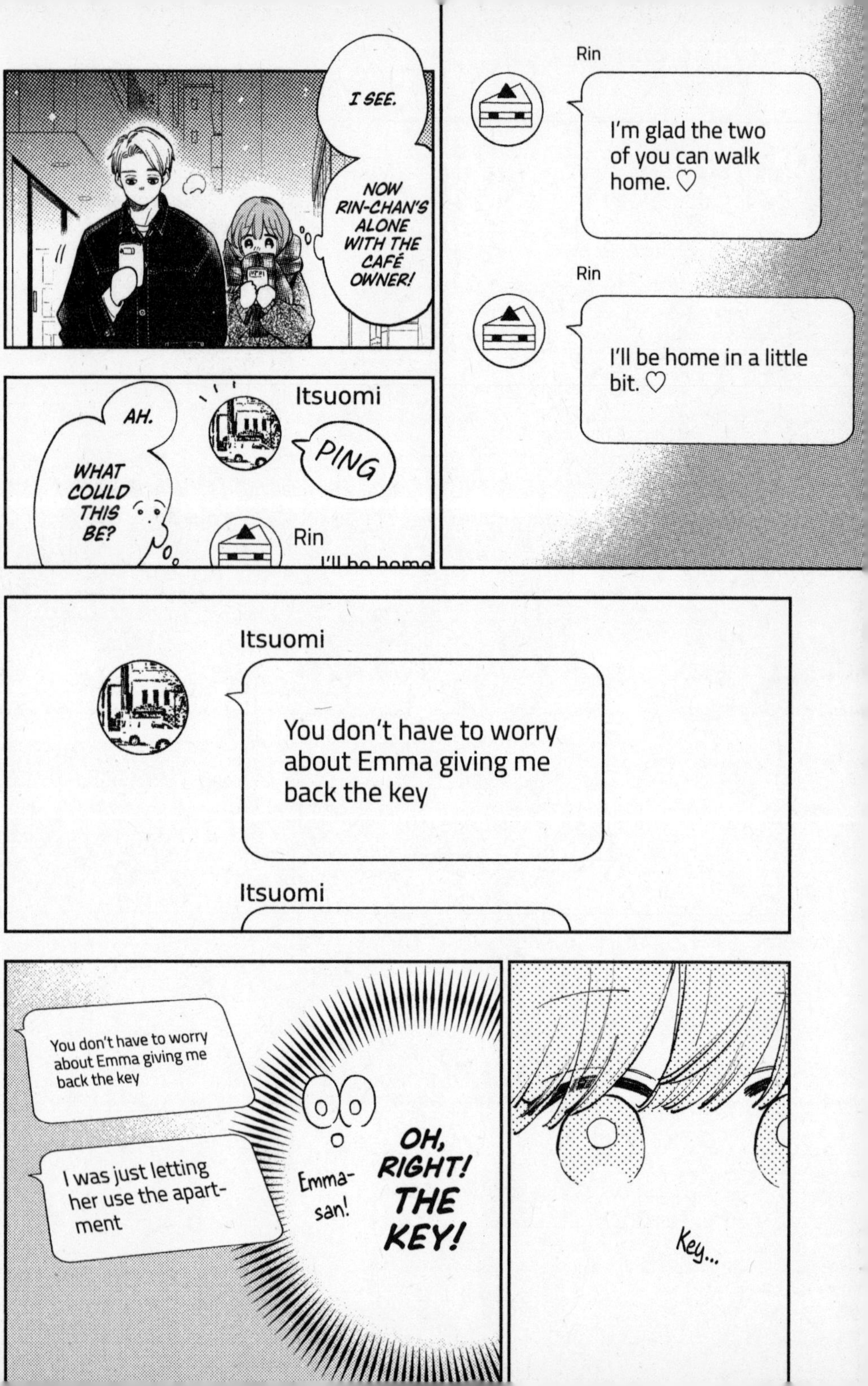

Rin
I'm glad the two of you can walk home. ♡
Rin
I'll be home in a little bit. ♡
I SEE.
NOW RIN-CHAN'S ALONE WITH THE CAFÉ OWNER!
Itsuomi
PING
AH.
WHAT COULD THIS BE?
Rin
Itsuomi
You don't have to worry about Emma giving me back the key
Itsuomi
Key...
You don't have to worry about Emma giving me back the key
I was just letting her use the apart-ment
Emma-san!
OH, RIGHT! THE KEY!

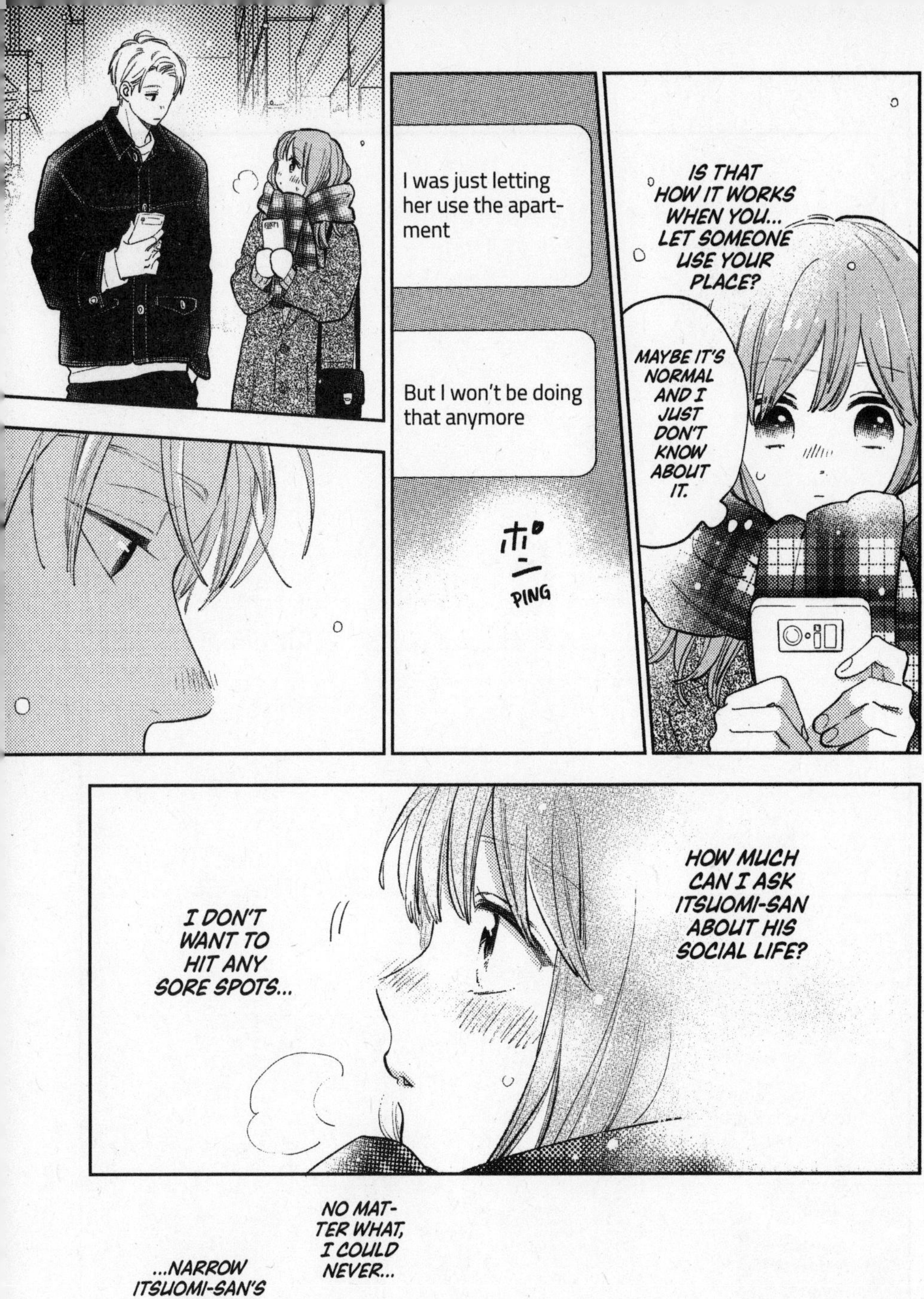
IS THAT HOW IT WORKS WHEN YOU... LET SOMEONE USE YOUR PLACE?
MAYBE IT'S NORMAL AND I JUST DON'T KNOW ABOUT IT.
I was just letting her use the apart-ment
But I won't be doing that anymore
PING
HOW MUCH CAN I ASK ITSUOMI-SAN ABOUT HIS SOCIAL LIFE?
I DON'T WANT TO HIT ANY SORE SPOTS...
NO MAT-TER WHAT, I COULD NEVER...
...NARROW ITSUOMI-SAN'S WORLD.

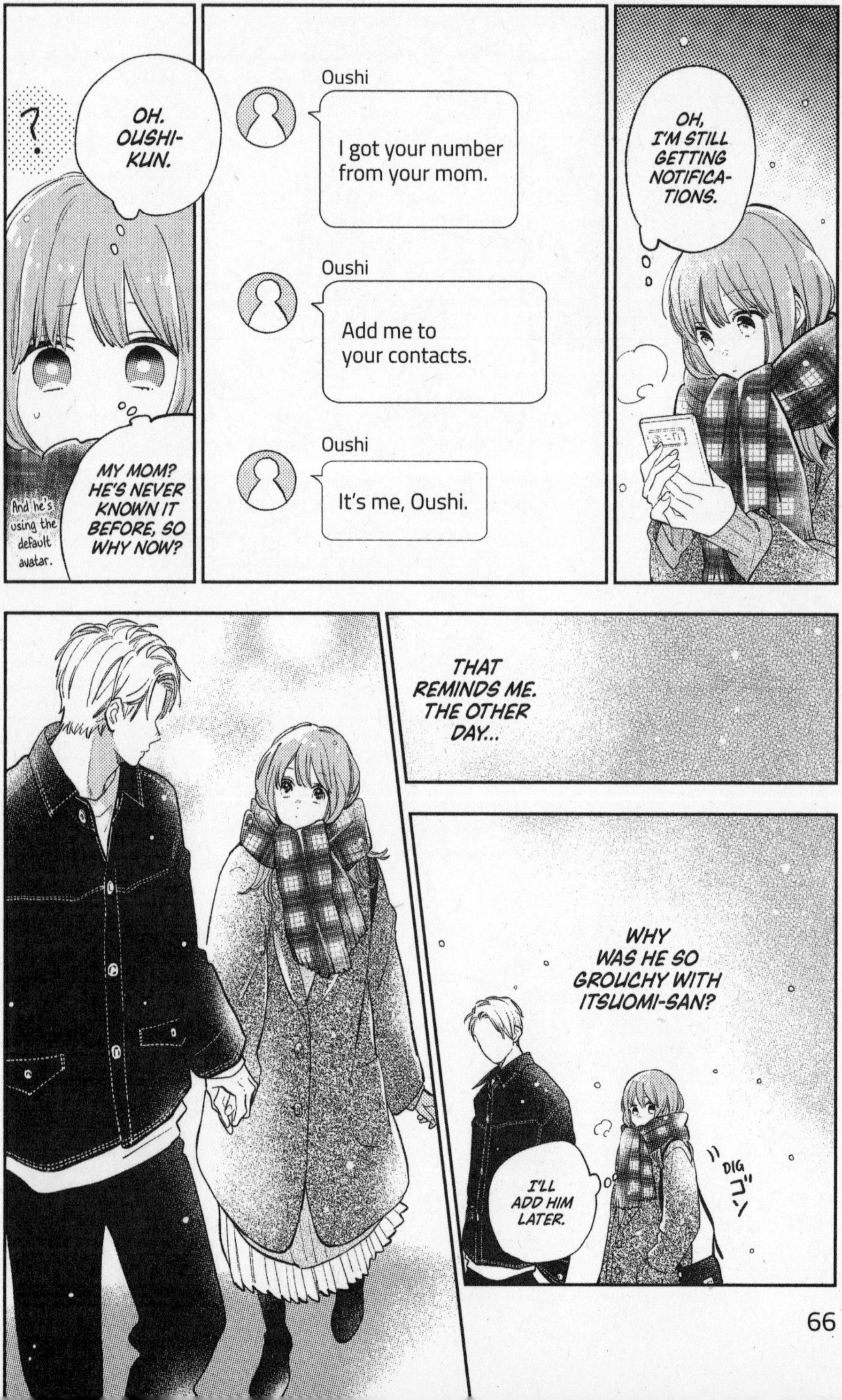
OH, I'M STILL GETTING NOTIFICATIONS.
Oushi
I got your number from your mom.
Oushi
Add me to your contacts.
Oushi
It's me, Oushi.
OH. OUSHI-KUN.
?
MY MOM? HE'S NEVER KNOWN IT BEFORE, SO WHY NOW?
And he's using the default avatar.
THAT REMINDS ME. THE OTHER DAY...
WHY WAS HE SO GROUCHY WITH ITSUOMI-SAN?
I'LL ADD HIM LATER.
DIG

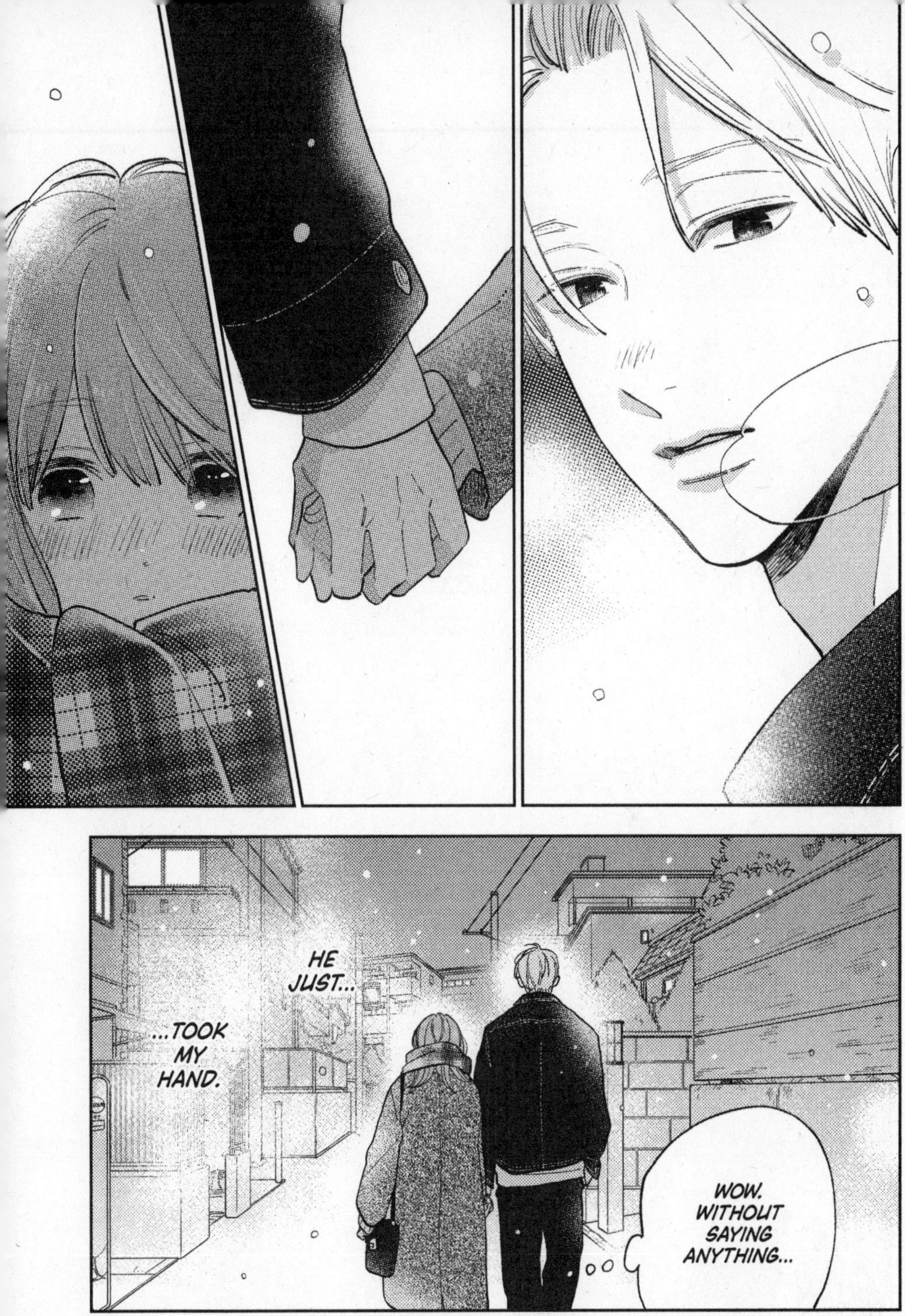
WOW. WITHOUT SAYING ANYTHING...
HE JUST...
...TOOK MY HAND.

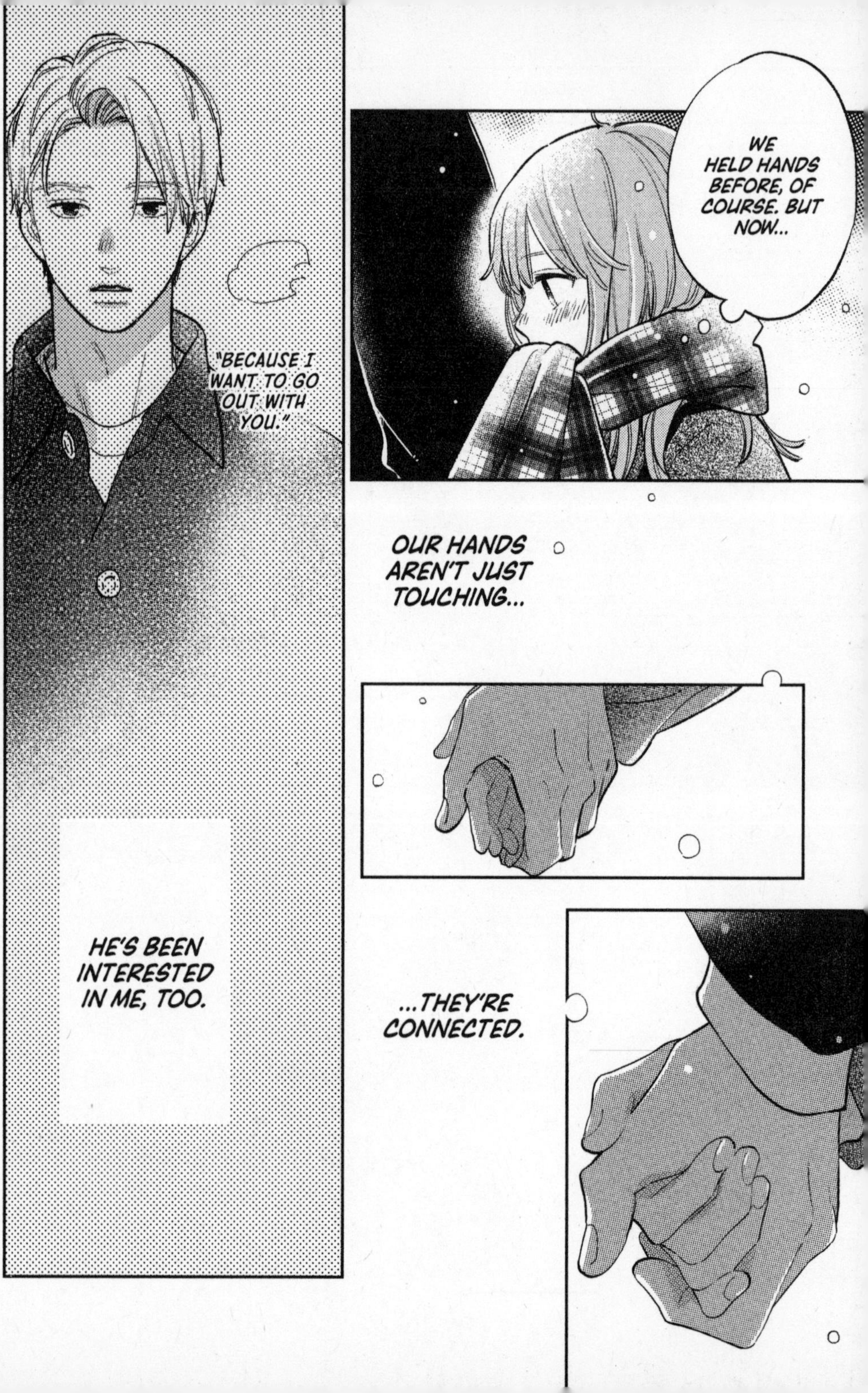
WE HELD HANDS BEFORE, OF COURSE. BUT NOW...
OUR HANDS AREN'T JUST TOUCHING...
...THEY'RE CONNECTED.
"BECAUSE I WANT TO GO OUT WITH YOU."
HE'S BEEN INTERESTED IN ME, TOO.

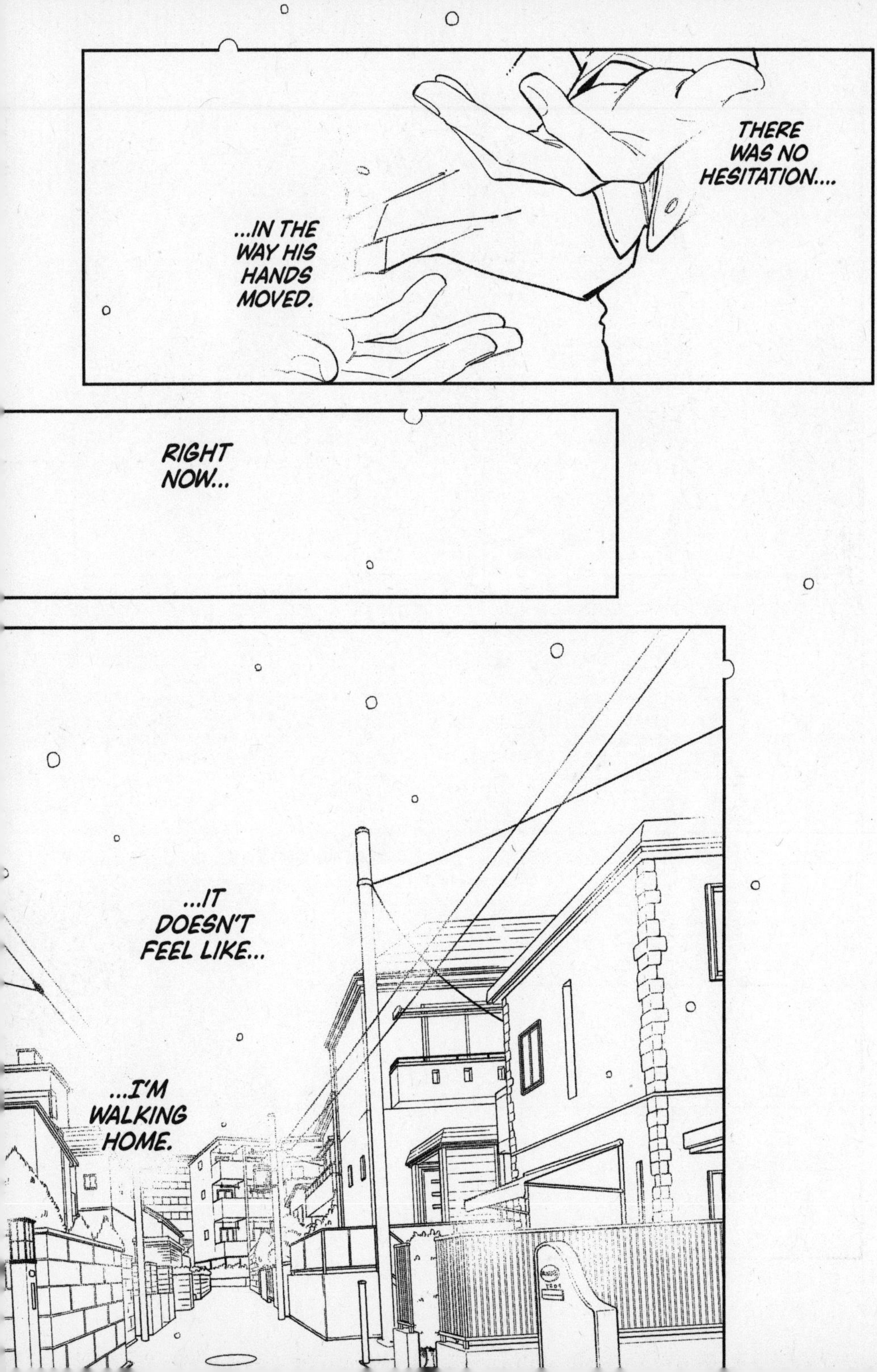
THERE WAS NO HESITATION....
...IN THE WAY HIS HANDS MOVED.
RIGHT NOW...
...IT DOESN'T FEEL LIKE...
...I'M WALKING HOME.

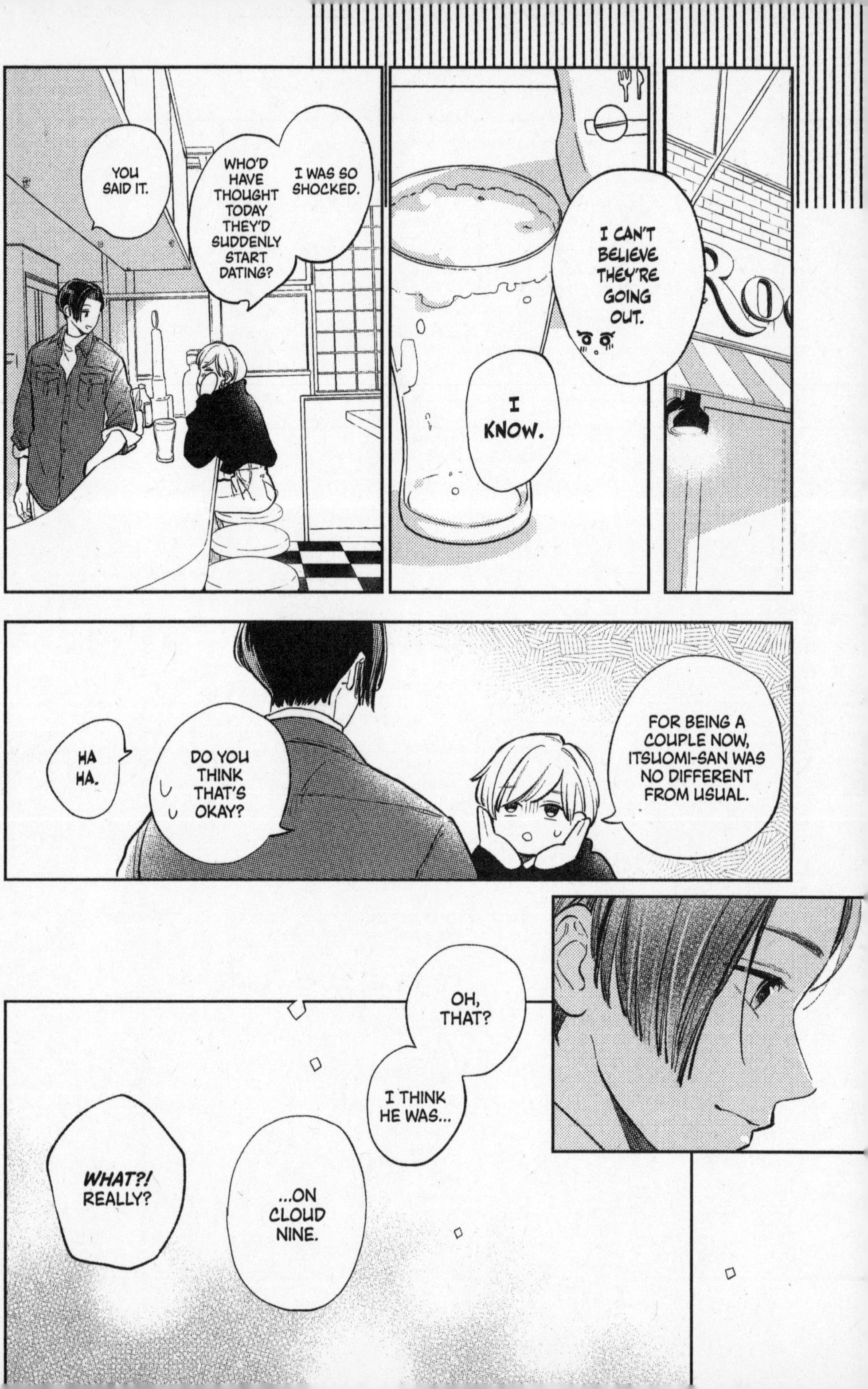

I CAN'T BELIEVE THEY'RE GOING OUT.
I KNOW.
I WAS SO SHOCKED.
WHO'D HAVE THOUGHT TODAY THEY'D SUDDENLY START DATING?
YOU SAID IT.
FOR BEING A COUPLE NOW, ITSUOMI-SAN WAS NO DIFFERENT FROM USUAL.
DO YOU THINK THAT'S OKAY?
HA HA.
OH, THAT?
I THINK HE WAS...
...ON CLOUD NINE.
WHAT?! REALLY?

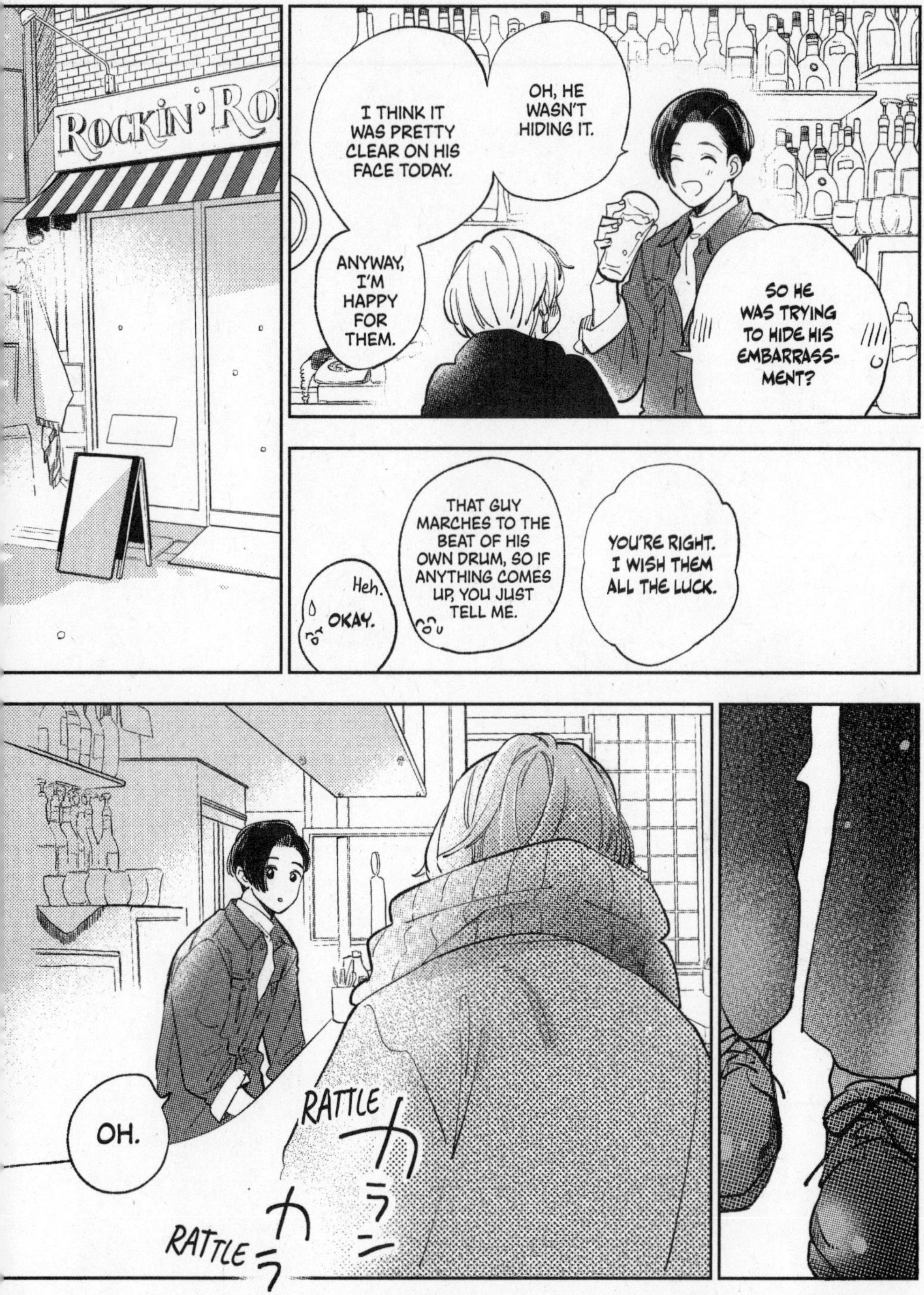
OH, HE WASN'T HIDING IT.
I THINK IT WAS PRETTY CLEAR ON HIS FACE TODAY.
SO HE WAS TRYING TO HIDE HIS EMBARRASS-MENT?
ANYWAY, I'M HAPPY FOR THEM.
ROCKIN' RO
YOU'RE RIGHT. I WISH THEM ALL THE LUCK.
THAT GUY MARCHES TO THE BEAT OF HIS OWN DRUM, SO IF ANYTHING COMES UP, YOU JUST TELL ME.
Heh. OKAY.
RATTLE
カラー
OH.
RATTLE
カラー

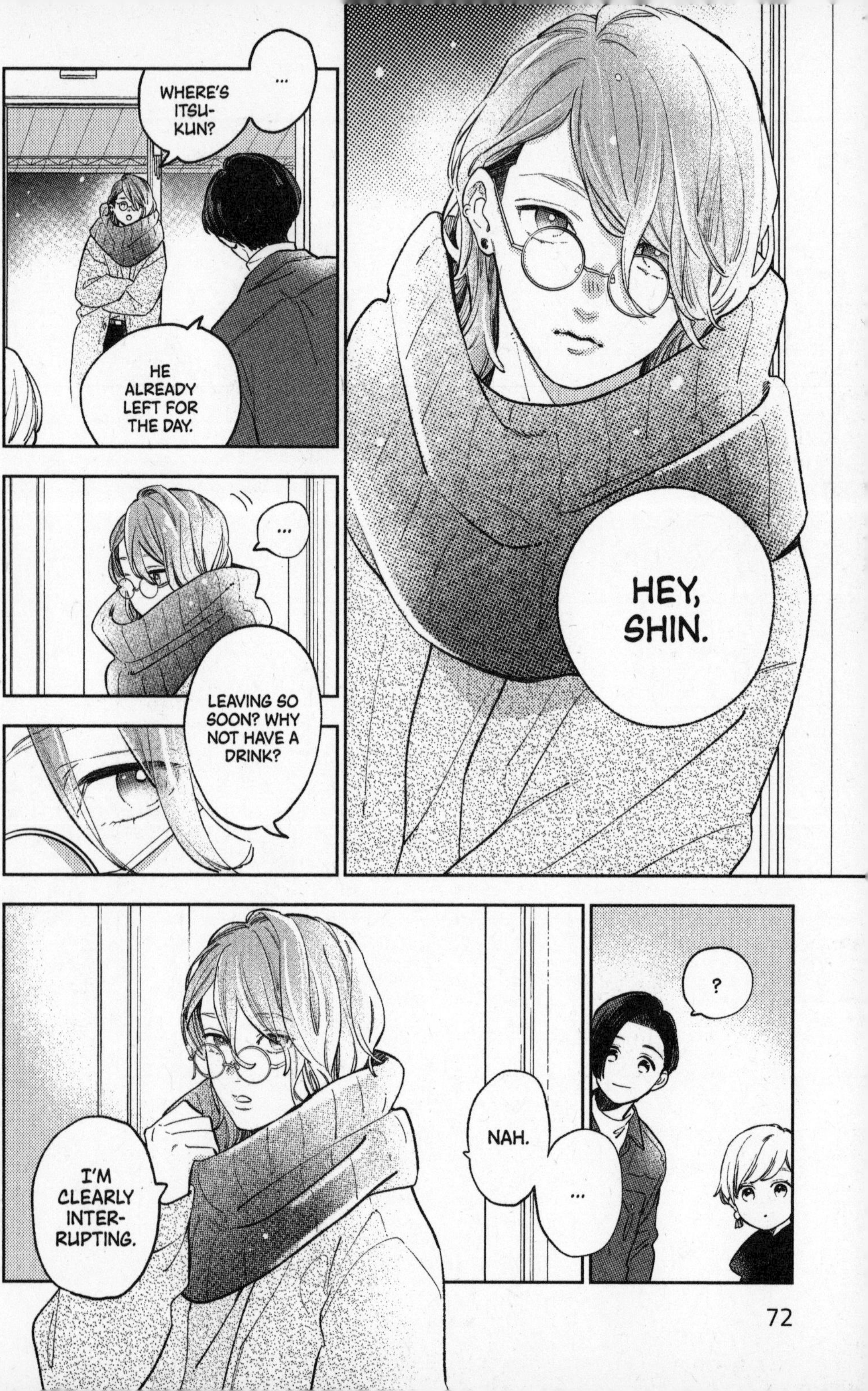
HEY, SHIN.
...
WHERE'S ITSU-KUN?
HE ALREADY LEFT FOR THE DAY.
...
LEAVING SO SOON? WHY NOT HAVE A DRINK?
?
NAH.
...
I'M CLEARLY INTERRUPTING.

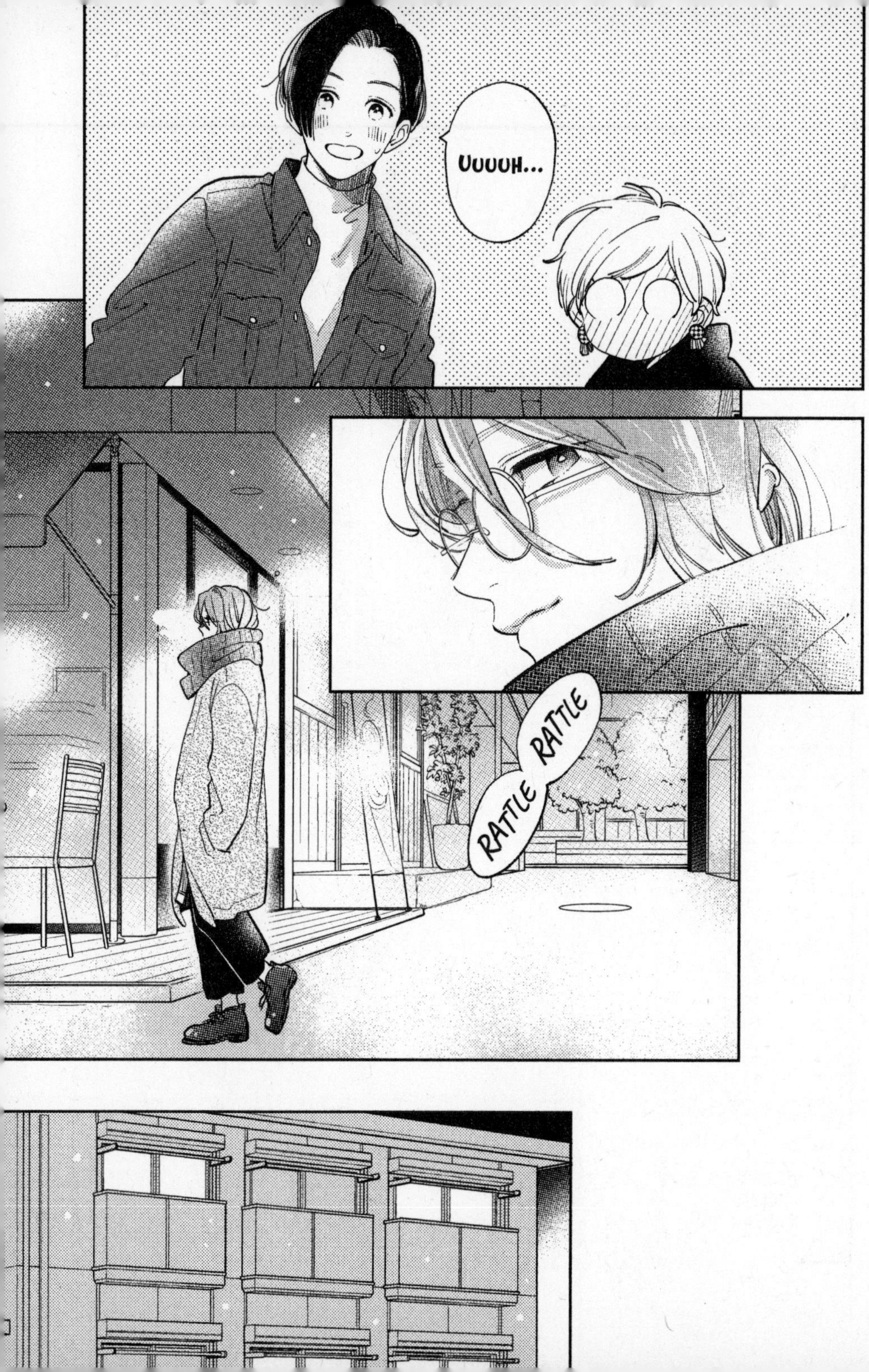
UUUUH...
RATTLE RATTLE

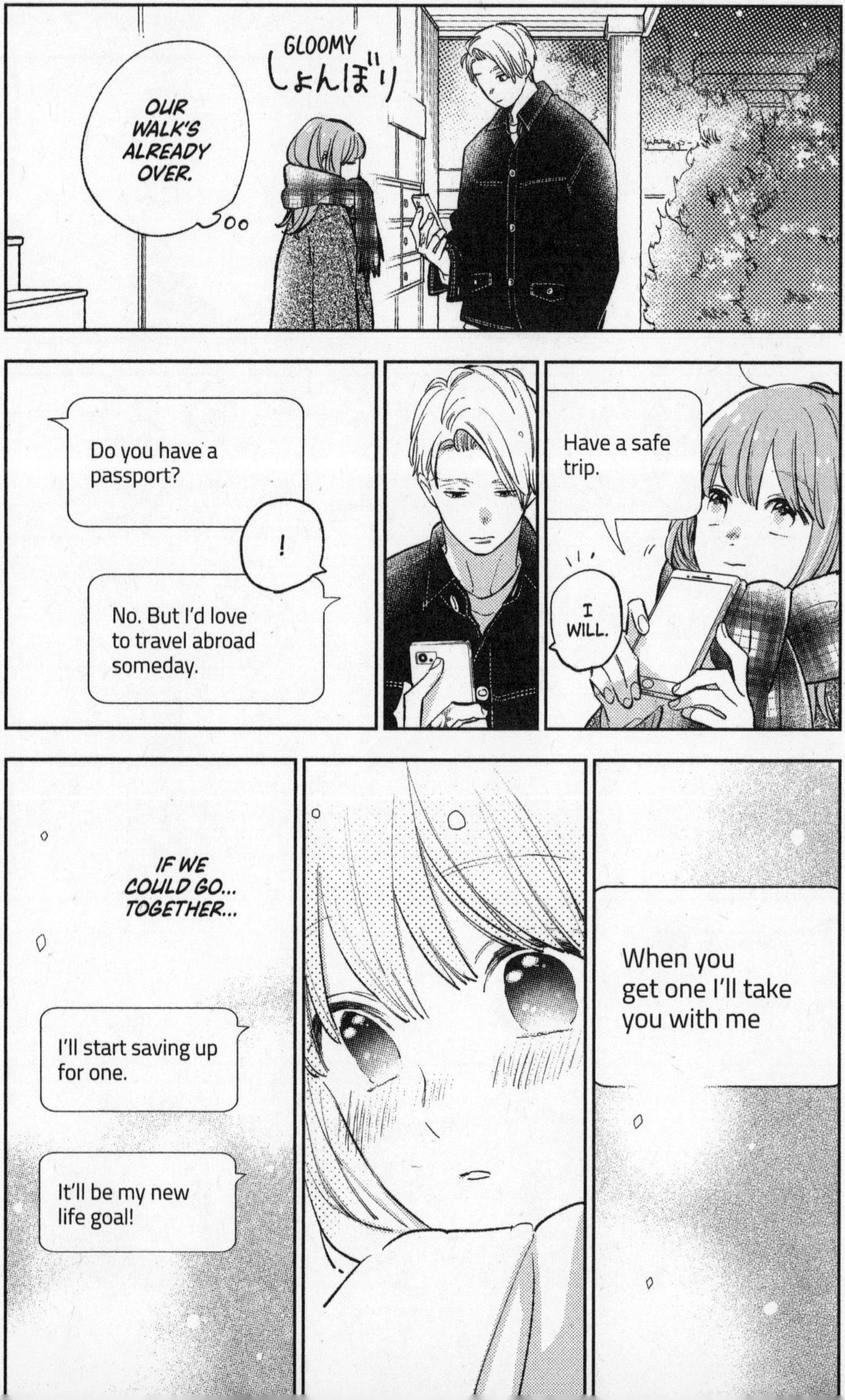
GLOOMY
しょんぼり
OUR WALK'S ALREADY OVER.
Have a safe trip.
I WILL.
Do you have a passport?
!
No. But I'd love to travel abroad someday.
When you get one I'll take you with me
IF WE COULD GO... TOGETHER...
I'll start saving up for one.
It'll be my new life goal!

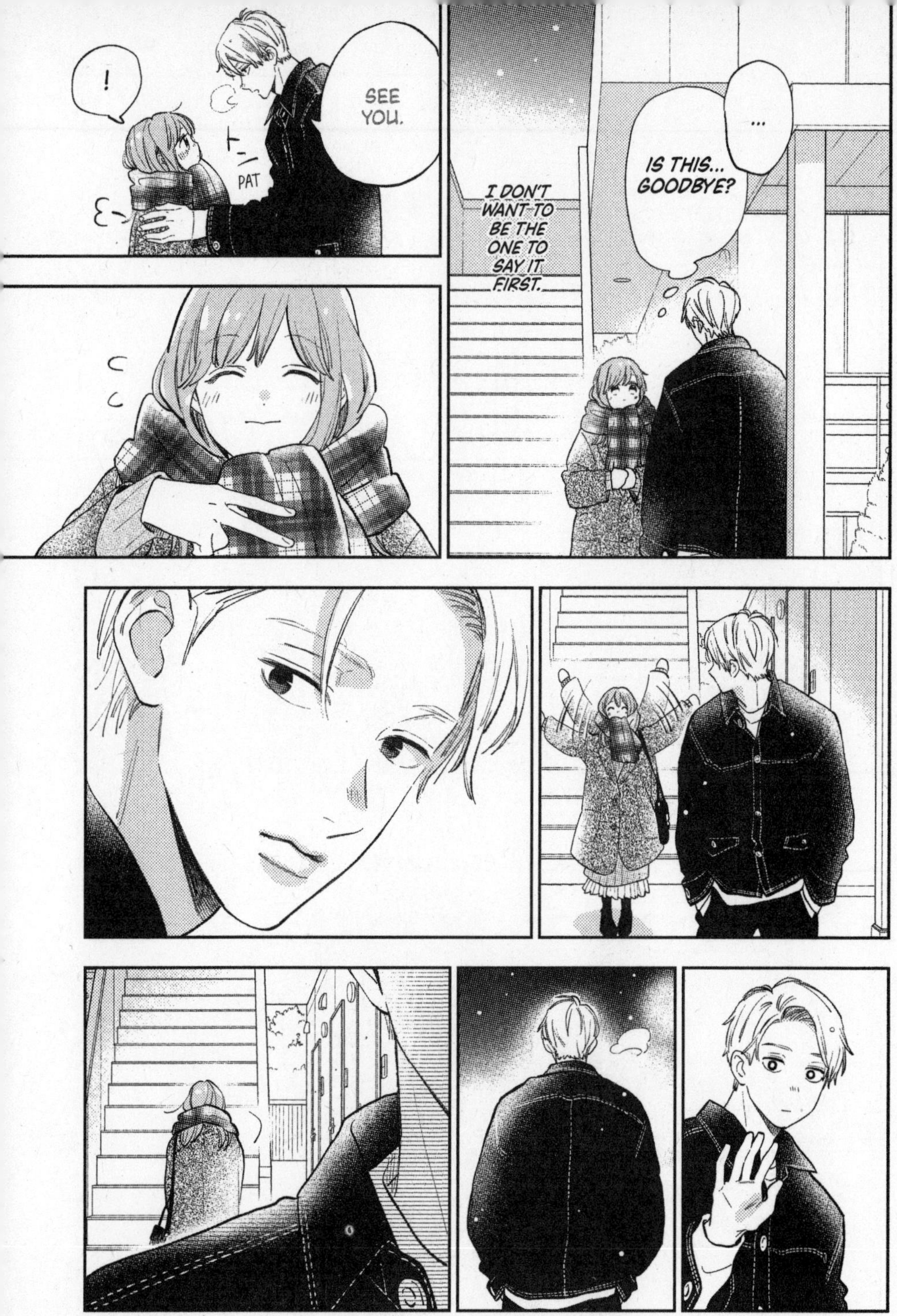
...
IS THIS... GOODBYE?
I DON'T WANT TO BE THE ONE TO SAY IT FIRST.
SEE YOU.
!
PAT

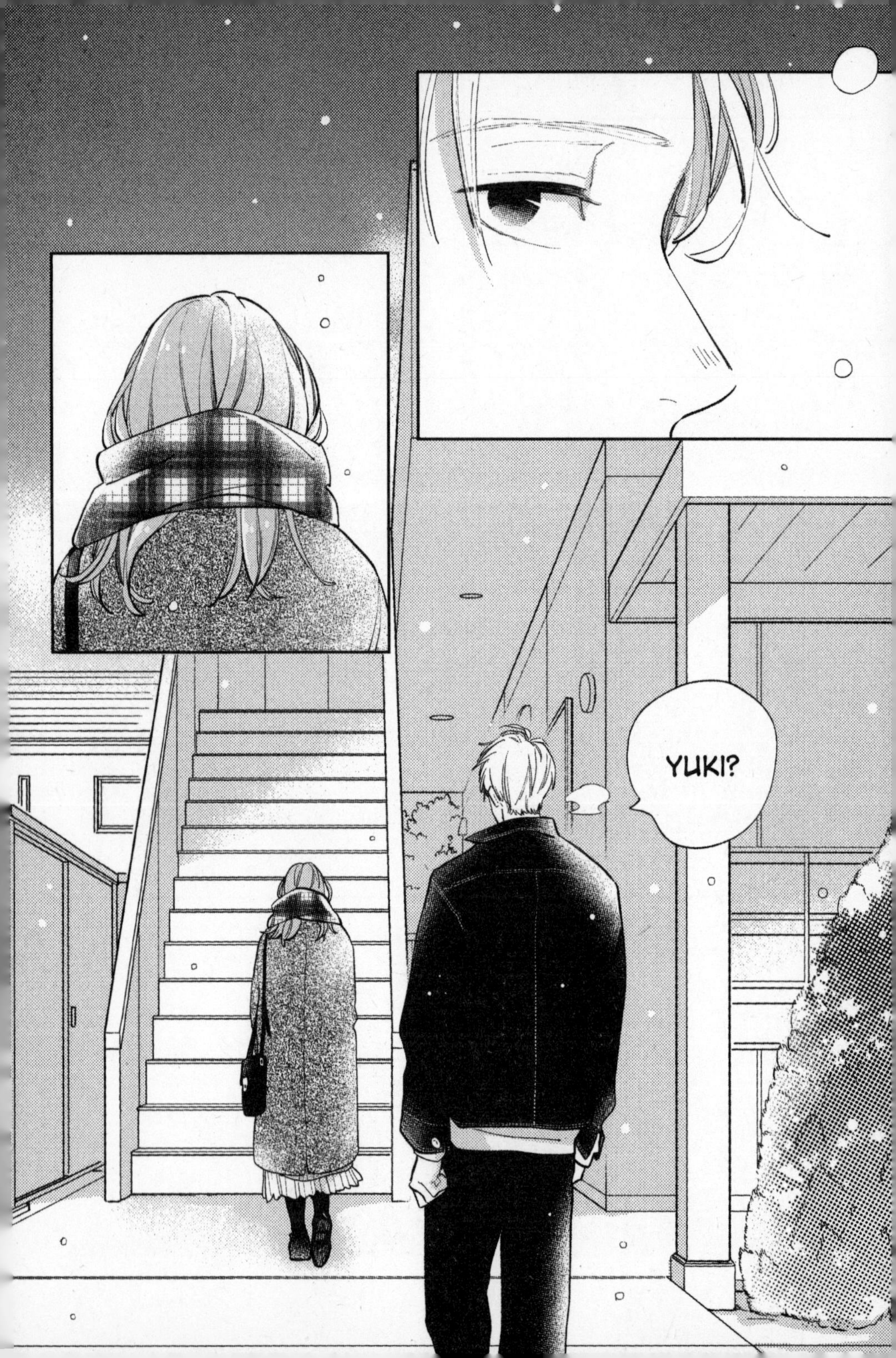
YUKI?

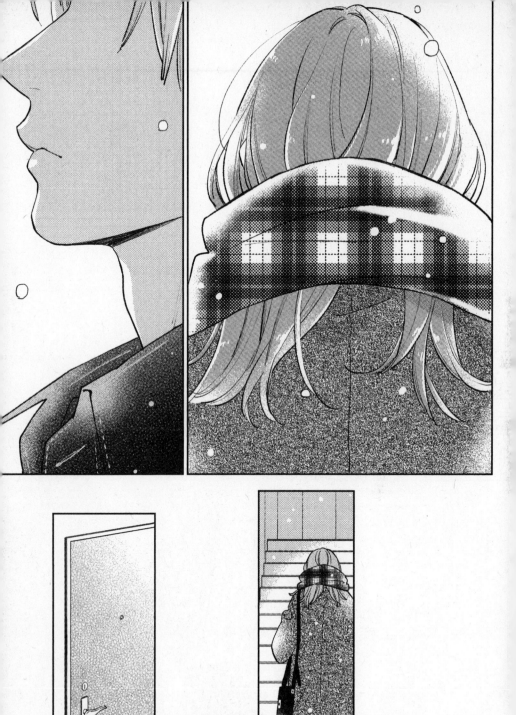

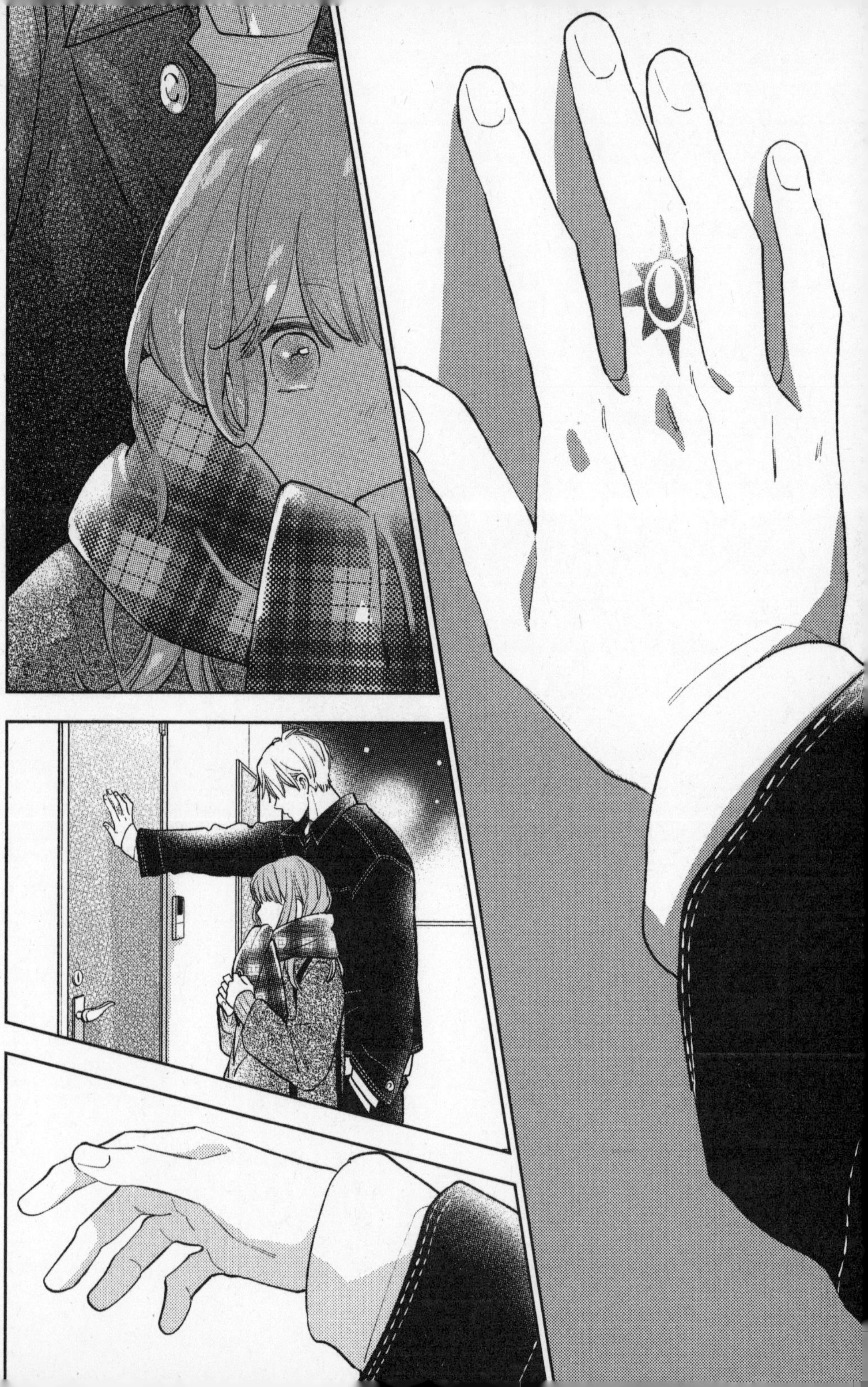

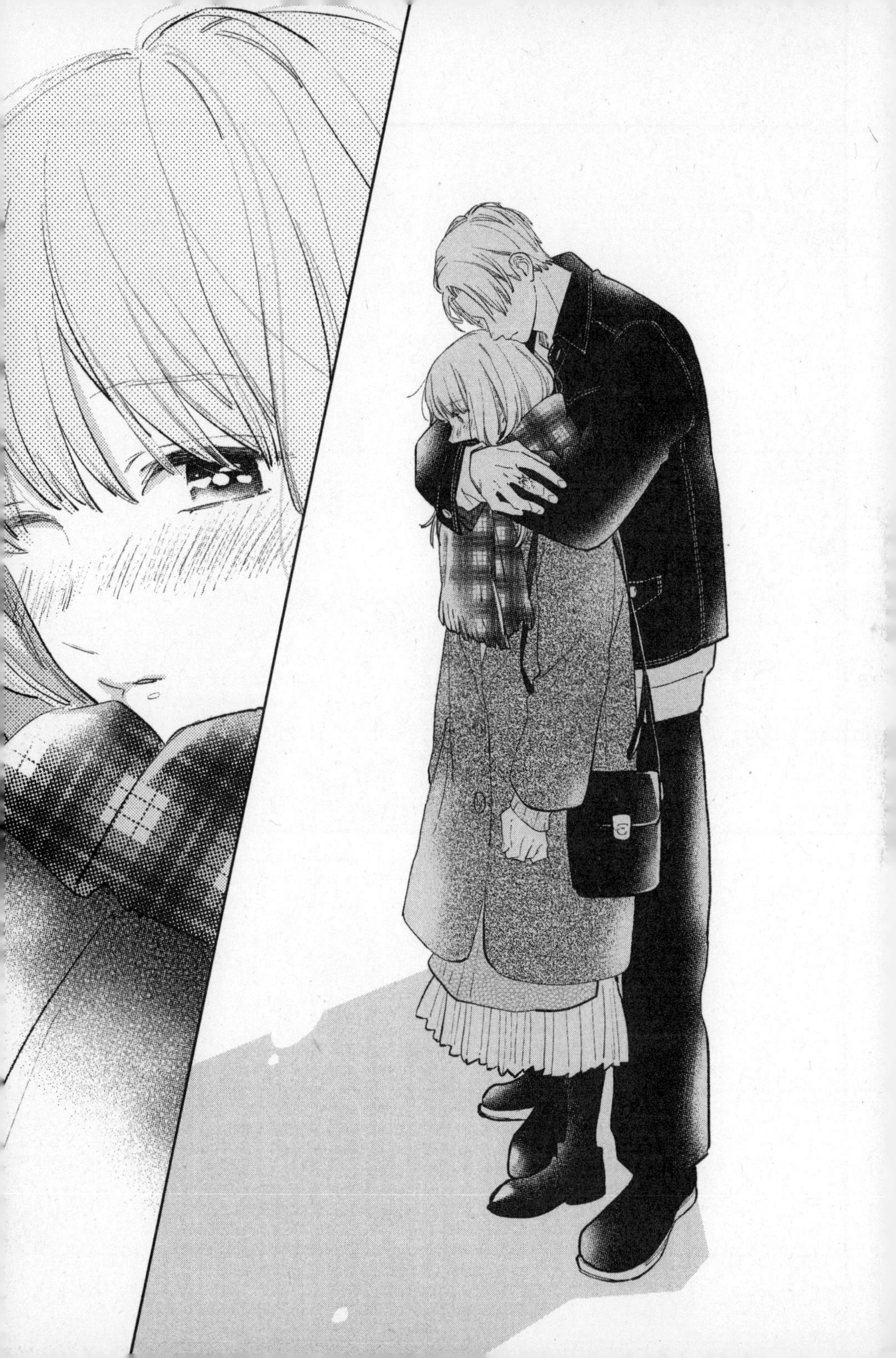

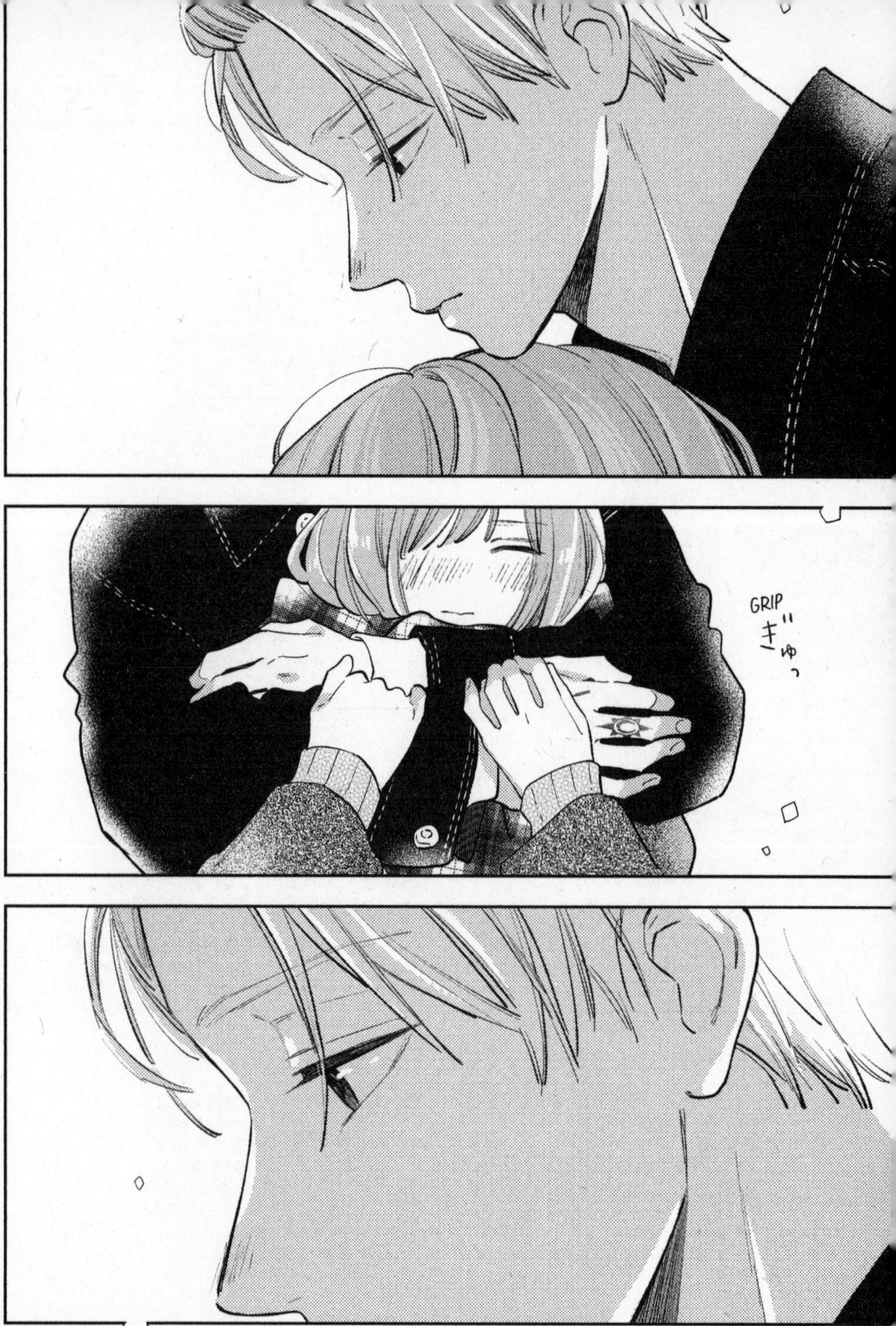
GRIP
ぎゅっ

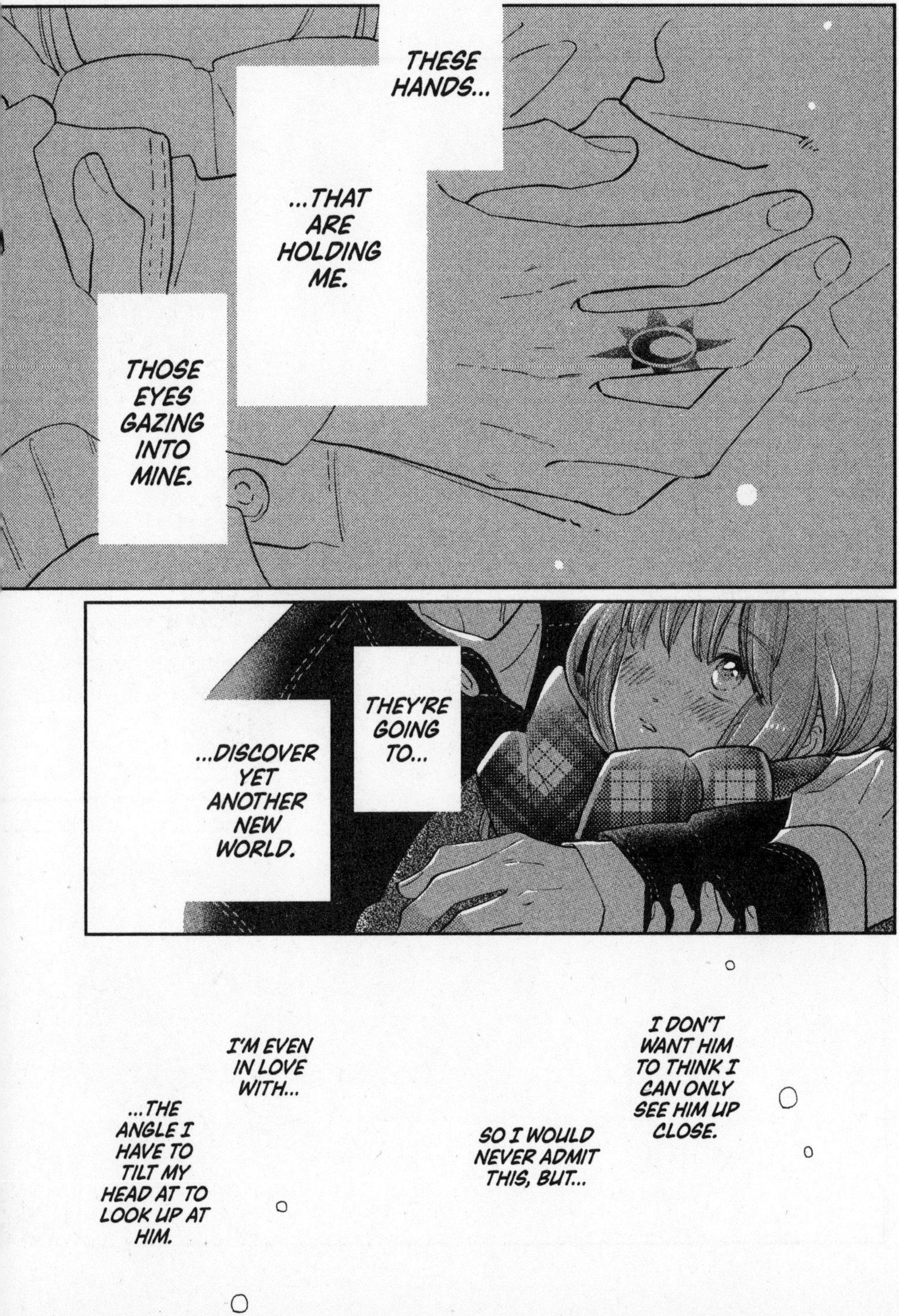
THESE HANDS...
...THAT ARE HOLDING ME.
THOSE EYES GAZING INTO MINE.
THEY'RE GOING TO...
...DISCOVER YET ANOTHER NEW WORLD.
I DON'T WANT HIM TO THINK I CAN ONLY SEE HIM UP CLOSE.
SO I WOULD NEVER ADMIT THIS, BUT...
I'M EVEN IN LOVE WITH...
...THE ANGLE I HAVE TO TILT MY HEAD AT TO LOOK UP AT HIM.

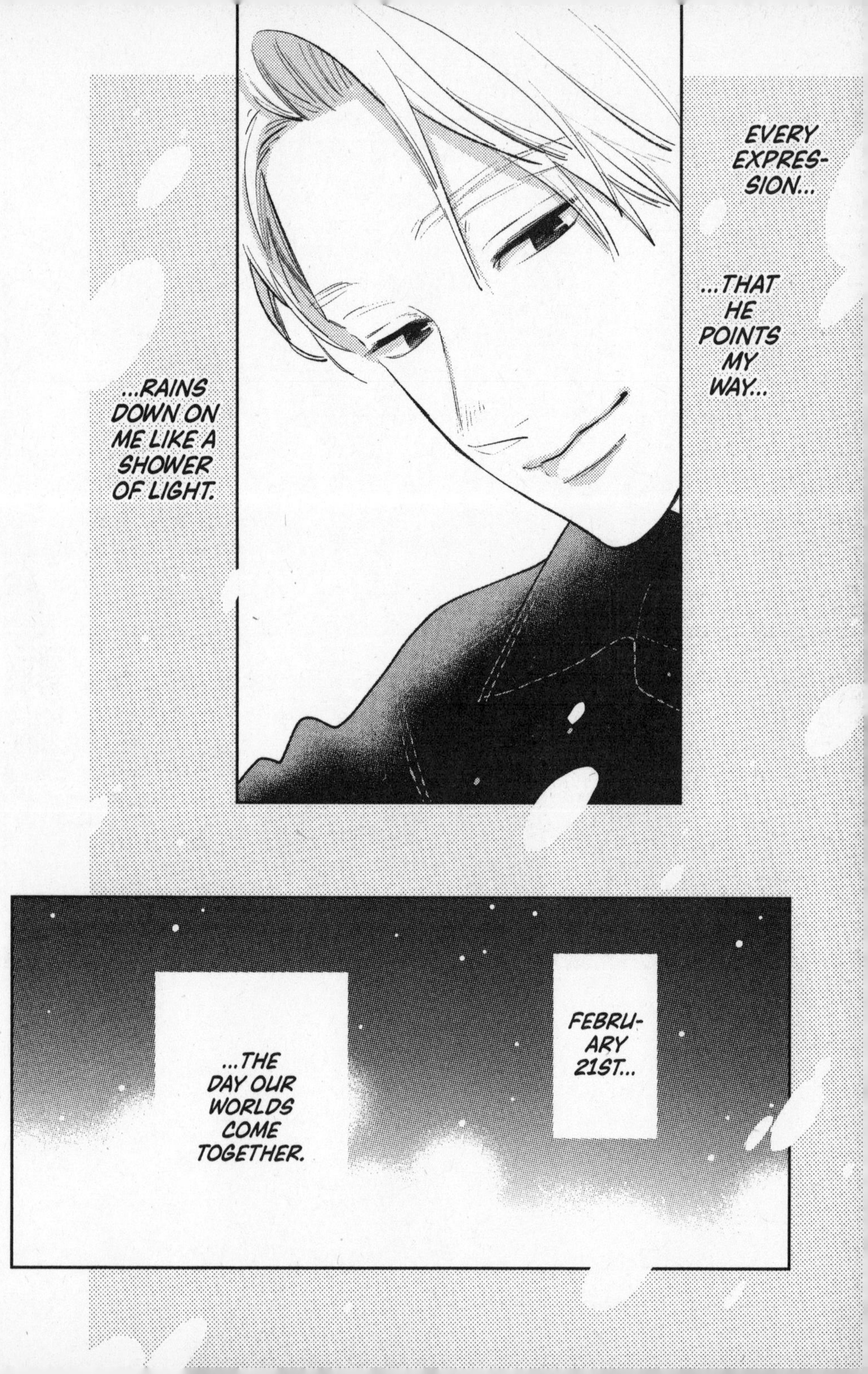
EVERY EXPRES-SION...
...THAT HE POINTS MY WAY...
...RAINS DOWN ON ME LIKE A SHOWER OF LIGHT.
FEBRU-ARY 21ST...
...THE DAY OUR WORLDS COME TOGETHER.

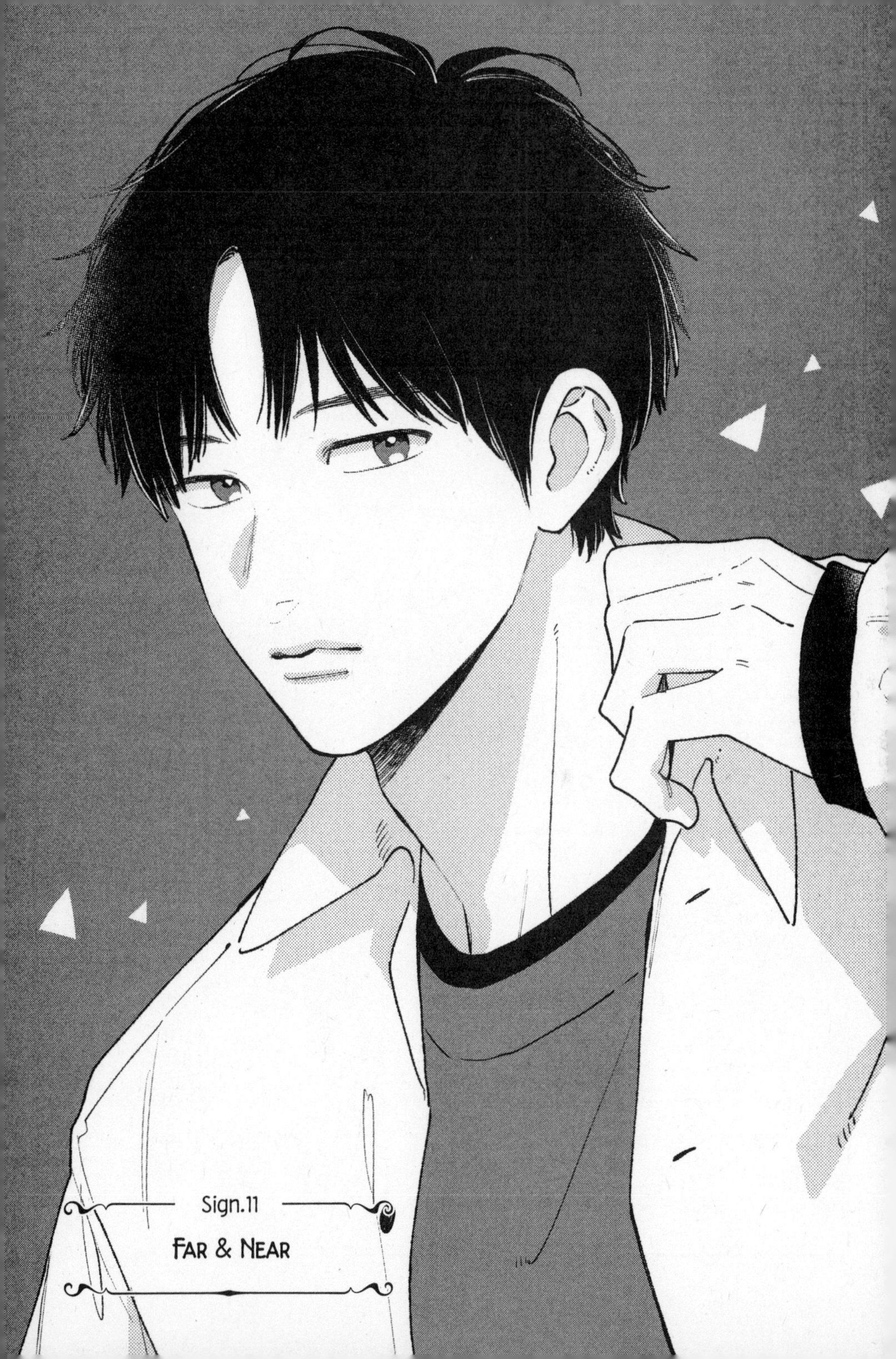
Sign.11
FAR & NEAR

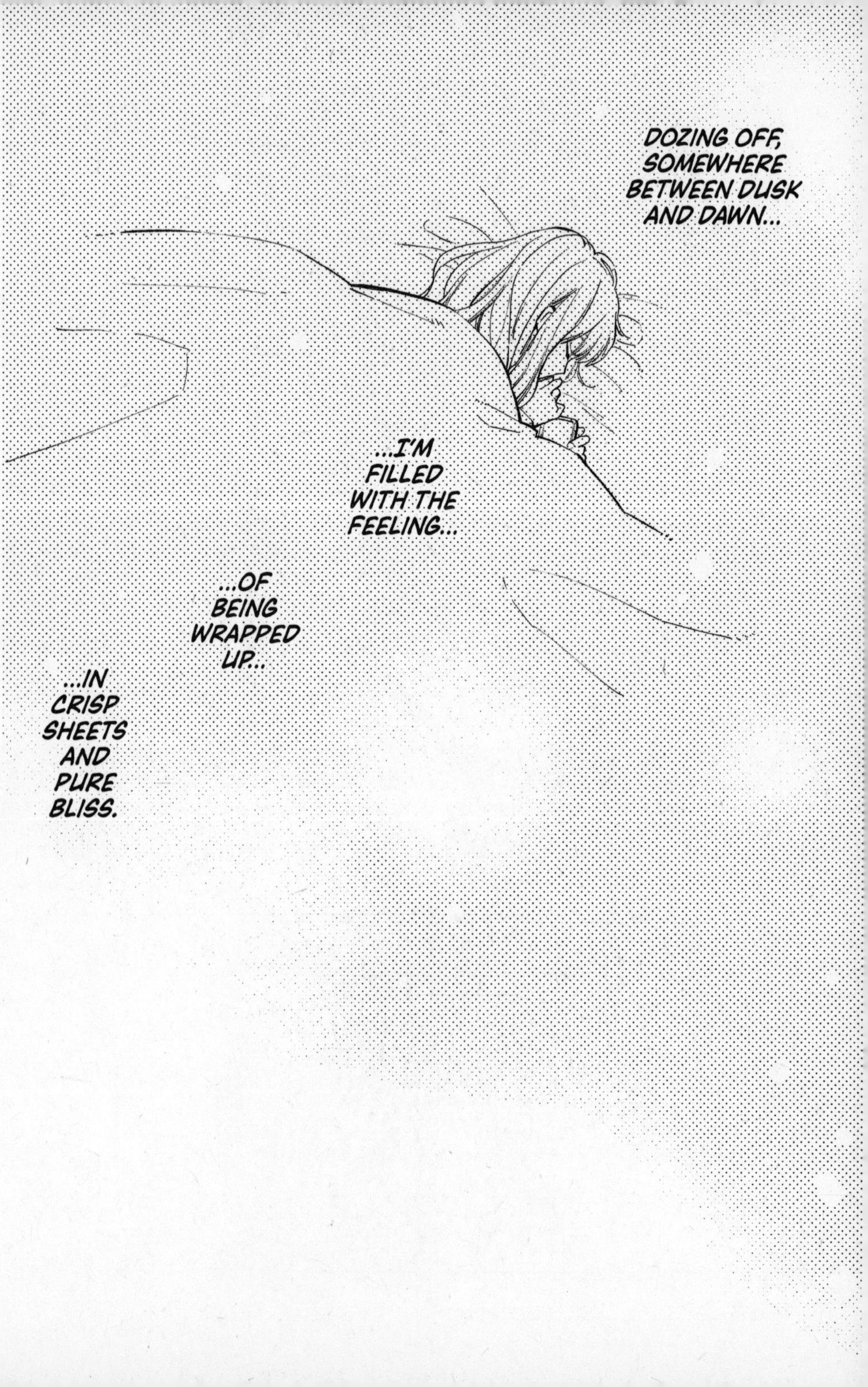
DOZING OFF, SOMEWHERE BETWEEN DUSK AND DAWN...
...I'M FILLED WITH THE FEELING...
...OF BEING WRAPPED UP...
...IN CRISP SHEETS AND PURE BLISS.

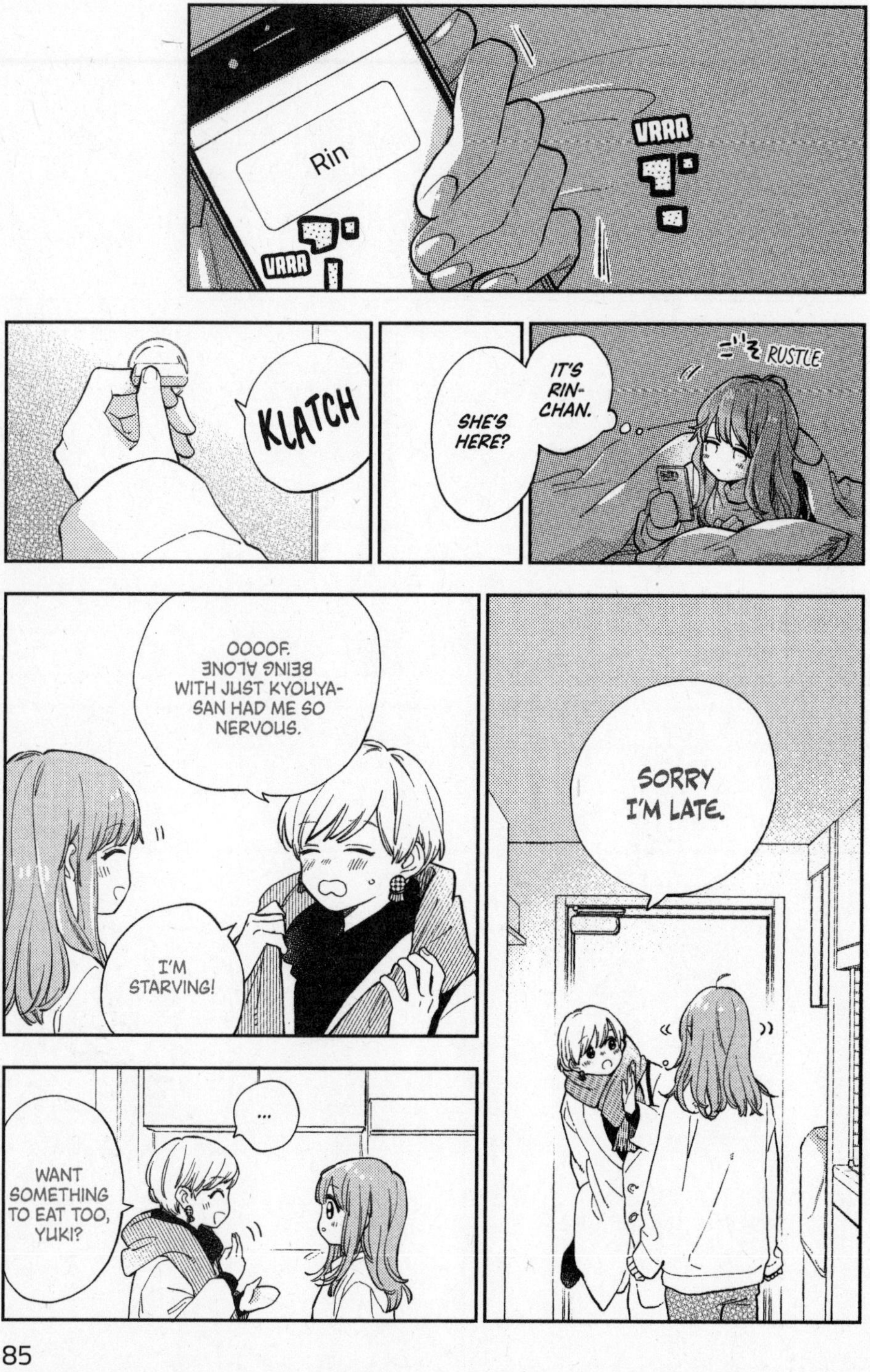
Rin
VRRR
VRRR
RUSTLE
IT'S RIN-CHAN.
SHE'S HERE?
KLATCH
SORRY I'M LATE.
OOOOF. BEING ALONE WITH JUST KYOUYA-SAN HAD ME SO NERVOUS.
I'M STARVING!
...
WANT SOMETHING TO EAT TOO, YUKI?

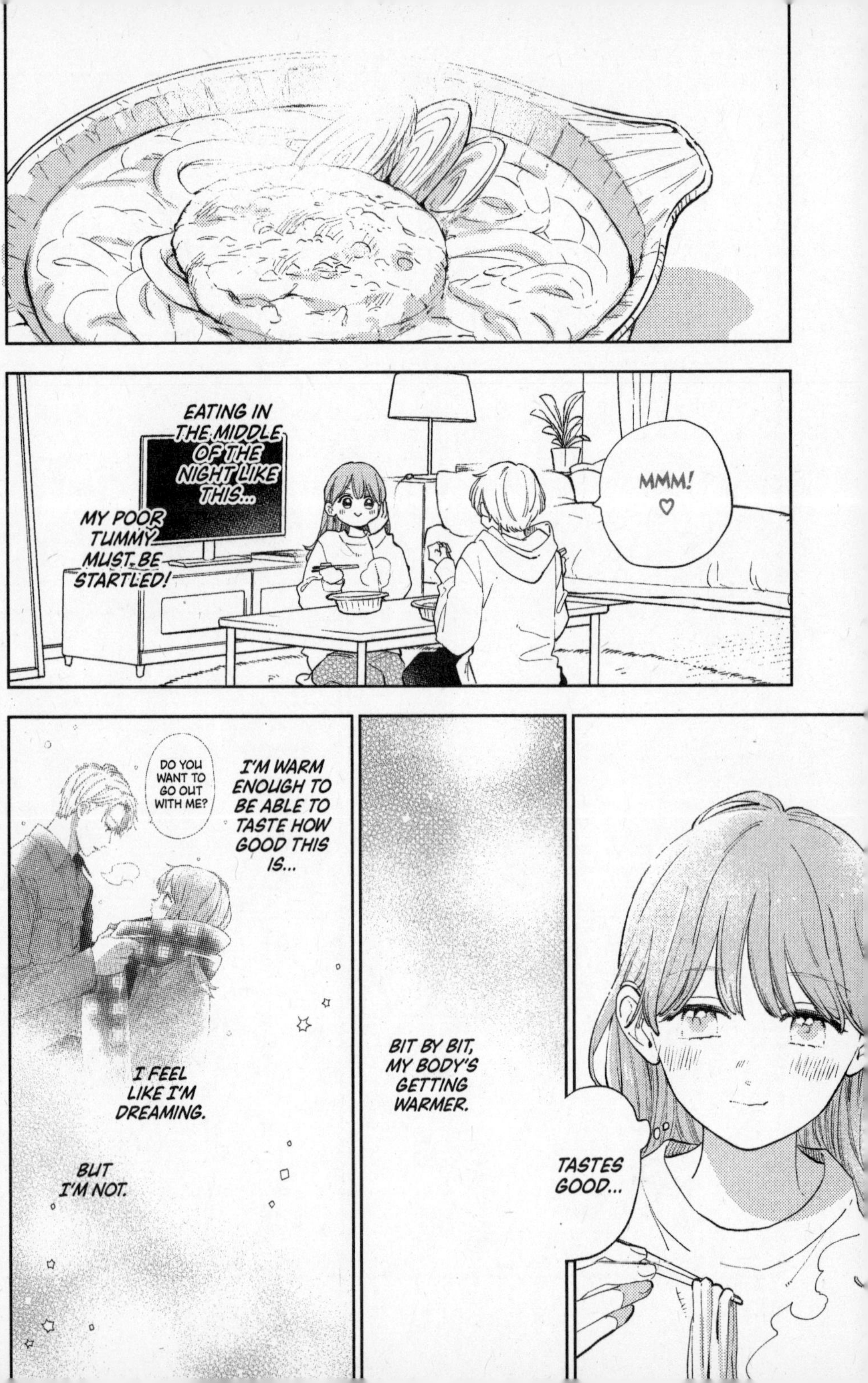
MMM! ♡
EATING IN THE MIDDLE OF THE NIGHT LIKE THIS...
MY POOR TUMMY MUST BE STARTLED!
TASTES GOOD...
BIT BY BIT, MY BODY'S GETTING WARMER.
I'M WARM ENOUGH TO BE ABLE TO TASTE HOW GOOD THIS IS...
DO YOU WANT TO GO OUT WITH ME?
I FEEL LIKE I'M DREAMING.
BUT I'M NOT.

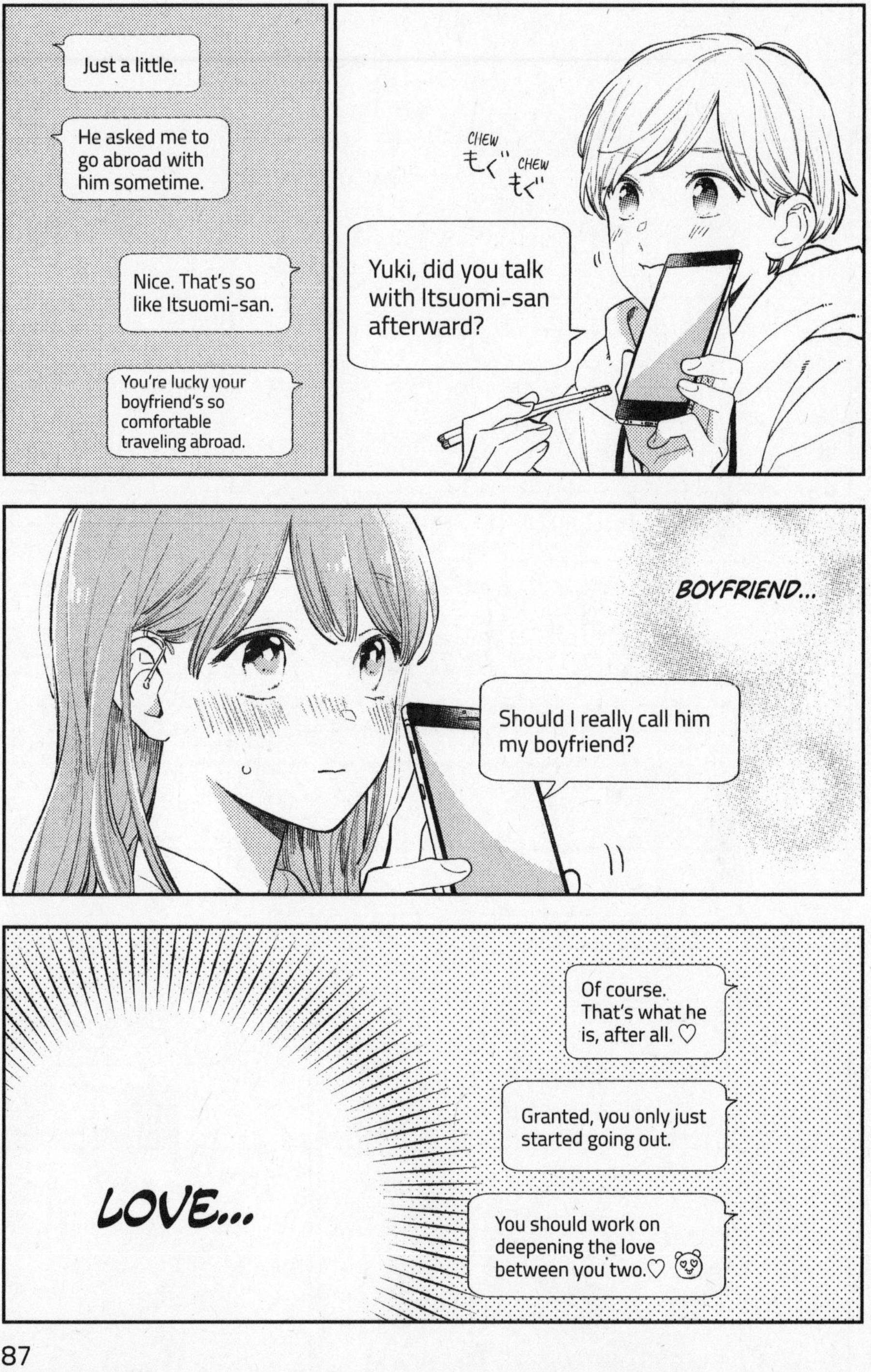
CHEW
もぐ
CHEW
もぐ
Yuki, did you talk with Itsuomi-san afterward?
Just a little.
He asked me to go abroad with him sometime.
Nice. That's so like Itsuomi-san.
You're lucky your boyfriend's so comfortable traveling abroad.
BOYFRIEND...
Should I really call him my boyfriend?
Of course. That's what he is, after all. ♡
Granted, you only just started going out.
You should work on deepening the love between you two.♡
LOVE...

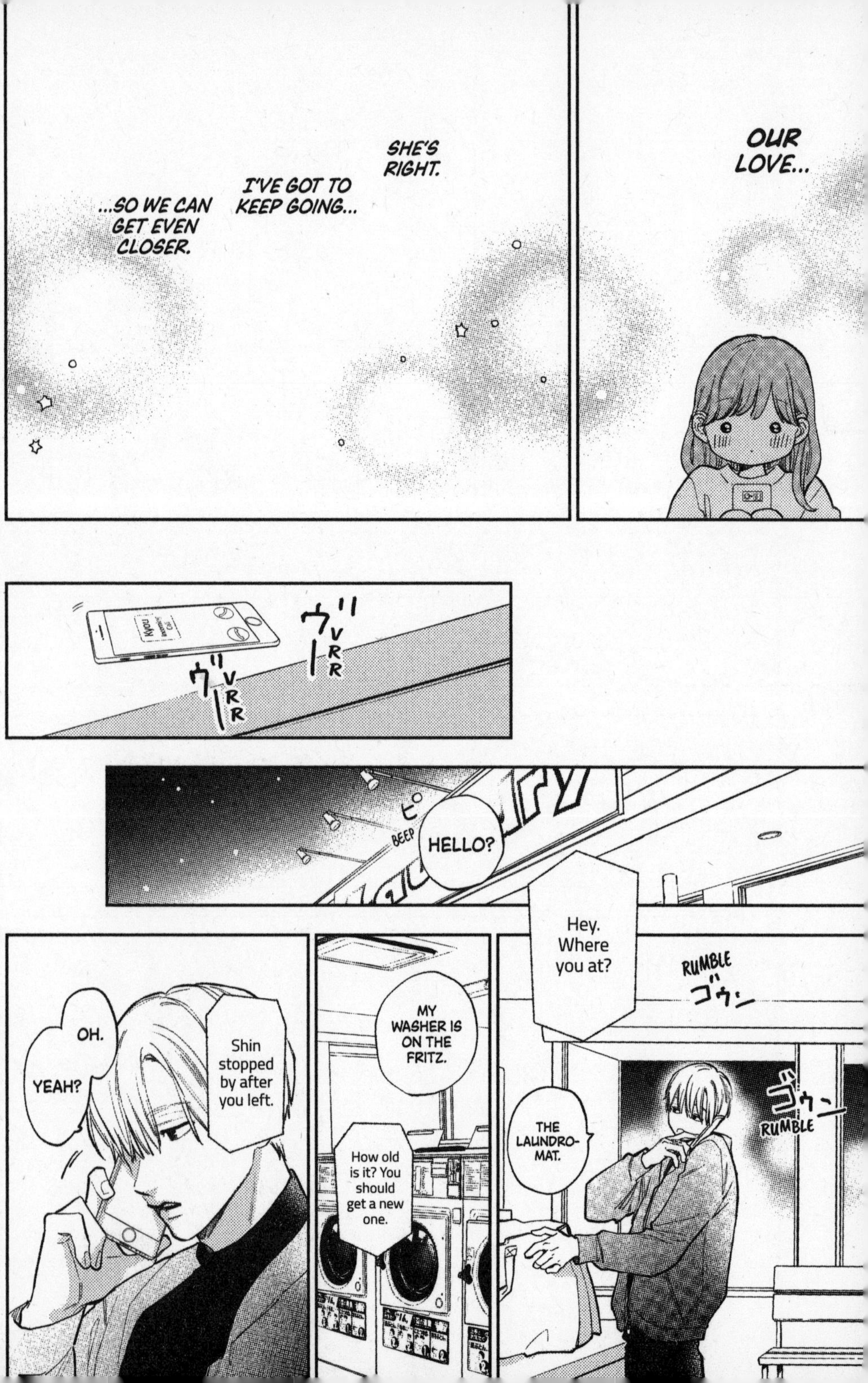
OUR LOVE...
SHE'S RIGHT.
I'VE GOT TO KEEP GOING...
...SO WE CAN GET EVEN CLOSER.
ヴー VRR
ヴー VRR
ピ BEEP
HELLO?
Hey. Where you at?
RUMBLE ゴウン
ゴウン RUMBLE
THE LAUNDROMAT.
MY WASHER IS ON THE FRITZ.
How old is it? You should get a new one.
Shin stopped by after you left.
OH.
YEAH?

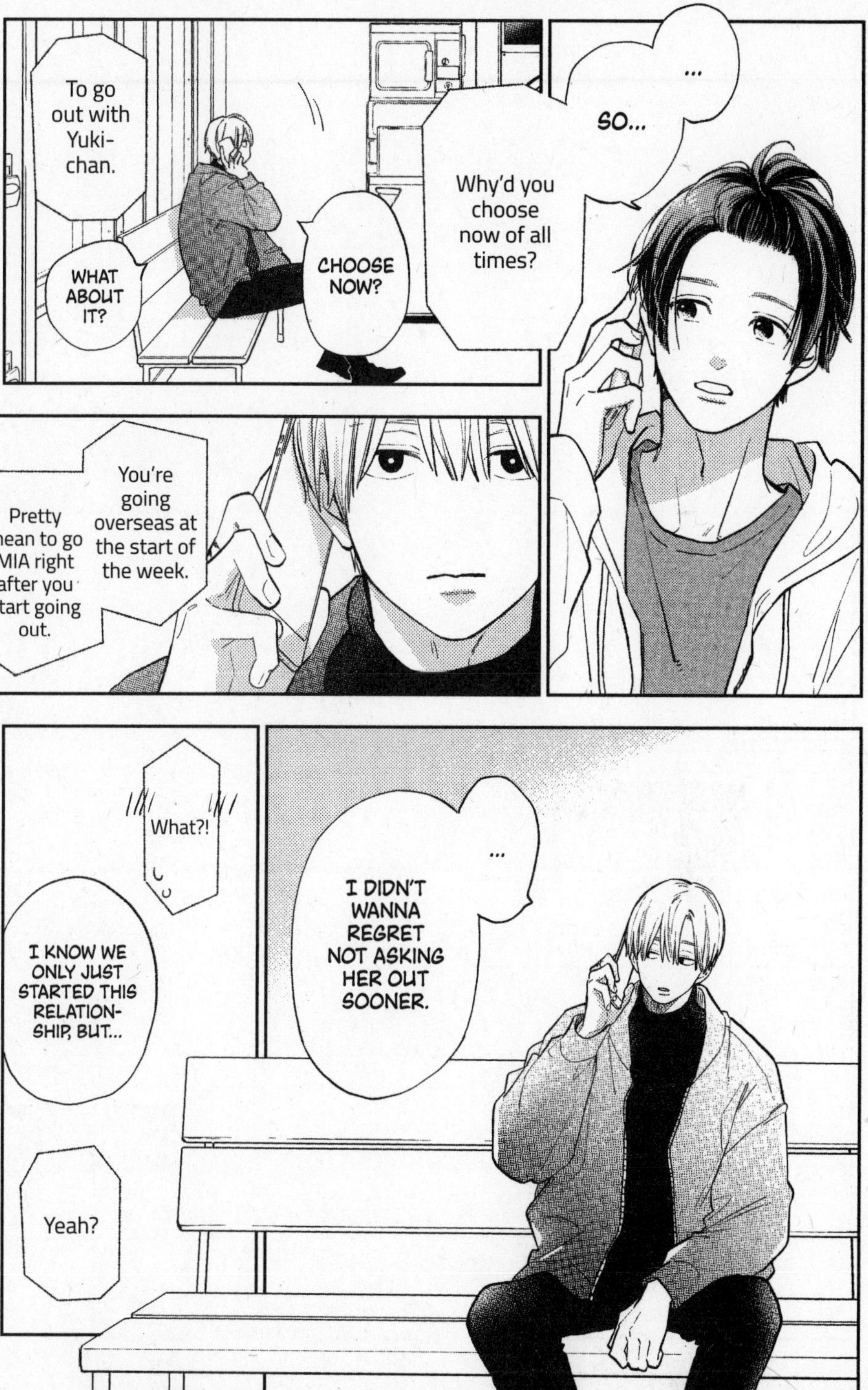
...
SO...
Why'd you choose now of all times?
CHOOSE NOW?
To go out with Yuki-chan.
WHAT ABOUT IT?
You're going overseas at the start of the week.
Pretty mean to go MIA right after you start going out.
...
I DIDN'T WANNA REGRET NOT ASKING HER OUT SOONER.
What?!
I KNOW WE ONLY JUST STARTED THIS RELATION-SHIP, BUT...
Yeah?

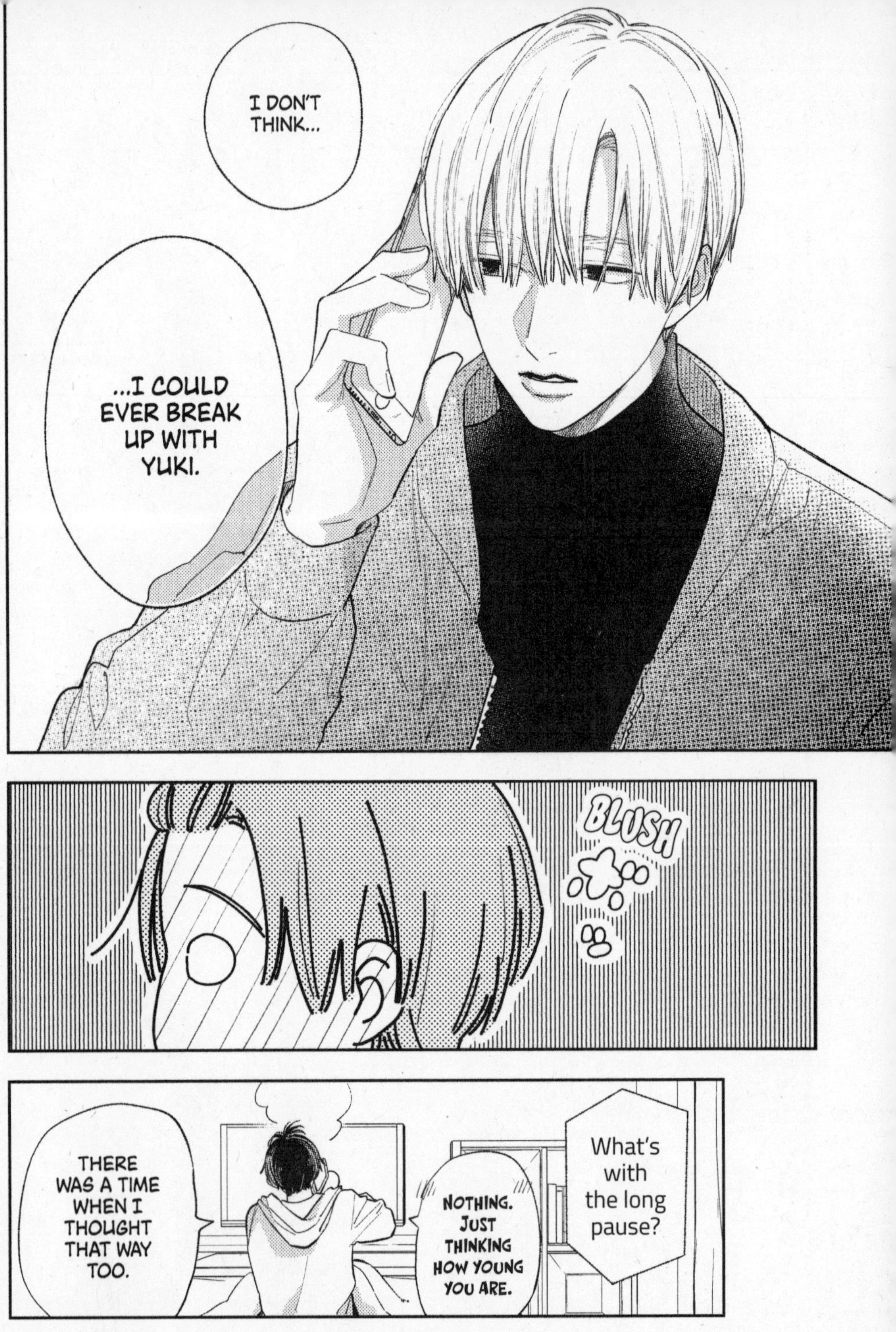
I DON'T THINK...
...I COULD EVER BREAK UP WITH YUKI.
BLUSH
What's with the long pause?
NOTHING. JUST THINKING HOW YOUNG YOU ARE.
THERE WAS A TIME WHEN I THOUGHT THAT WAY TOO.

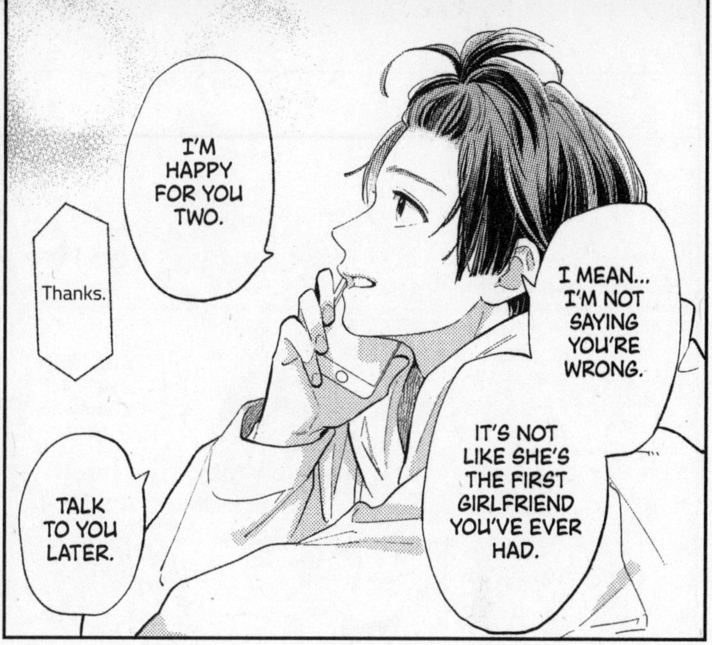
I MEAN... I'M NOT SAYING YOU'RE WRONG.
IT'S NOT LIKE SHE'S THE FIRST GIRLFRIEND YOU'VE EVER HAD.
I'M HAPPY FOR YOU TWO.
Thanks.
TALK TO YOU LATER.
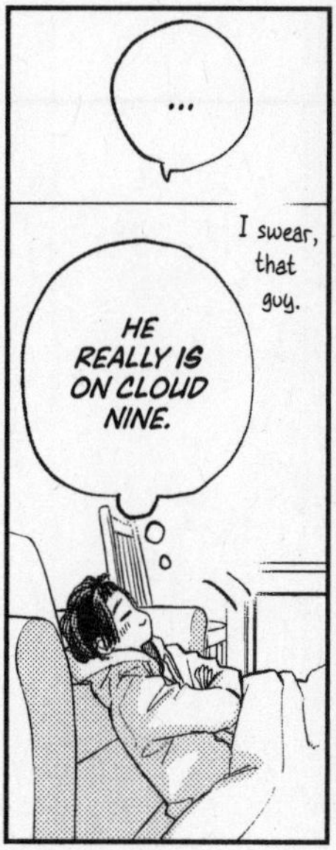
...
I swear, that guy.
HE REALLY IS ON CLOUD NINE.
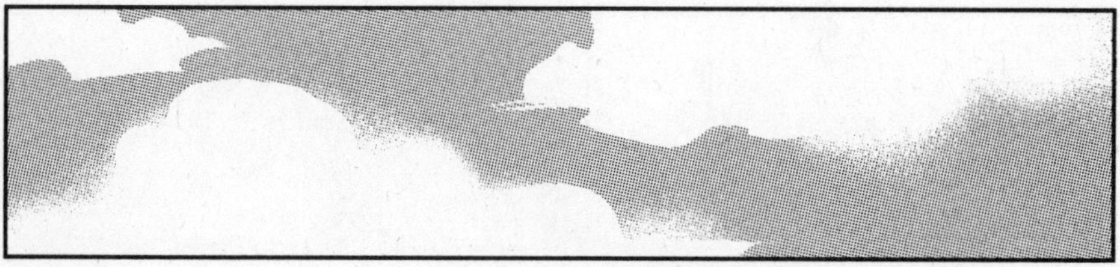
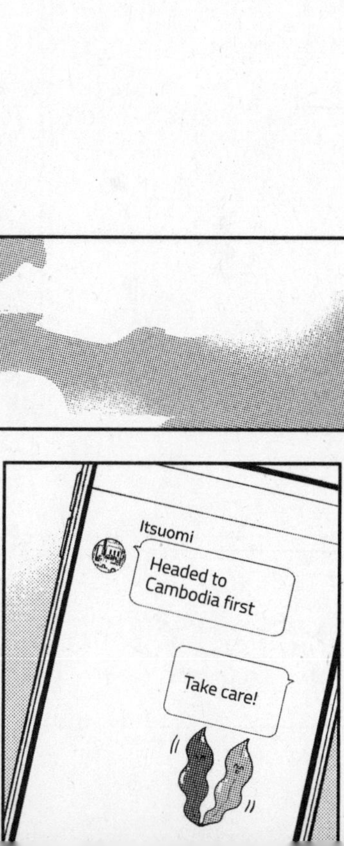
Itsuomi
Headed to Cambodia first
Take care!
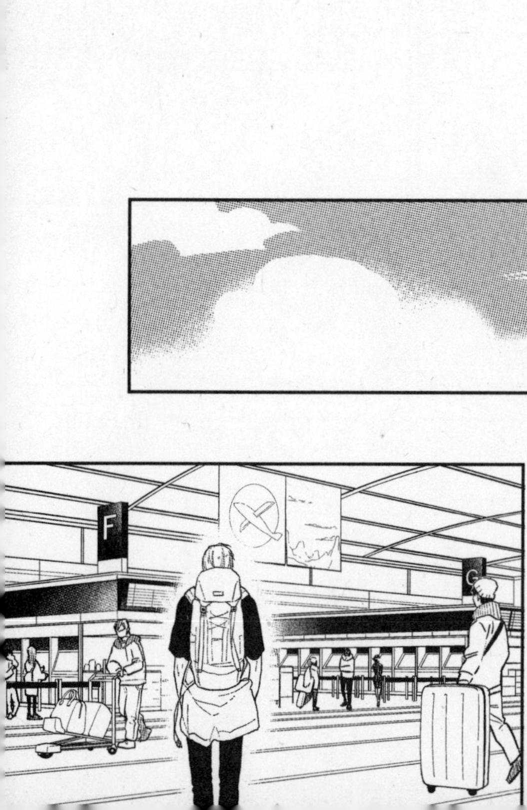
F
G

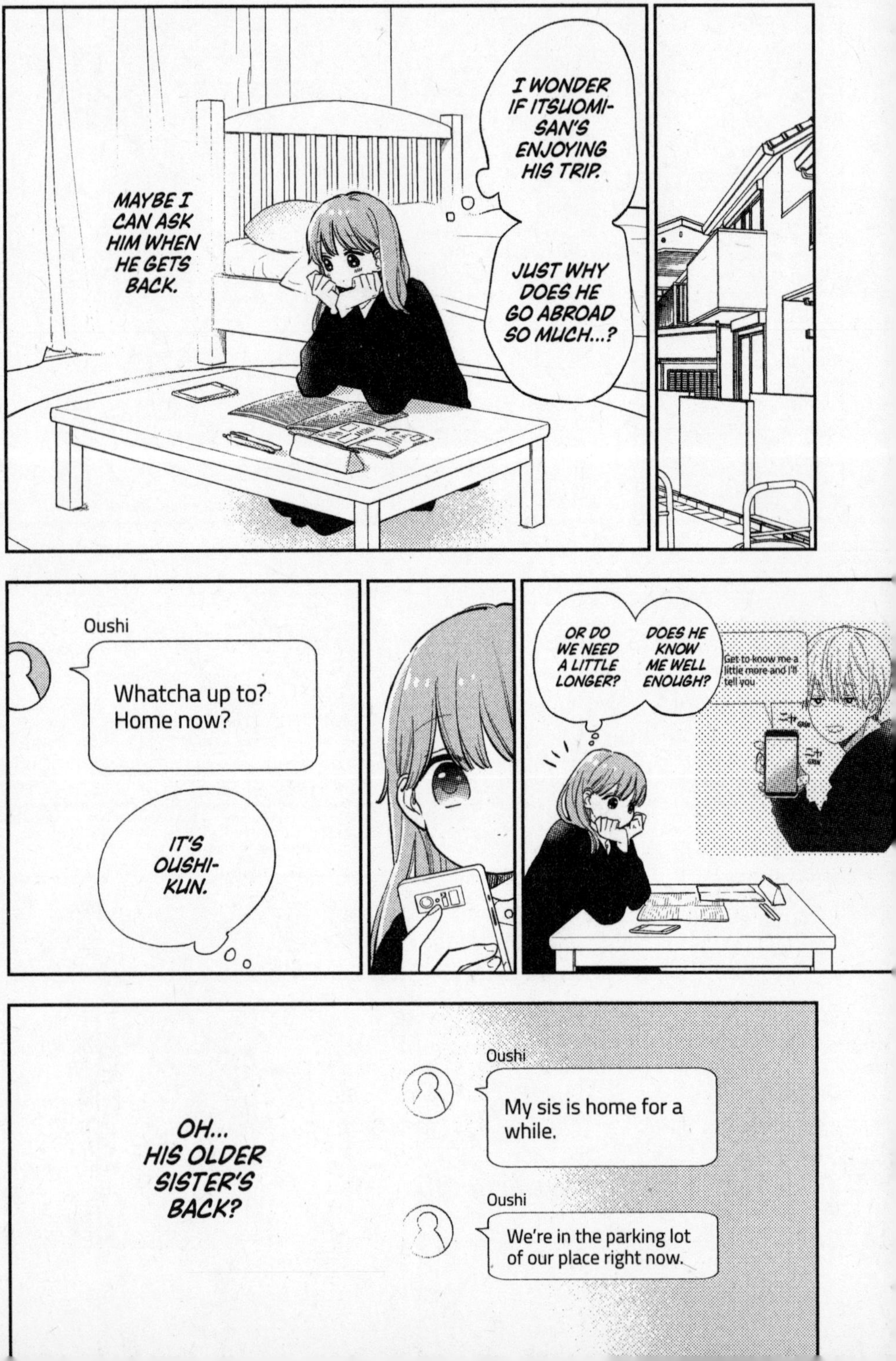
I WONDER IF ITSUOMI-SAN'S ENJOYING HIS TRIP.
JUST WHY DOES HE GO ABROAD SO MUCH...?
MAYBE I CAN ASK HIM WHEN HE GETS BACK.
DOES HE KNOW ME WELL ENOUGH?
OR DO WE NEED A LITTLE LONGER?
Get to know me a little more and I'll tell you
Oushi
Whatcha up to? Home now?
IT'S OUSHI-KUN.
Oushi
My sis is home for a while.
Oushi
We're in the parking lot of our place right now.
OH... HIS OLDER SISTER'S BACK?

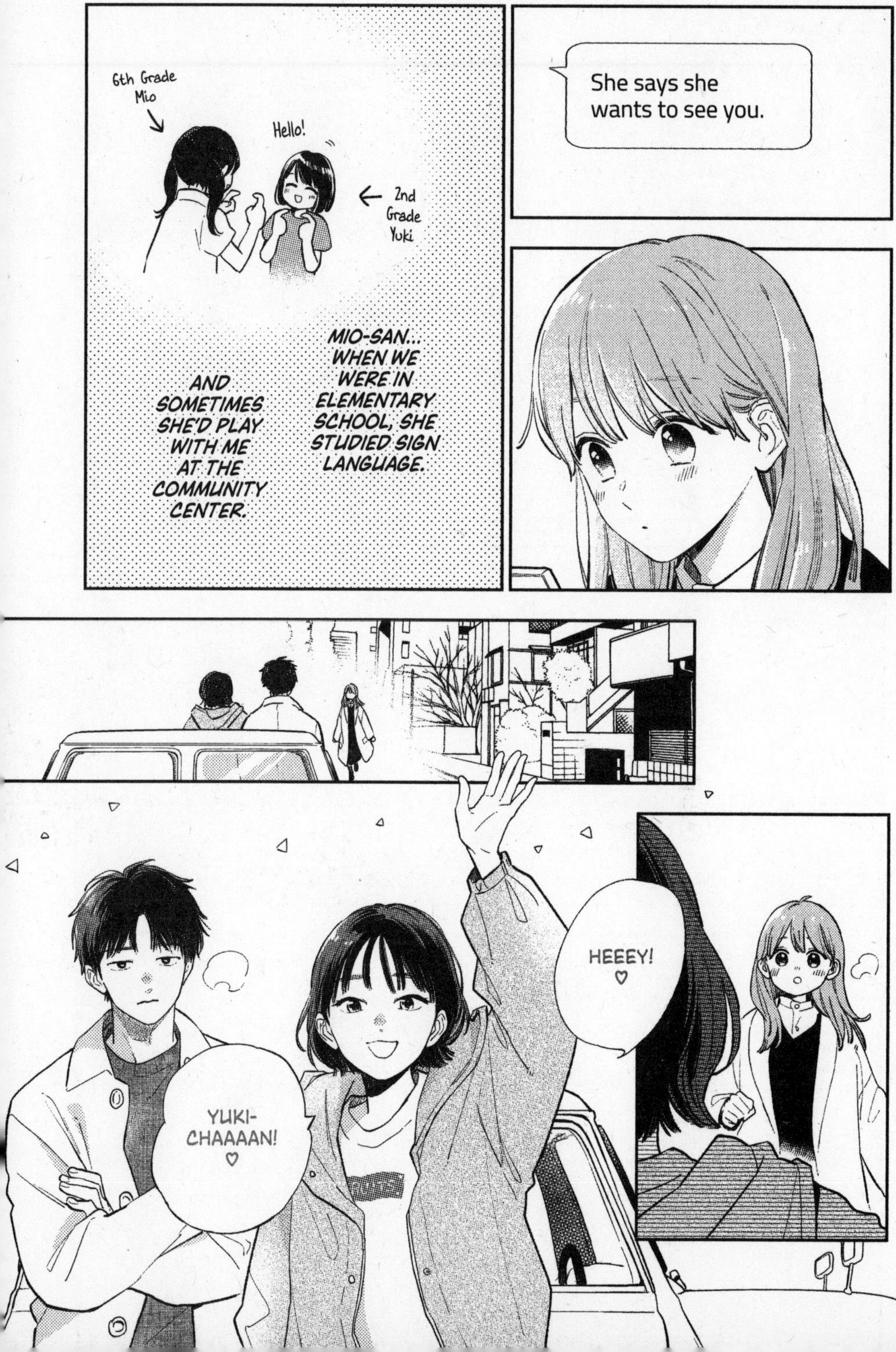
She says she wants to see you.
MIO-SAN... WHEN WE WERE IN ELEMENTARY SCHOOL, SHE STUDIED SIGN LANGUAGE.
AND SOMETIMES SHE'D PLAY WITH ME AT THE COMMUNITY CENTER.
6th Grade Mio
Hello!
2nd Grade Yuki
HEEEY! ♡
YUKI-CHAAAAN! ♡

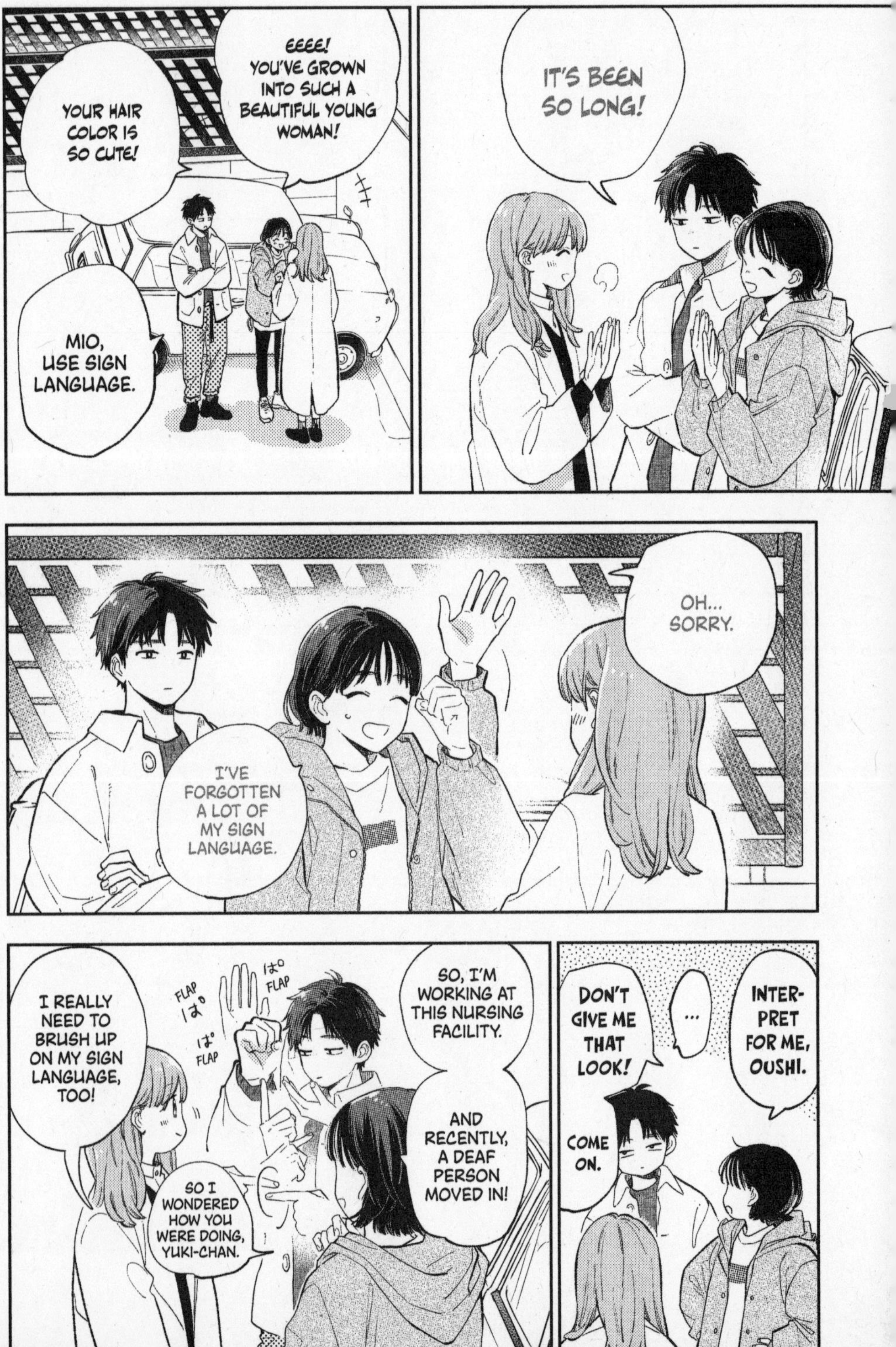
IT'S BEEN SO LONG!
EEEE! YOU'VE GROWN INTO SUCH A BEAUTIFUL YOUNG WOMAN!
YOUR HAIR COLOR IS SO CUTE!
MIO, USE SIGN LANGUAGE.
OH... SORRY.
I'VE FORGOTTEN A LOT OF MY SIGN LANGUAGE.
INTERPRET FOR ME, OUSHI.
...
DON'T GIVE ME THAT LOOK!
COME ON.
SO, I'M WORKING AT THIS NURSING FACILITY.
AND RECENTLY, A DEAF PERSON MOVED IN!
ぱ FLAP
ぱ FLAP
ぱ FLAP
I REALLY NEED TO BRUSH UP ON MY SIGN LANGUAGE, TOO!
SO I WONDERED HOW YOU WERE DOING, YUKI-CHAN.

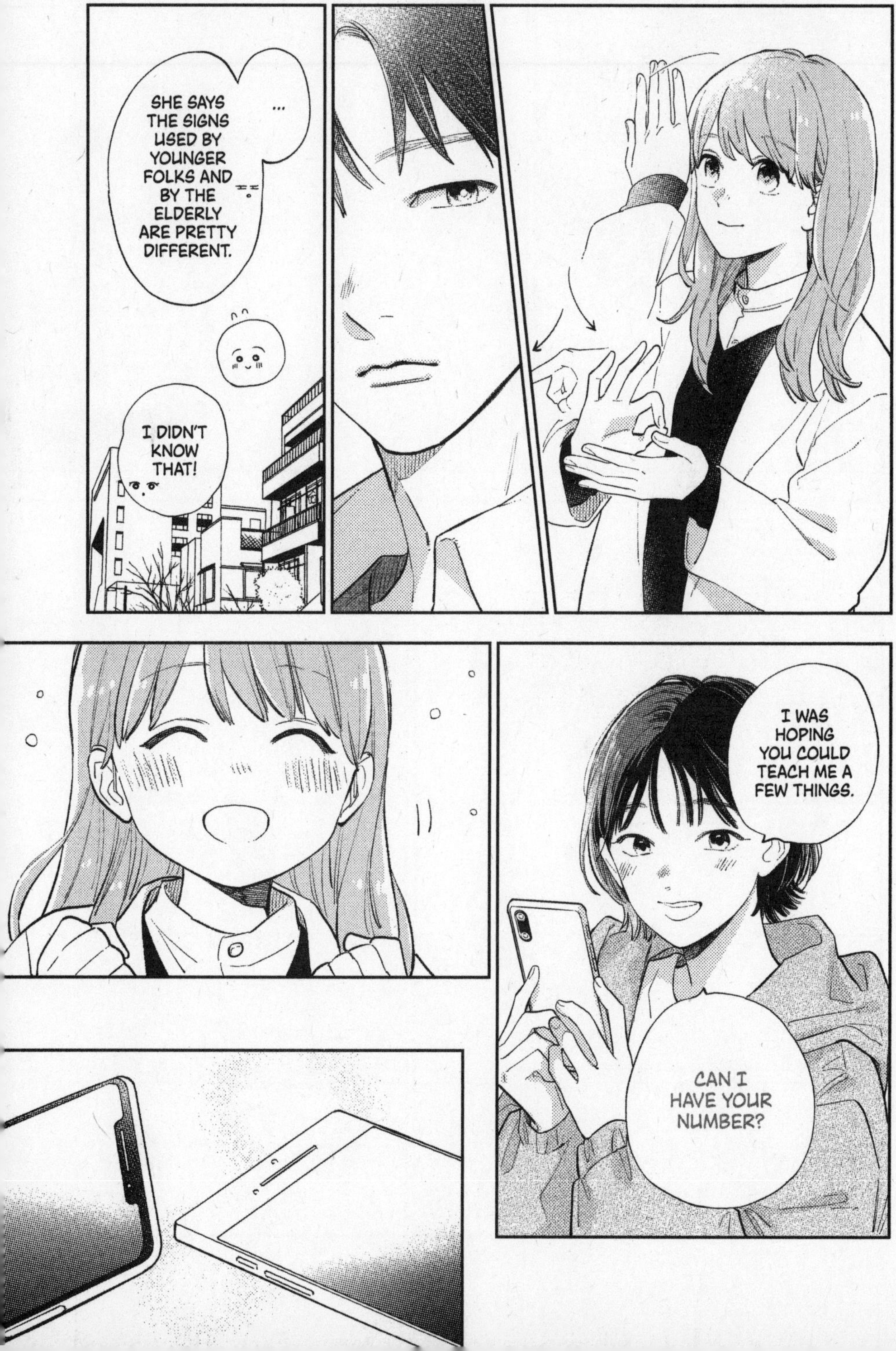
SHE SAYS THE SIGNS USED BY YOUNGER FOLKS AND BY THE ELDERLY ARE PRETTY DIFFERENT.
...
I DIDN'T KNOW THAT!
I WAS HOPING YOU COULD TEACH ME A FEW THINGS.
CAN I HAVE YOUR NUMBER?

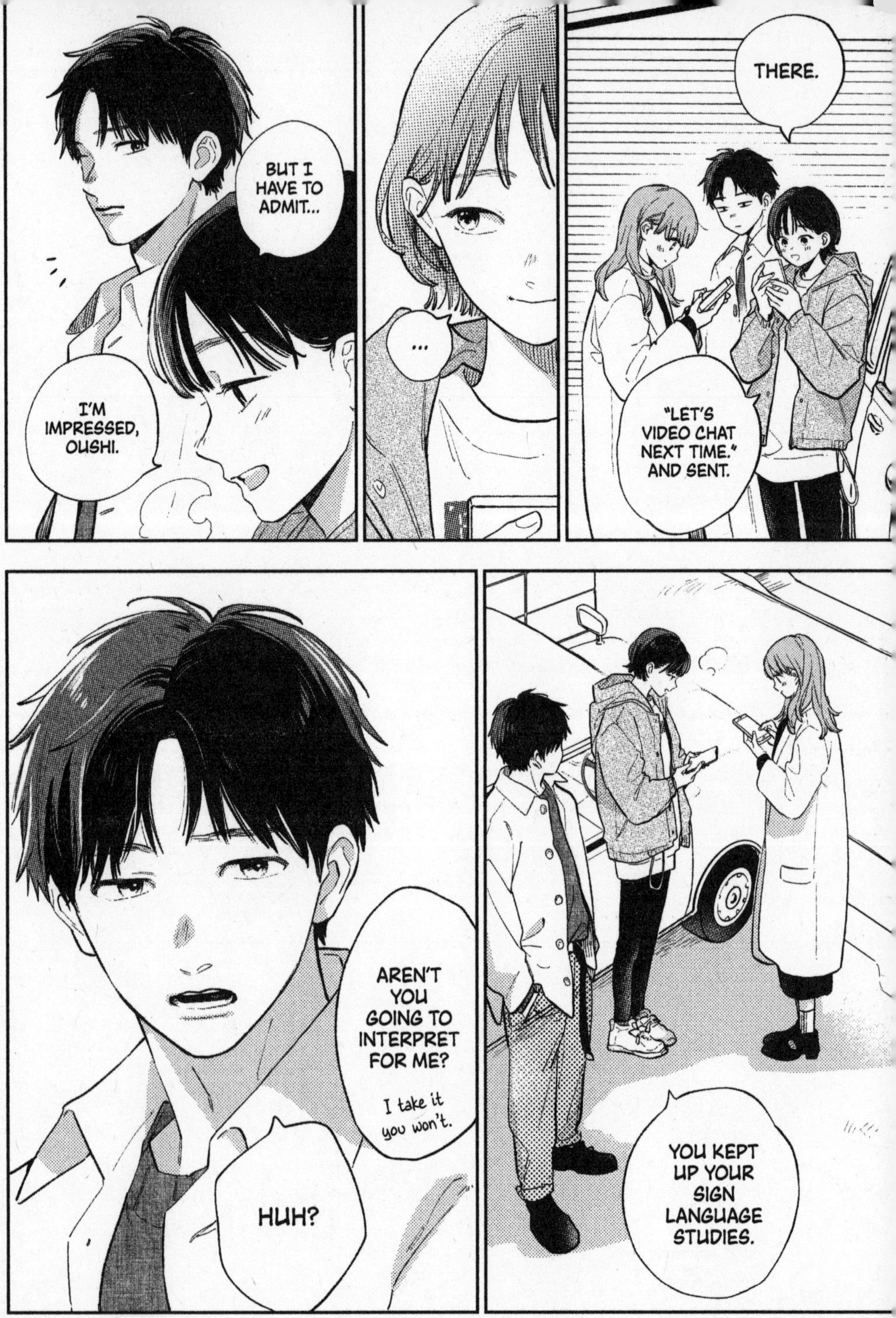
THERE.
"LET'S VIDEO CHAT NEXT TIME." AND SENT.
...
BUT I HAVE TO ADMIT...
I'M IMPRESSED, OUSHI.
YOU KEPT UP YOUR SIGN LANGUAGE STUDIES.
AREN'T YOU GOING TO INTERPRET FOR ME?
I take it you won't.
HUH?

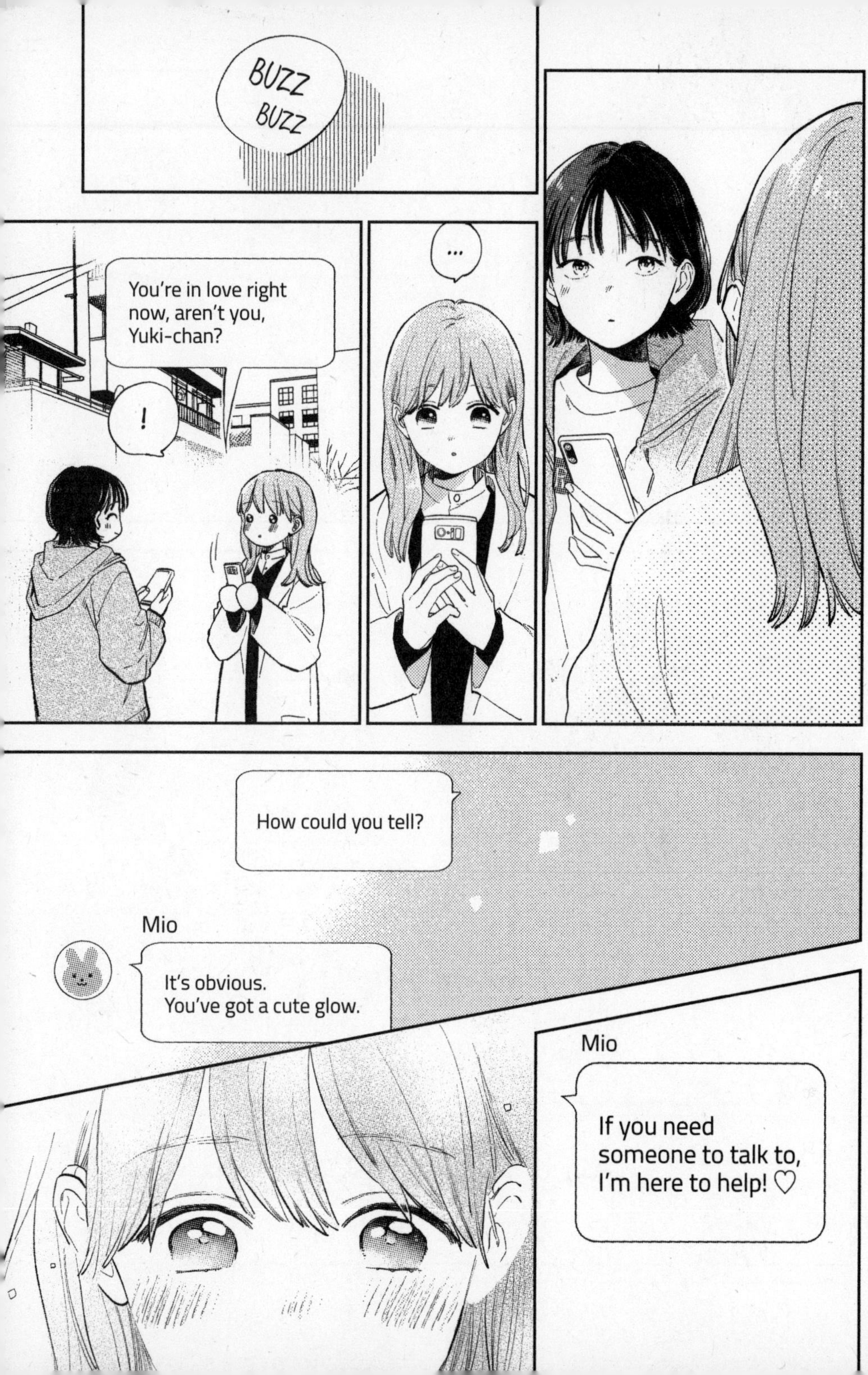
BUZZ BUZZ
...
You're in love right now, aren't you, Yuki-chan?
!
How could you tell?
Mio
It's obvious. You've got a cute glow.
Mio
If you need someone to talk to, I'm here to help! ♡

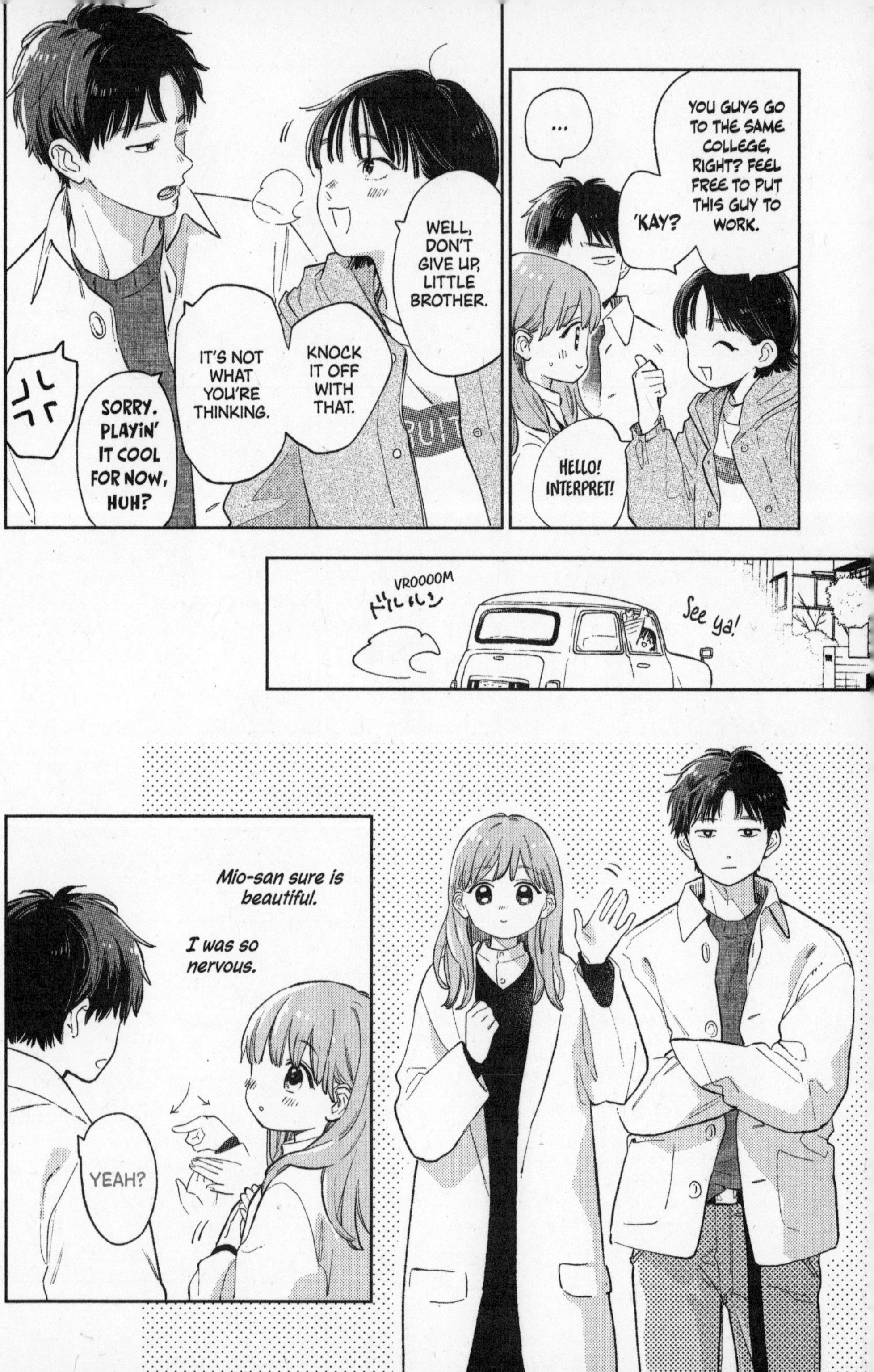
YOU GUYS GO TO THE SAME COLLEGE, RIGHT? FEEL FREE TO PUT THIS GUY TO WORK.
'KAY?
...
HELLO! INTERPRET!
WELL, DON'T GIVE UP, LITTLE BROTHER.
KNOCK IT OFF WITH THAT.
IT'S NOT WHAT YOU'RE THINKING.
SORRY. PLAYIN' IT COOL FOR NOW, HUH?
See ya!
VROOOOM
ドルルルン
Mio-san sure is beautiful.
I was so nervous.
YEAH?

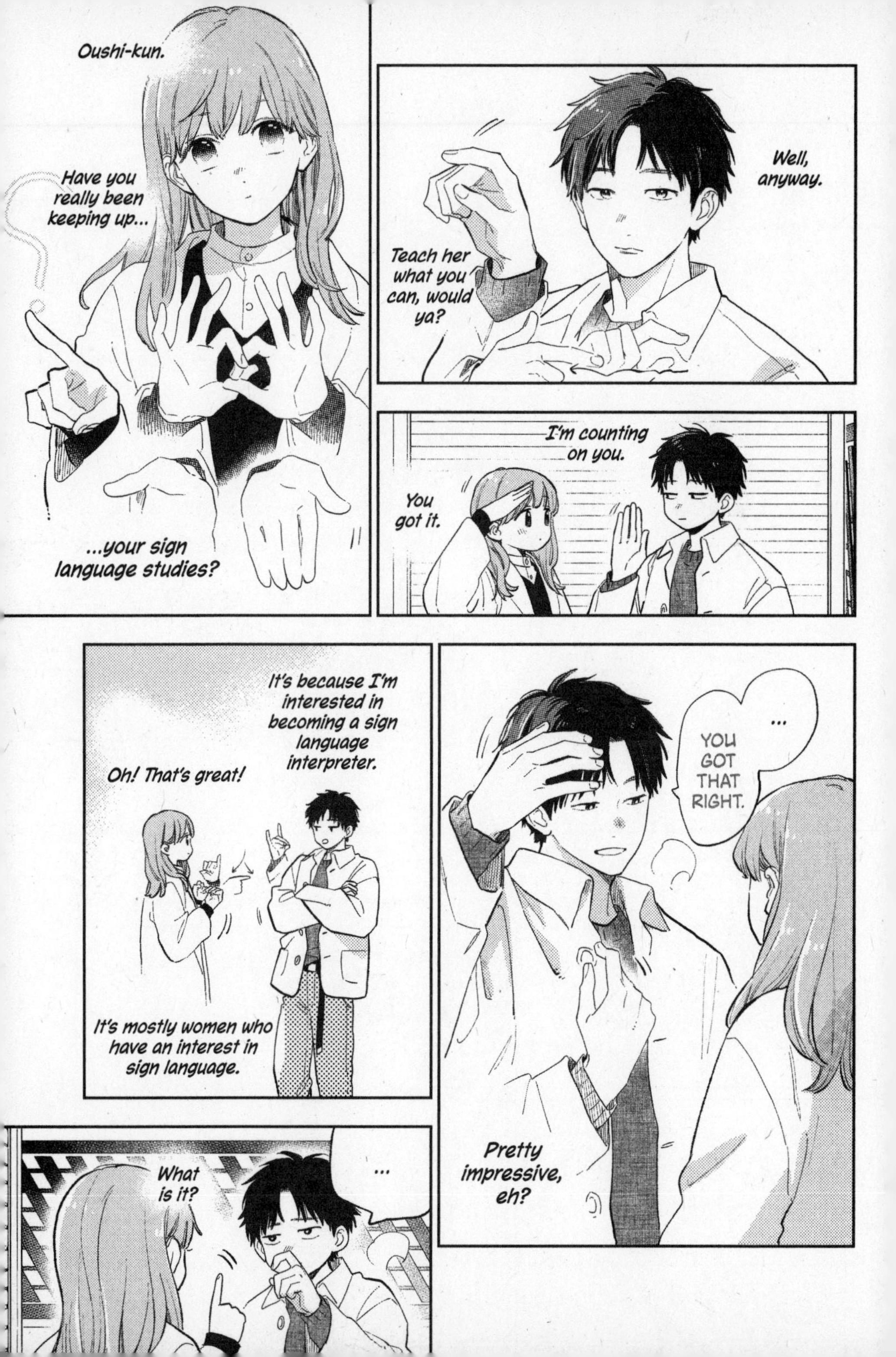

Well, anyway.
Teach her what you can, would ya?
I'm counting on you.
You got it.
Oushi-kun.
Have you really been keeping up...
...your sign language studies?
...
YOU GOT THAT RIGHT.
Pretty impressive, eh?
It's because I'm interested in becoming a sign language interpreter.
Oh! That's great!
It's mostly women who have an interest in sign language.
...
What is it?

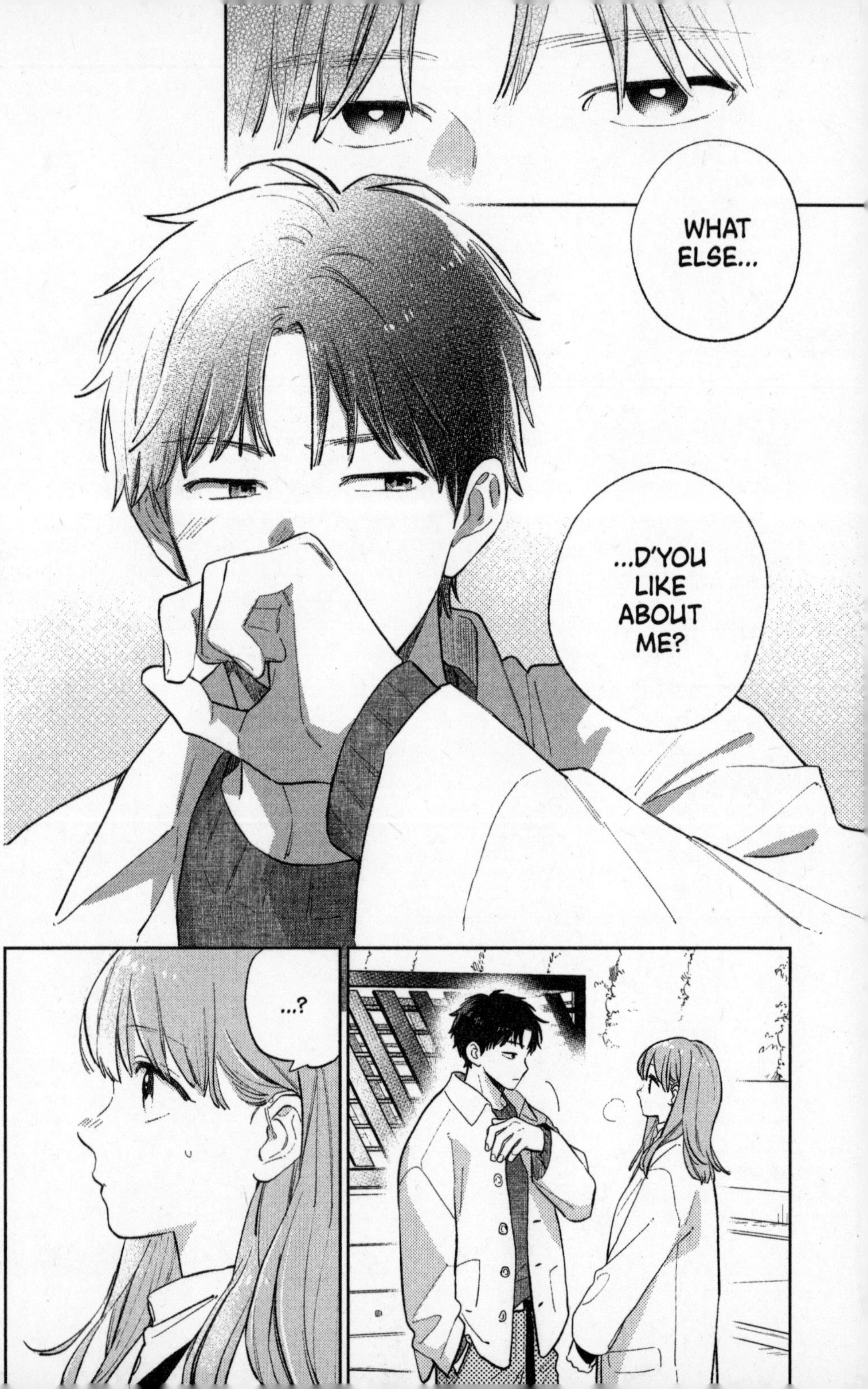
WHAT ELSE...
...D'YOU LIKE ABOUT ME?
...?

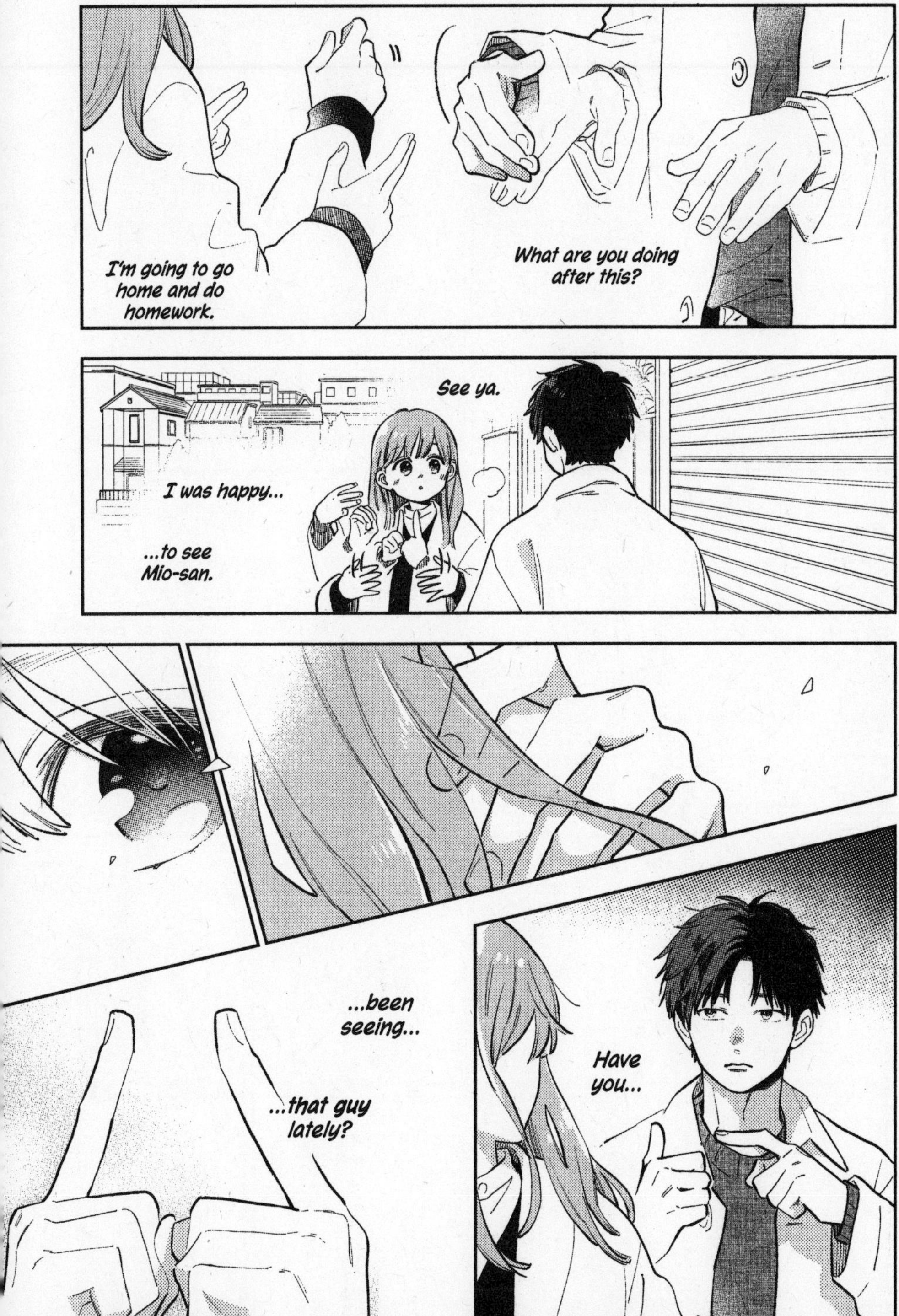
What are you doing after this?
I'm going to go home and do homework.
See ya.
I was happy...
...to see Mio-san.
Have you...
...been seeing...
...that guy lately?

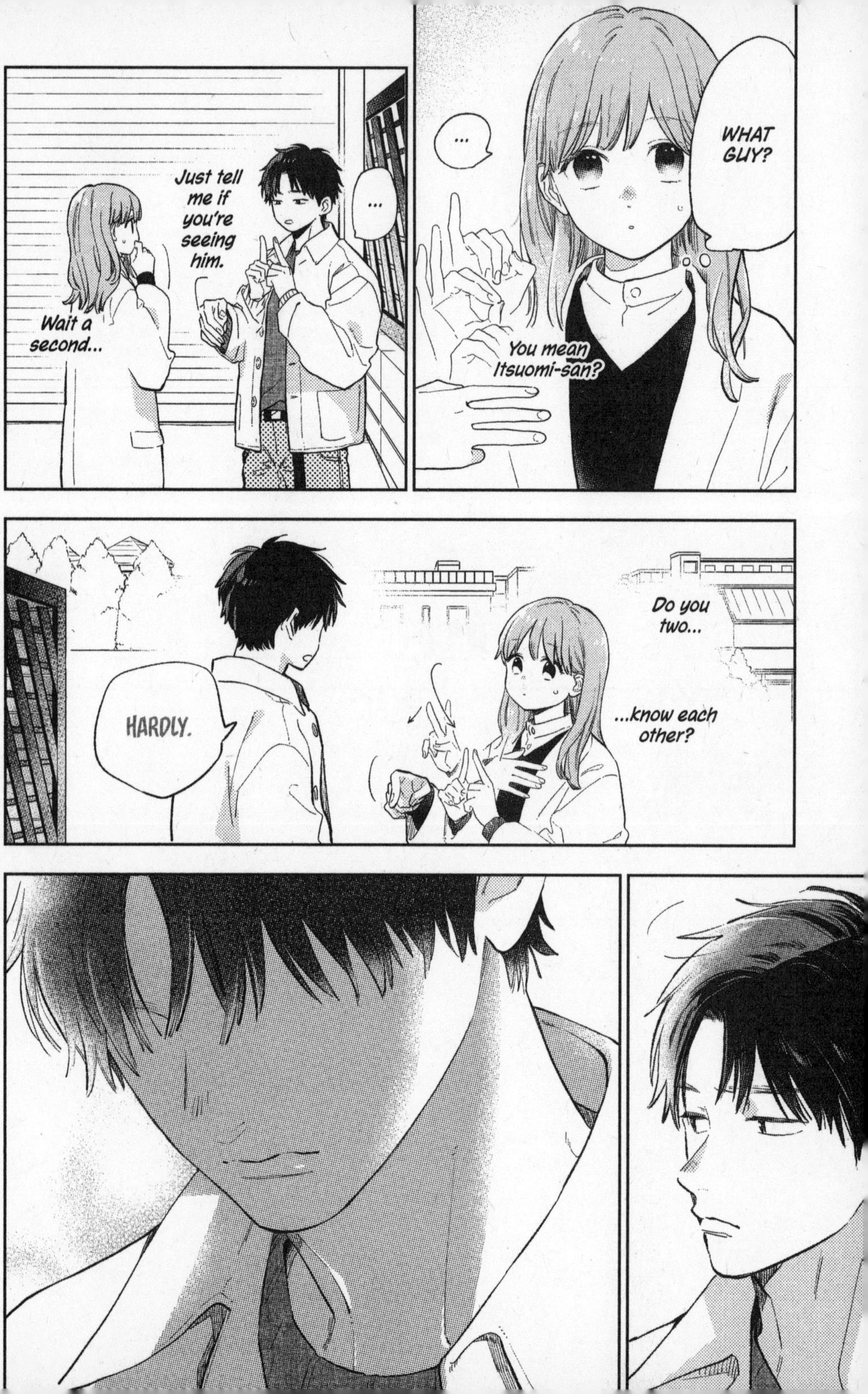
WHAT GUY?
...
You mean Itsuomi-san?
...
Just tell me if you're seeing him.
Wait a second...
Do you two...
...know each other?
HARDLY.

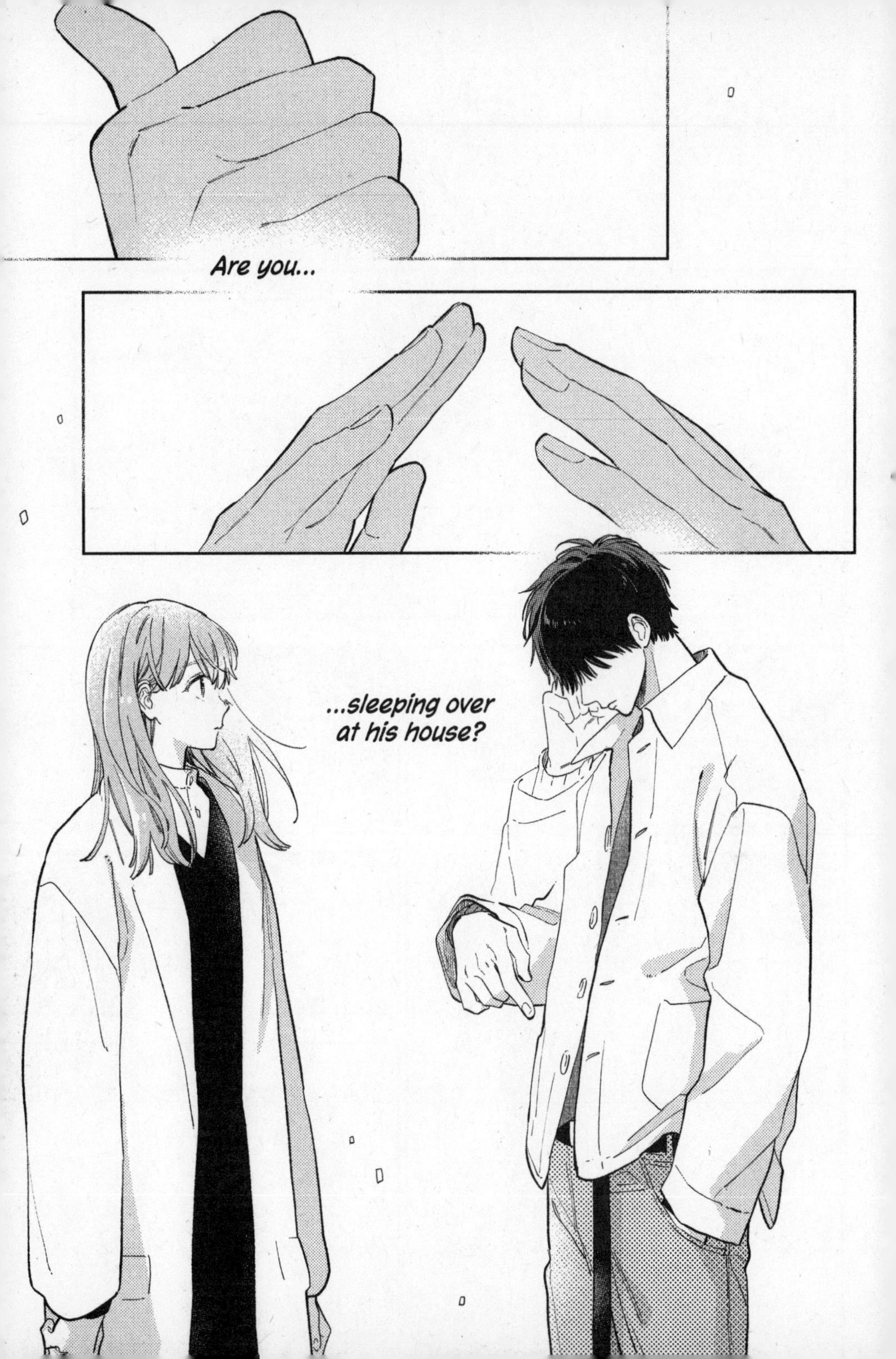
Are you...
...sleeping over at his house?

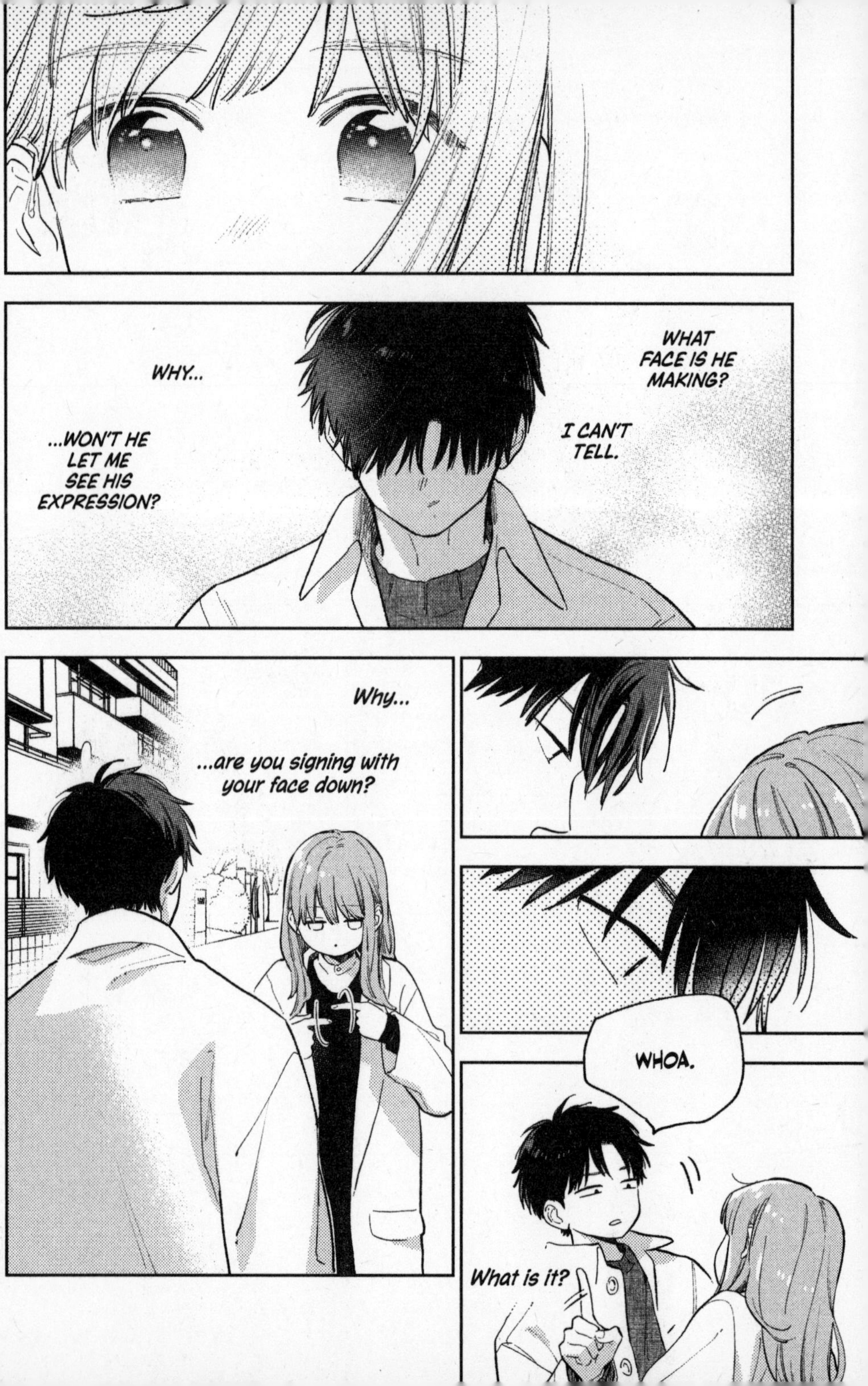
WHAT FACE IS HE MAKING?
I CAN'T TELL.
WHY...
...WON'T HE LET ME SEE HIS EXPRESSION?
WHOA.
What is it?
Why...
...are you signing with your face down?

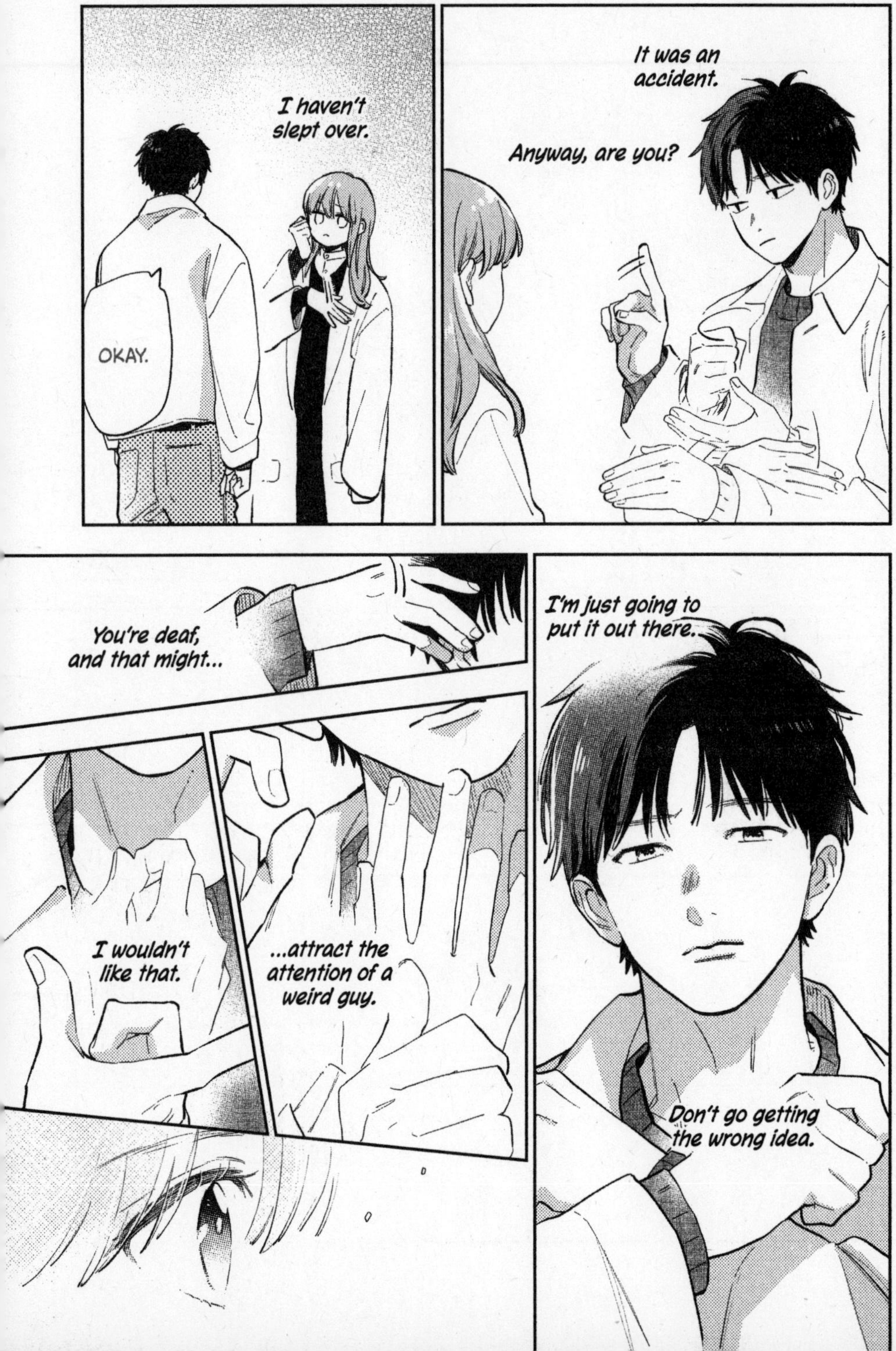
It was an accident.
Anyway, are you?
I haven't slept over.
OKAY.
I'm just going to put it out there.
Don't go getting the wrong idea.
You're deaf, and that might...
...attract the attention of a weird guy.
I wouldn't like that.

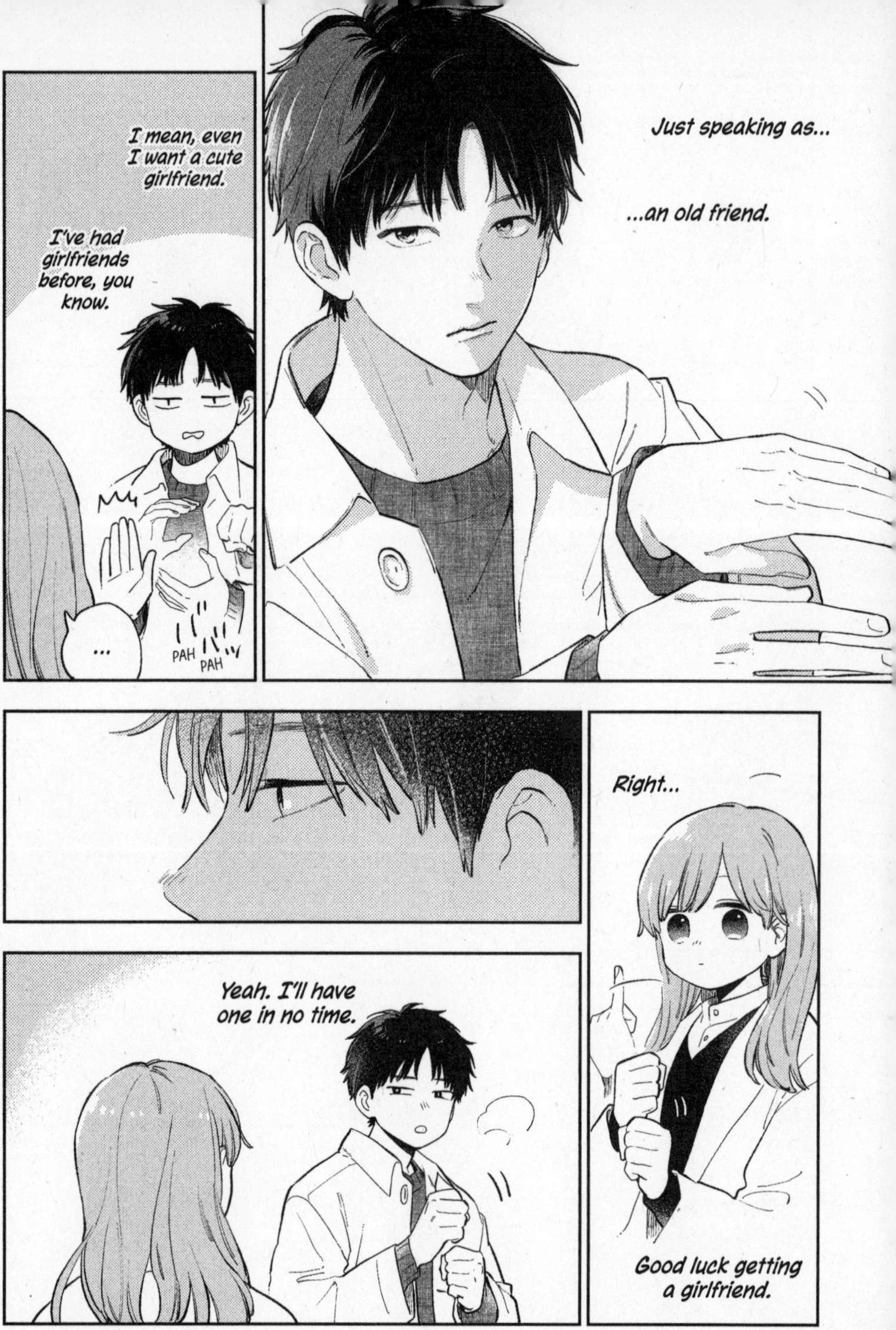
Just speaking as...
...an old friend.
I mean, even I want a cute girlfriend.
I've had girlfriends before, you know.
...
PAH
PAH
Right...
Good luck getting a girlfriend.
Yeah. I'll have one in no time.

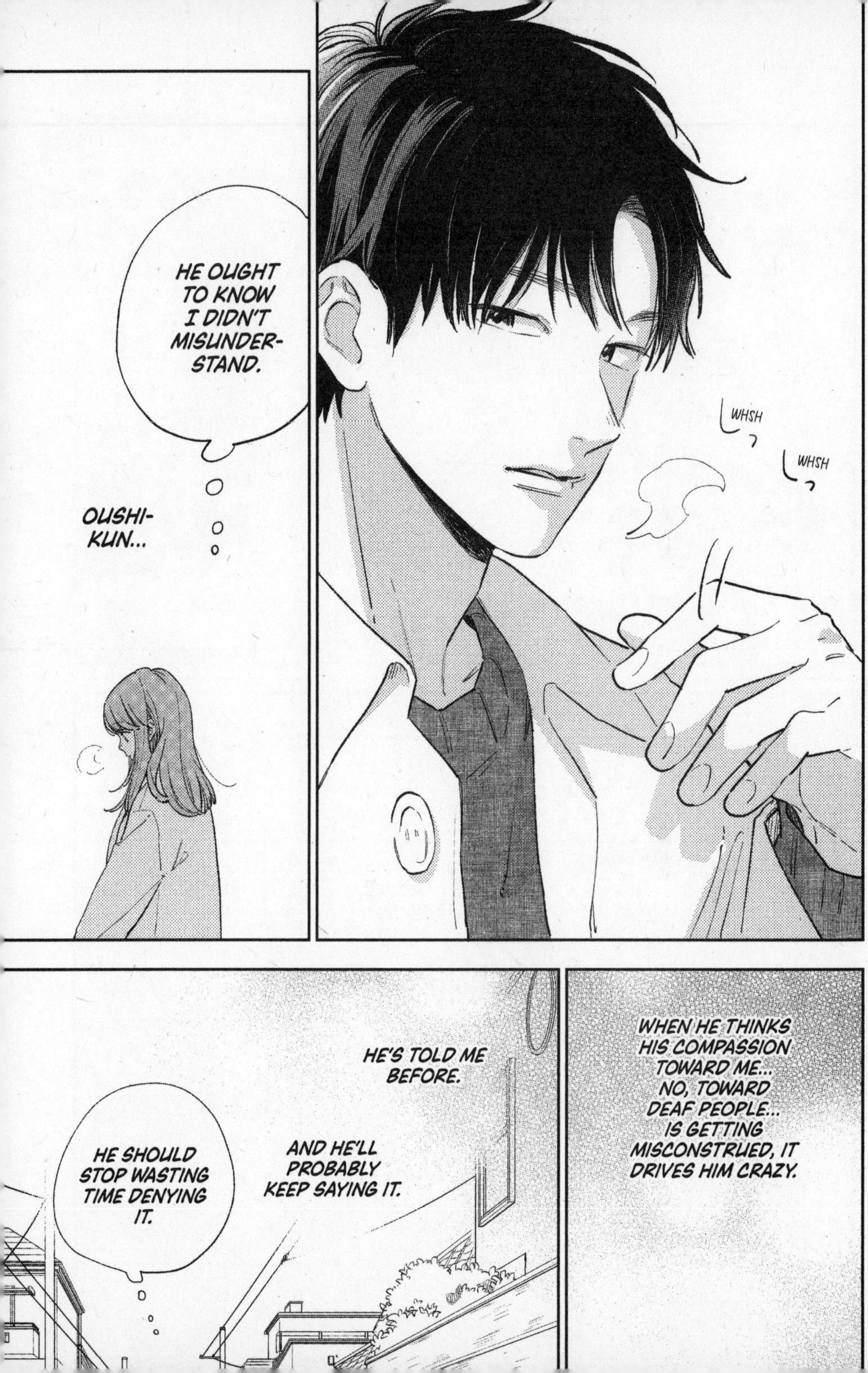
WHSH
WHSH
HE OUGHT TO KNOW I DIDN'T MISUNDER-STAND.
OUSHI-KUN...
WHEN HE THINKS HIS COMPASSION TOWARD ME... NO, TOWARD DEAF PEOPLE... IS GETTING MISCONSTRUED, IT DRIVES HIM CRAZY.
HE'S TOLD ME BEFORE.
AND HE'LL PROBABLY KEEP SAYING IT.
HE SHOULD STOP WASTING TIME DENYING IT.

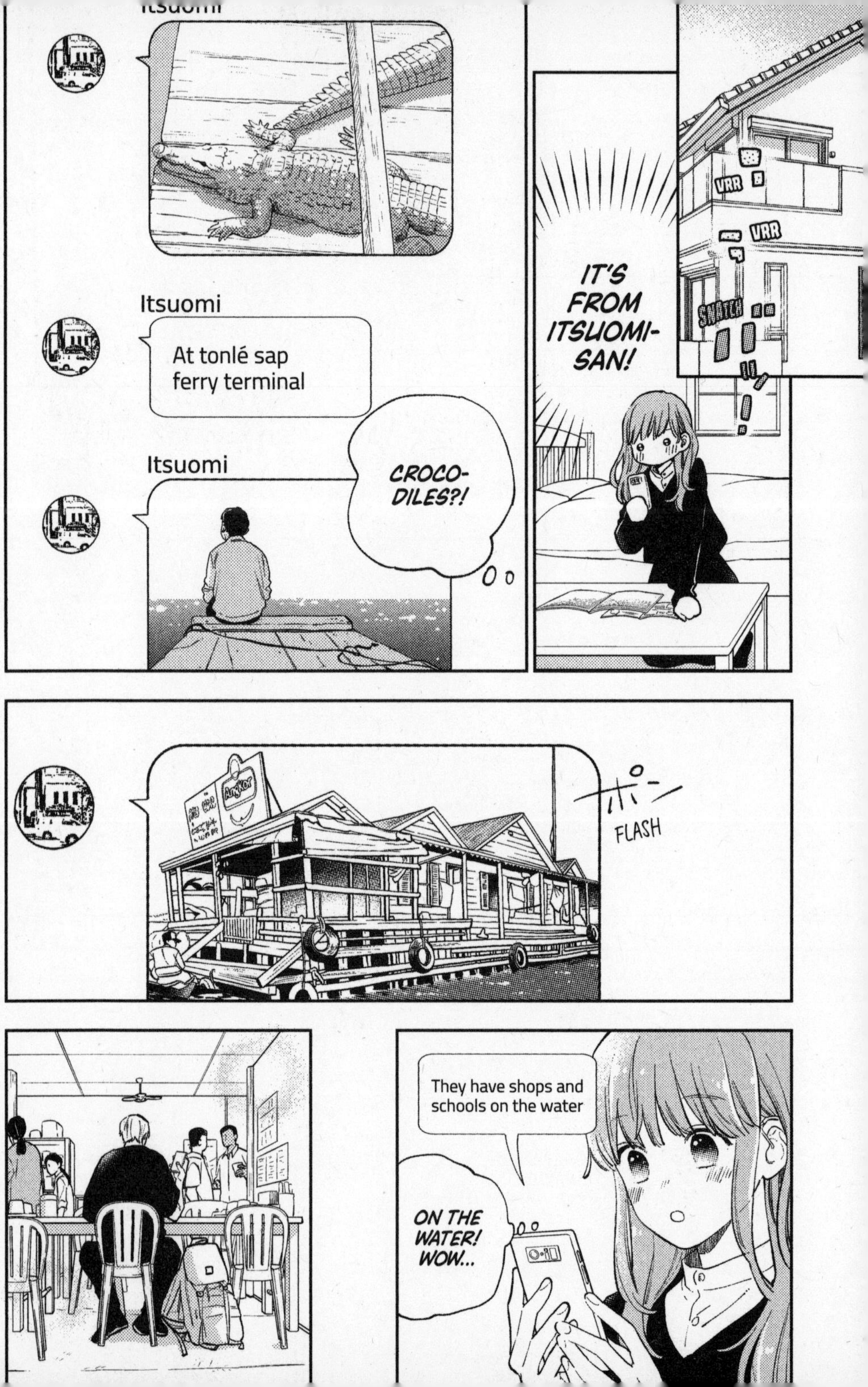
VRR
VRR
SNATCH
IT'S FROM ITSUOMI-SAN!
Itsuomi
Itsuomi
At tonlé sap ferry terminal
Itsuomi
CROCO-DILES?!
FLASH
They have shops and schools on the water
ON THE WATER! WOW...

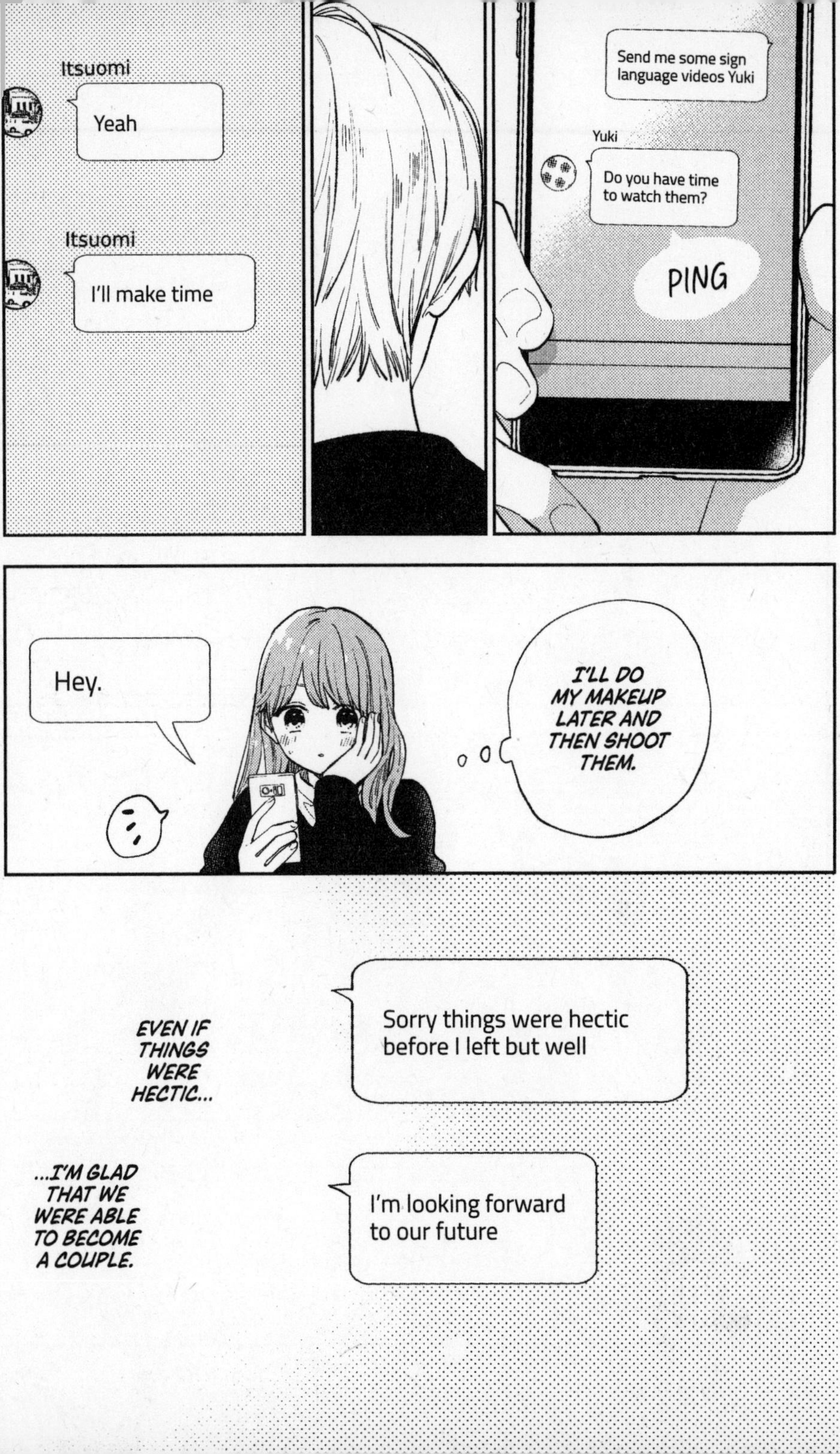
Send me some sign language videos Yuki
Yuki
Do you have time to watch them?
PING
Itsuomi
Yeah
Itsuomi
I'll make time
I'LL DO MY MAKEUP LATER AND THEN SHOOT THEM.
Hey.
Sorry things were hectic before I left but well
EVEN IF THINGS WERE HECTIC...
I'm looking forward to our future
...I'M GLAD THAT WE WERE ABLE TO BECOME A COUPLE.

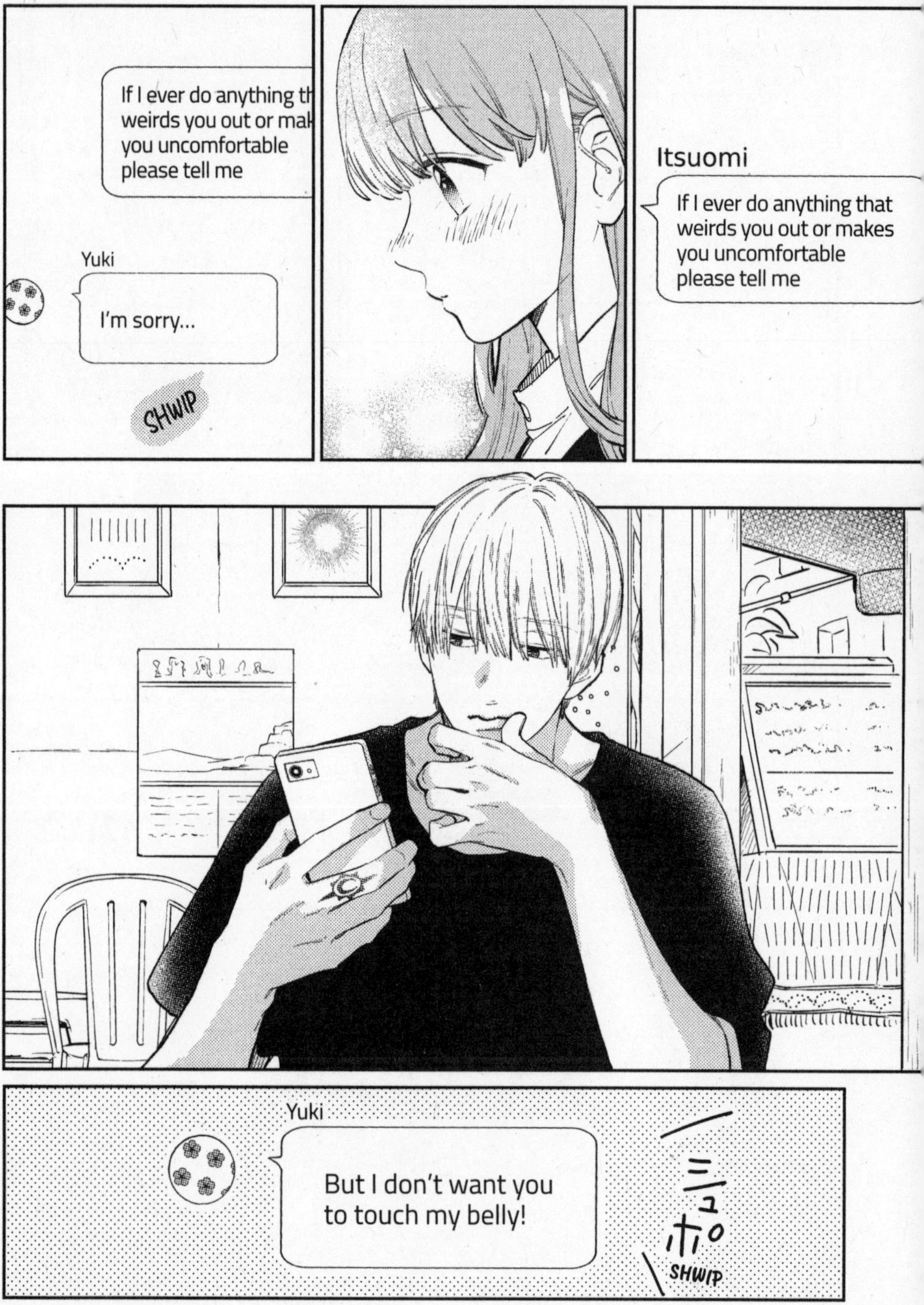
Itsuomi
If I ever do anything that weirds you out or makes you uncomfortable please tell me
If I ever do anything th weirds you out or mak you uncomfortable please tell me
Yuki
I'm sorry...
SHWIP
Yuki
But I don't want you to touch my belly!
SHWIP

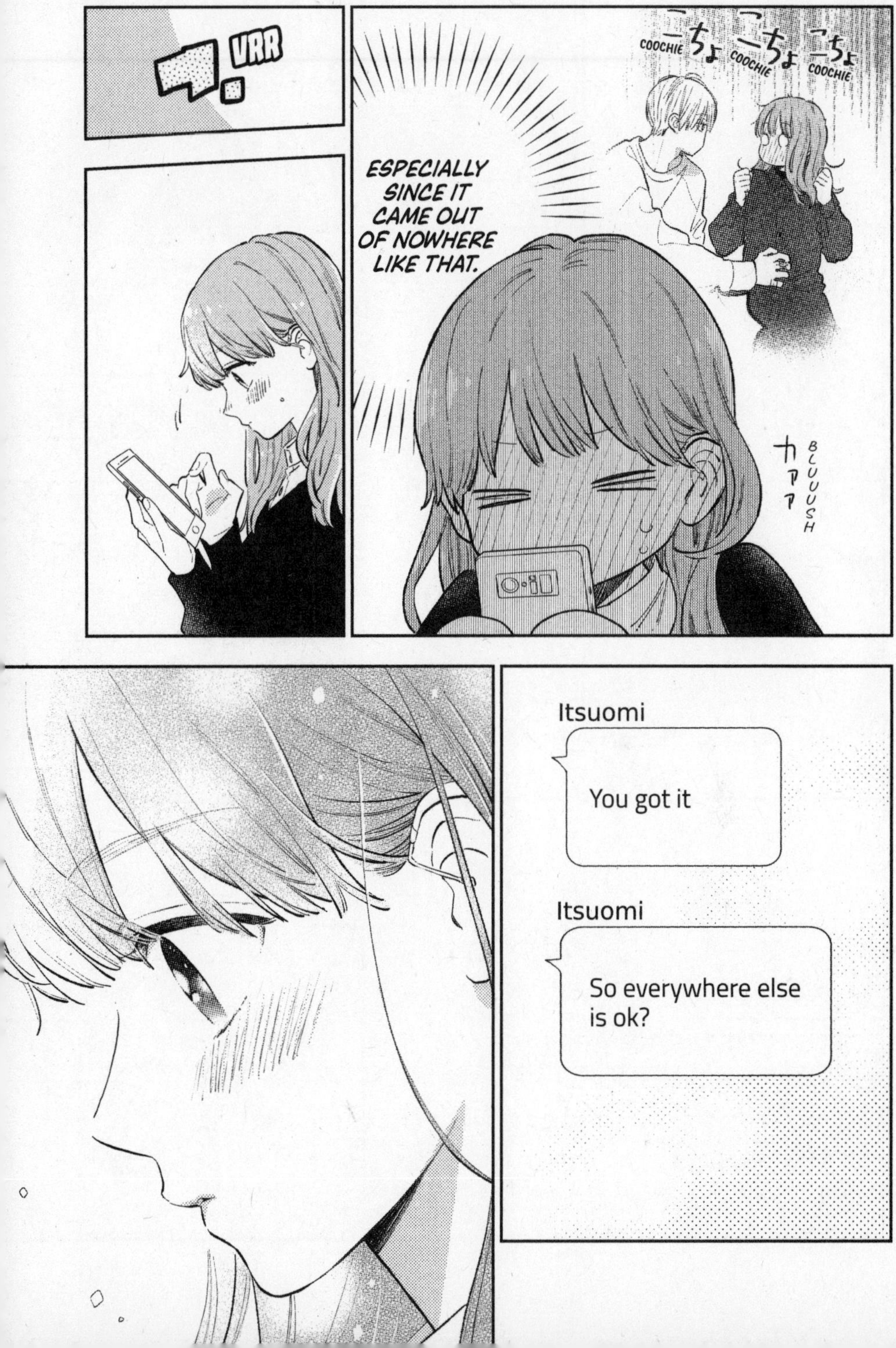
こちょ COOCHIE
こちょ COOCHIE
こちょ COOCHIE
ESPECIALLY SINCE IT CAME OUT OF NOWHERE LIKE THAT.
カァァ BLUUUSH
VRR
Itsuomi
You got it
Itsuomi
So everywhere else is ok?

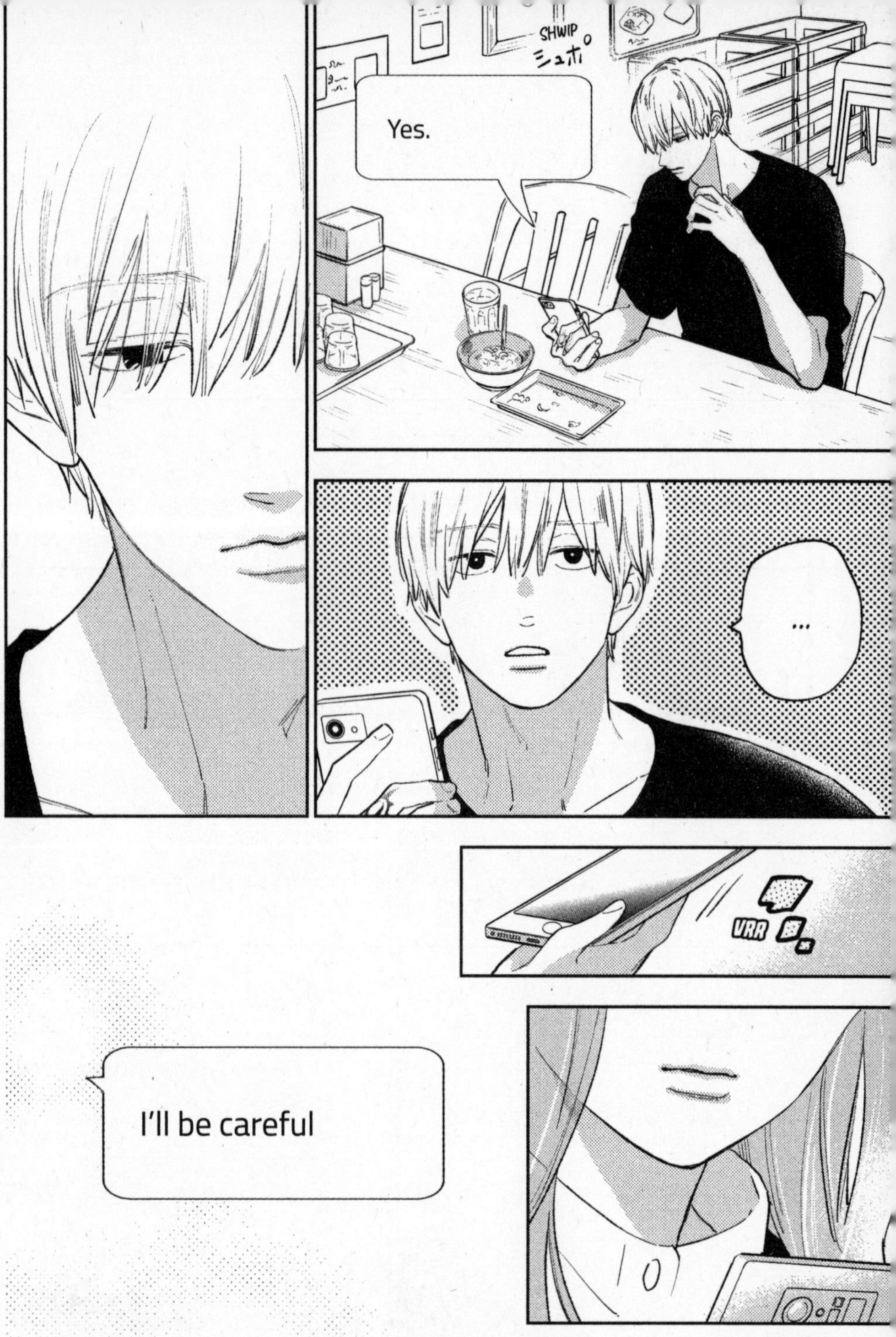
SHWIP
シュポ
Yes.
...
VRR
I'll be careful

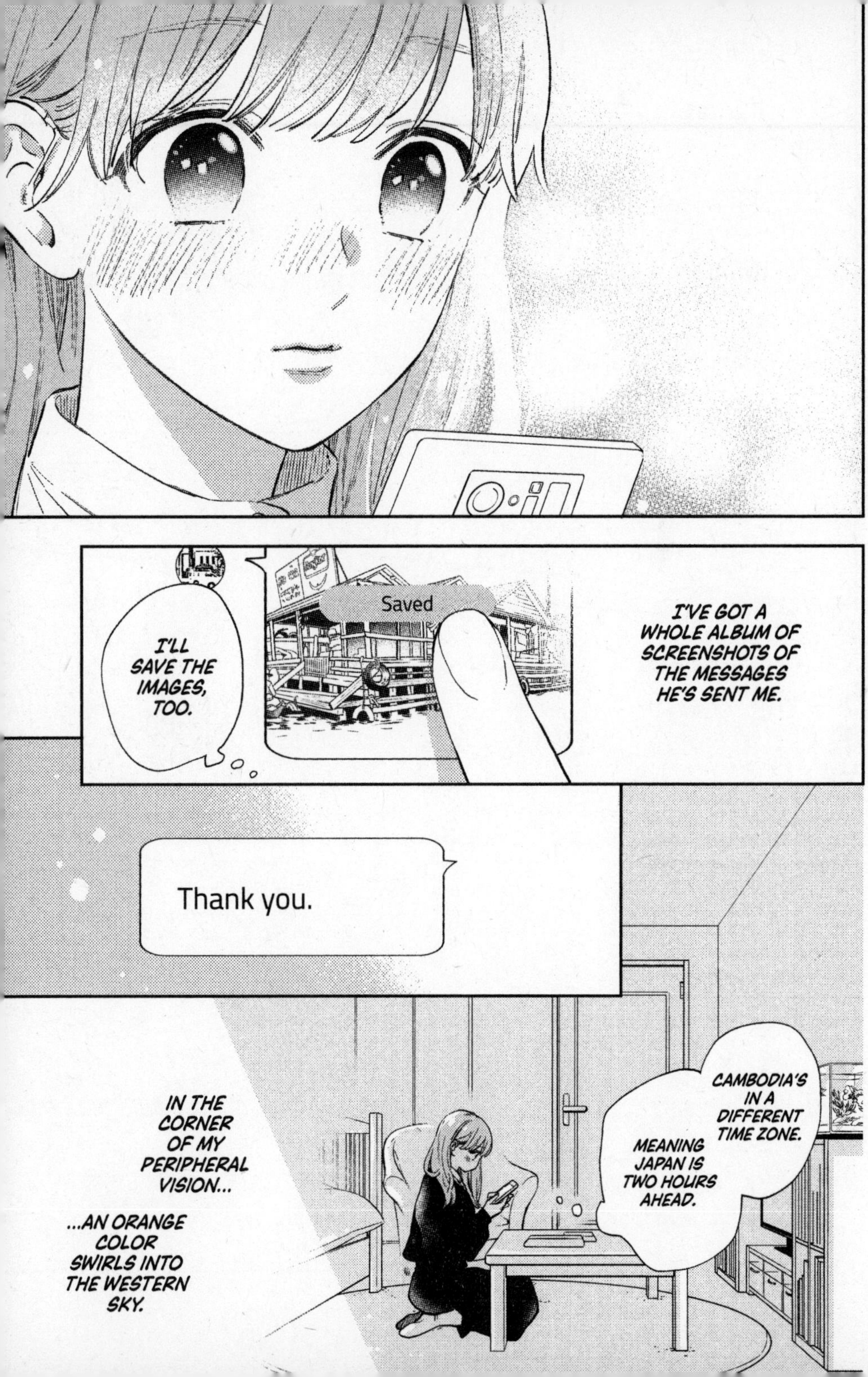
I'VE GOT A WHOLE ALBUM OF SCREENSHOTS OF THE MESSAGES HE'S SENT ME.
Saved
I'LL SAVE THE IMAGES, TOO.
Thank you.
CAMBODIA'S IN A DIFFERENT TIME ZONE.
MEANING JAPAN IS TWO HOURS AHEAD.
IN THE CORNER OF MY PERIPHERAL VISION...
...AN ORANGE COLOR SWIRLS INTO THE WESTERN SKY.

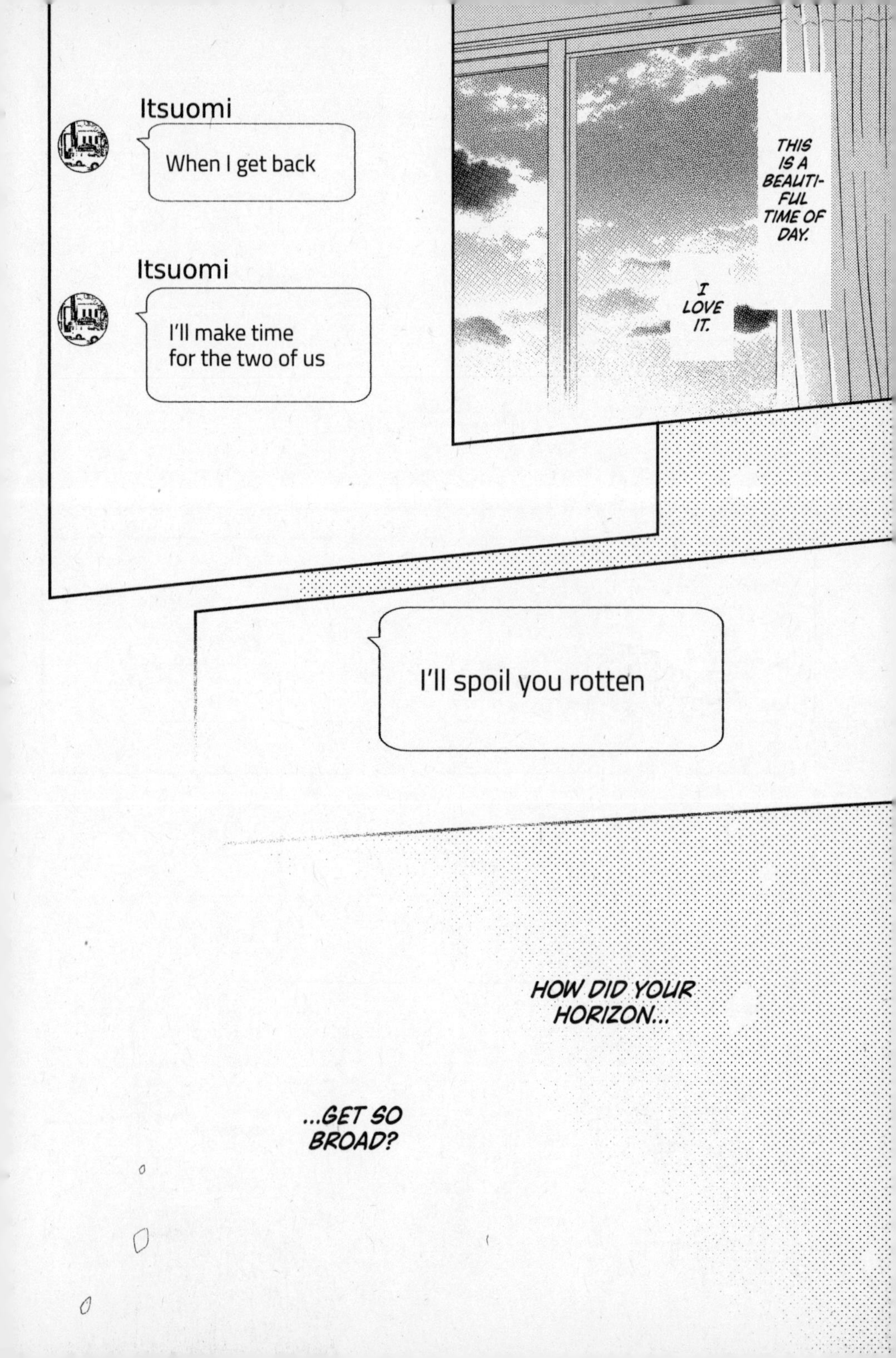
THIS IS A BEAUTIFUL TIME OF DAY.
I LOVE IT.
Itsuomi
When I get back
Itsuomi
I'll make time for the two of us
I'll spoil you rotten
HOW DID YOUR HORIZON...
...GET SO BROAD?

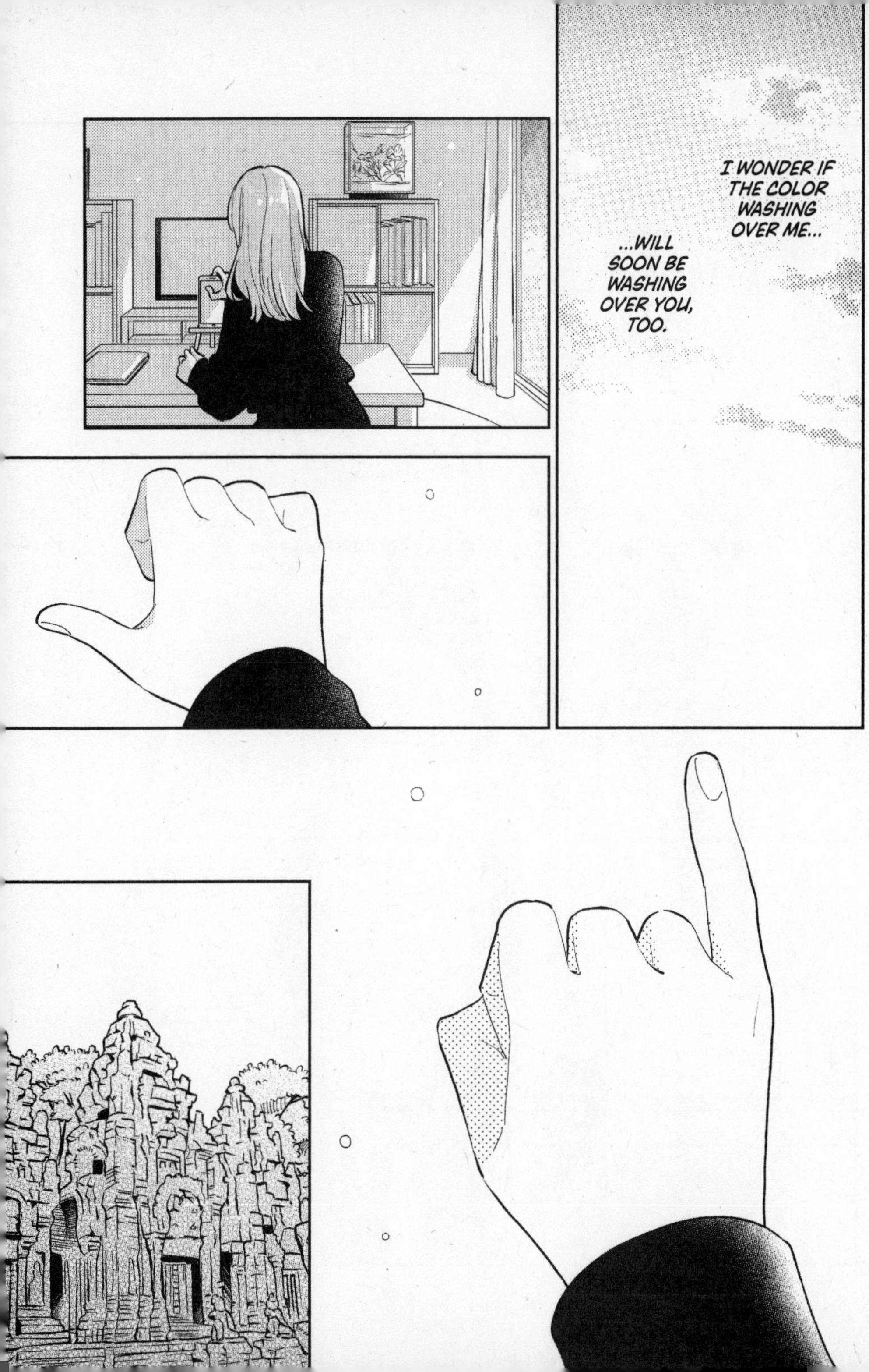
I WONDER IF THE COLOR WASHING OVER ME...
...WILL SOON BE WASHING OVER YOU, TOO.

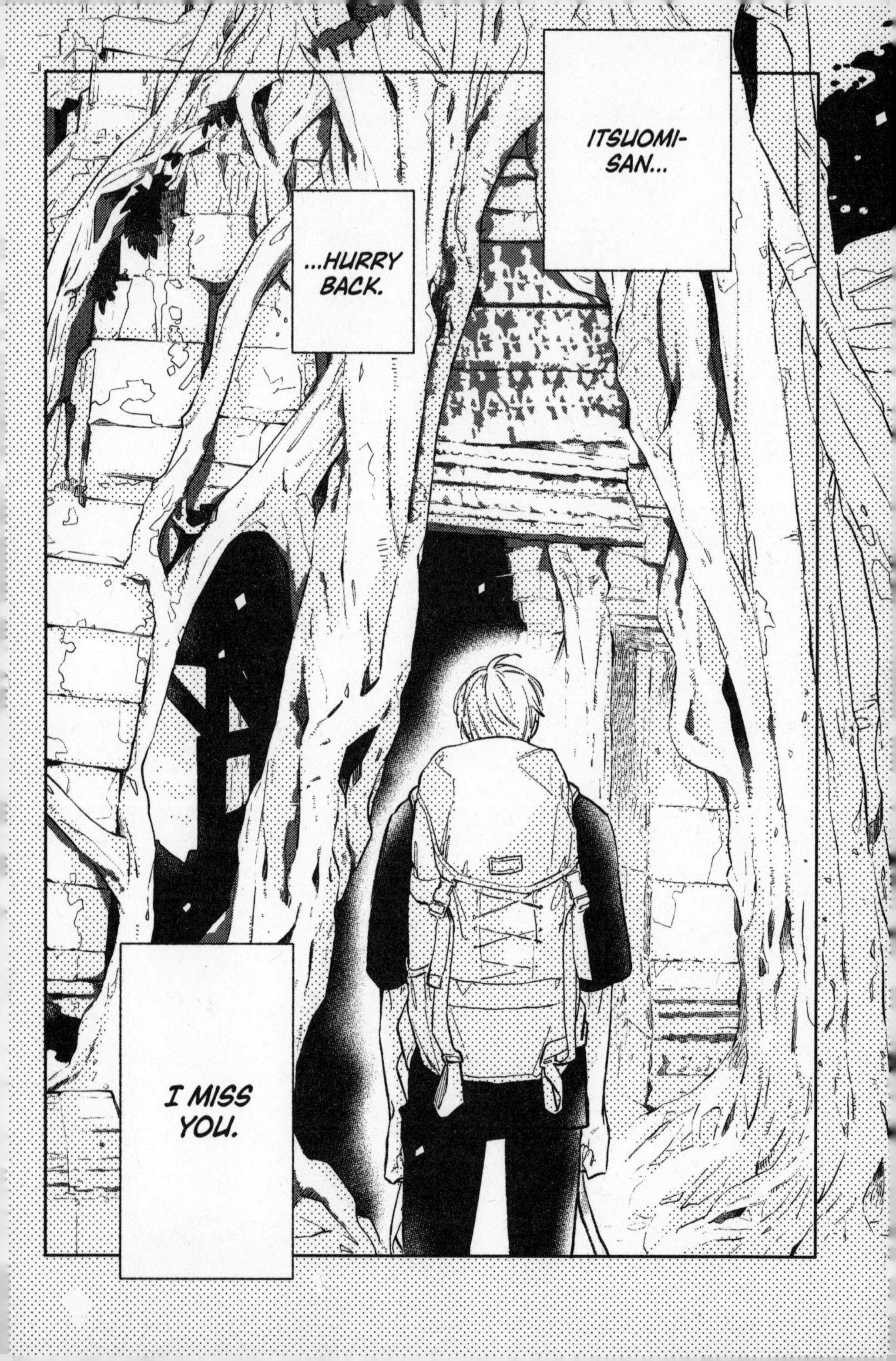
ITSUOMI-SAN...
...HURRY BACK.
I MISS YOU.

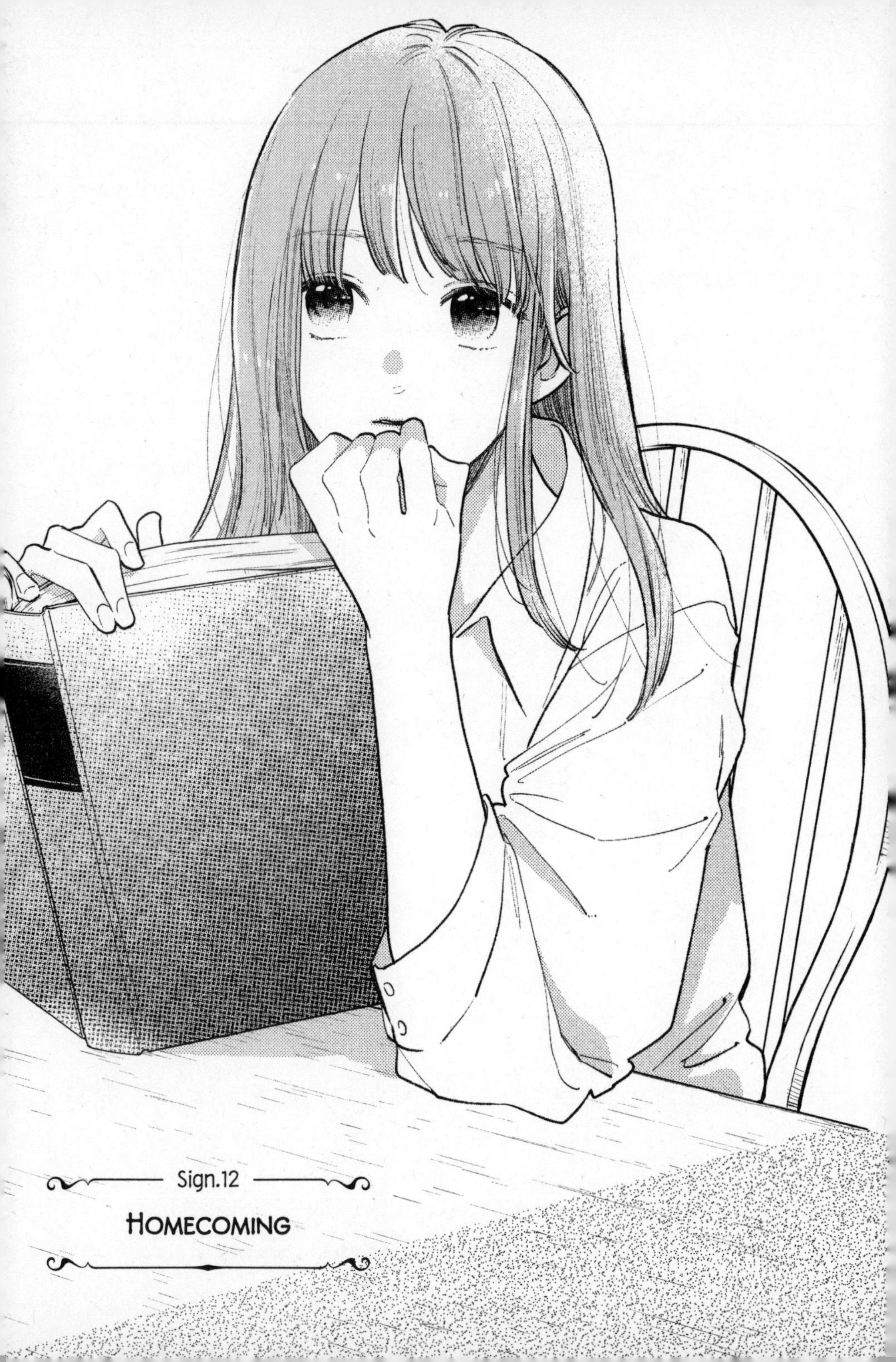
Sign.12
HOMECOMING

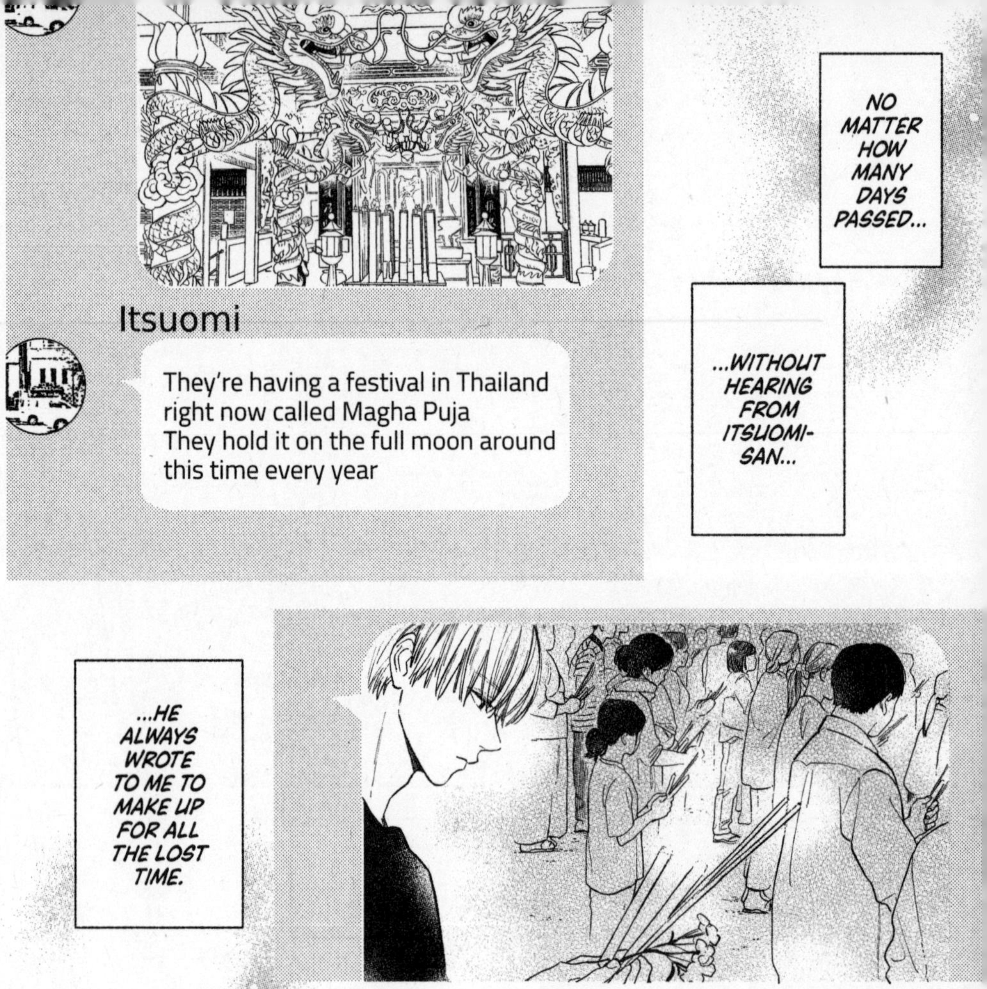
NO MATTER HOW MANY DAYS PASSED...
...WITHOUT HEARING FROM ITSUOMI-SAN...
Itsuomi
They're having a festival in Thailand right now called Magha Puja They hold it on the full moon around this time every year
...HE ALWAYS WROTE TO ME TO MAKE UP FOR ALL THE LOST TIME.

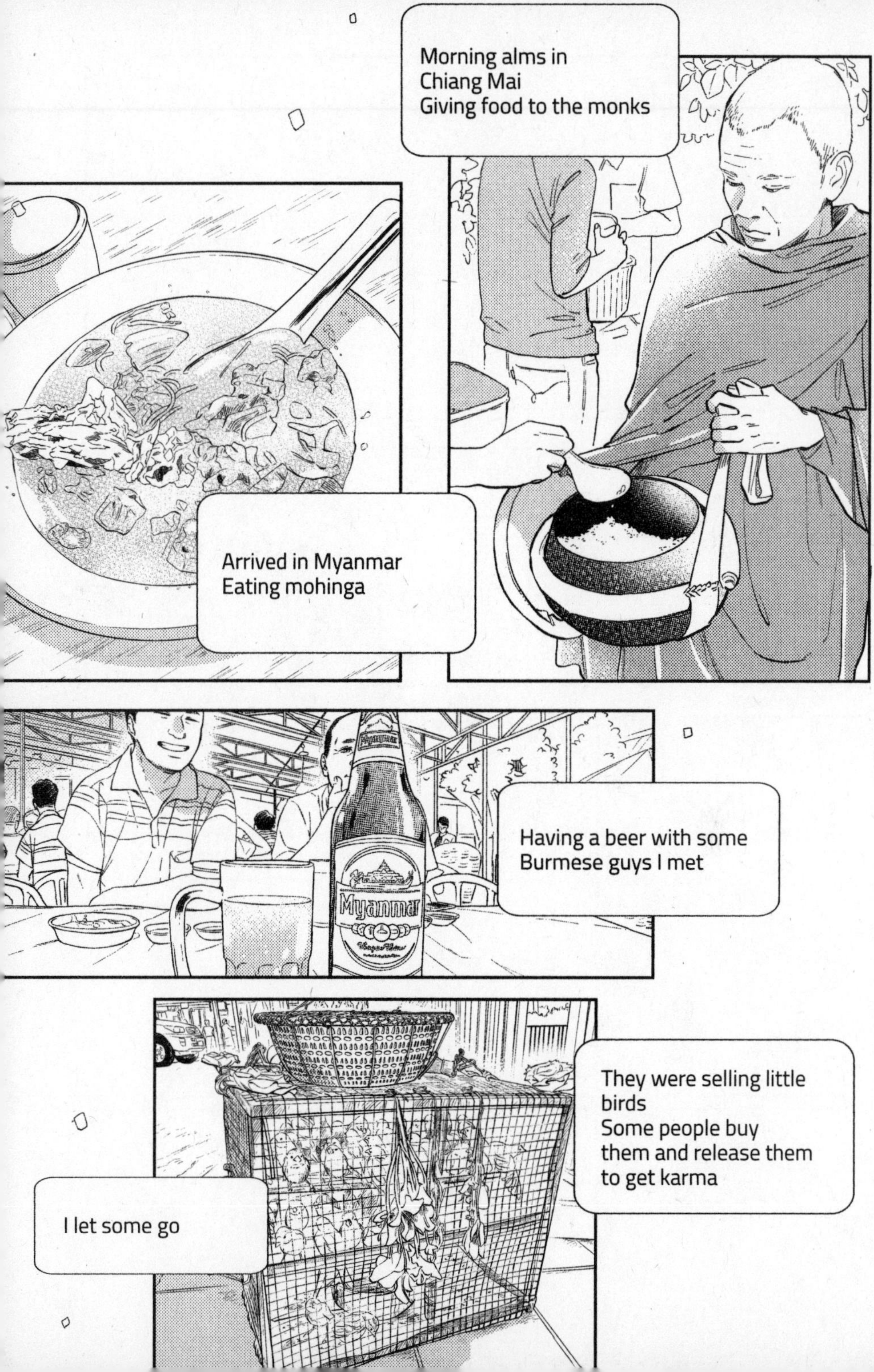
Morning alms in Chiang Mai
Giving food to the monks
Arrived in Myanmar
Eating mohinga
Having a beer with some Burmese guys I met
Myanmar
They were selling little birds
Some people buy them and release them to get karma
I let some go

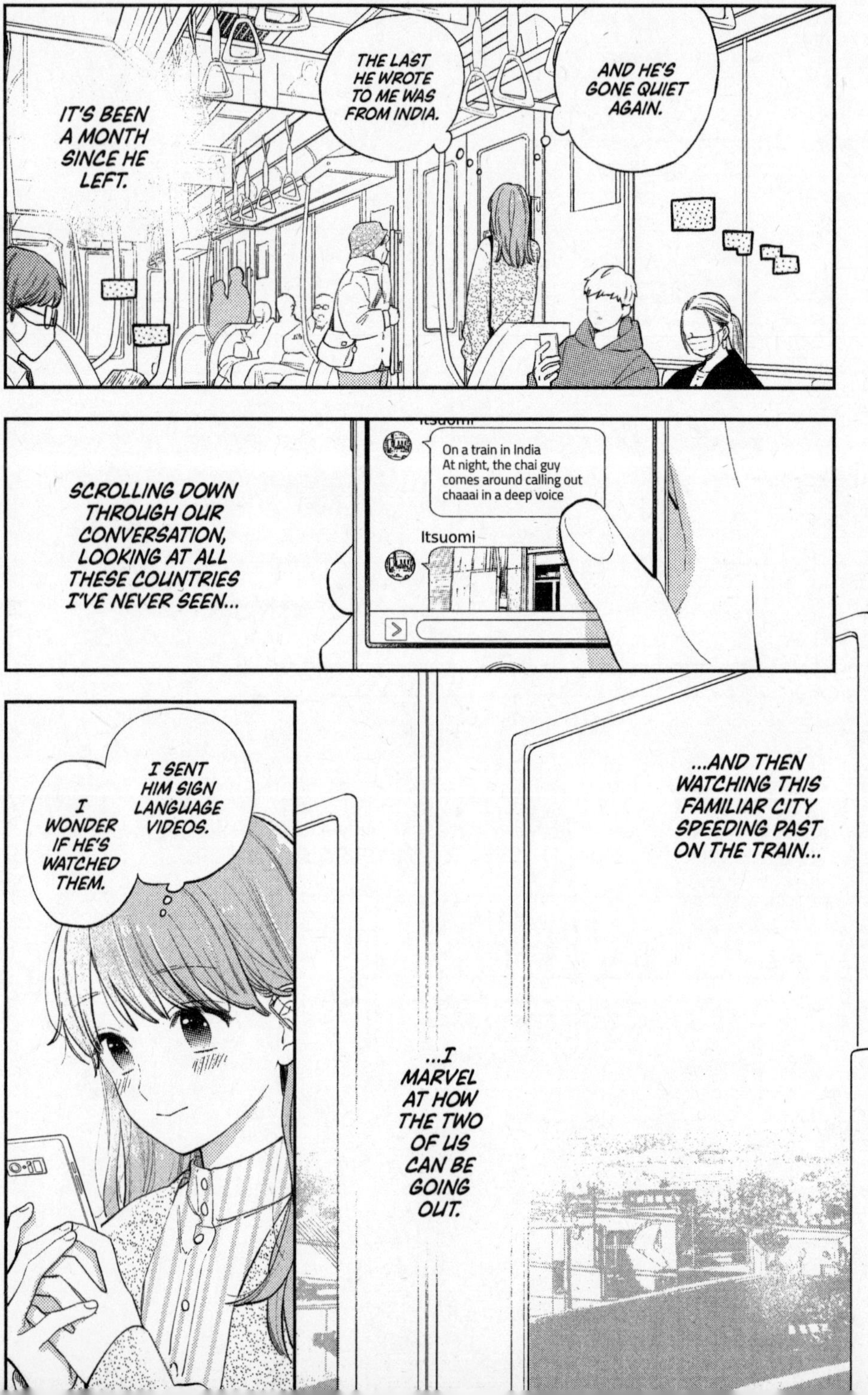
AND HE'S GONE QUIET AGAIN.
THE LAST HE WROTE TO ME WAS FROM INDIA.
IT'S BEEN A MONTH SINCE HE LEFT.
Itsuomi
On a train in India
At night, the chai guy comes around calling out chaaai in a deep voice
Itsuomi
SCROLLING DOWN THROUGH OUR CONVERSATION, LOOKING AT ALL THESE COUNTRIES I'VE NEVER SEEN...
...AND THEN WATCHING THIS FAMILIAR CITY SPEEDING PAST ON THE TRAIN...
...I MARVEL AT HOW THE TWO OF US CAN BE GOING OUT.
I SENT HIM SIGN LANGUAGE VIDEOS.
I WONDER IF HE'S WATCHED THEM.

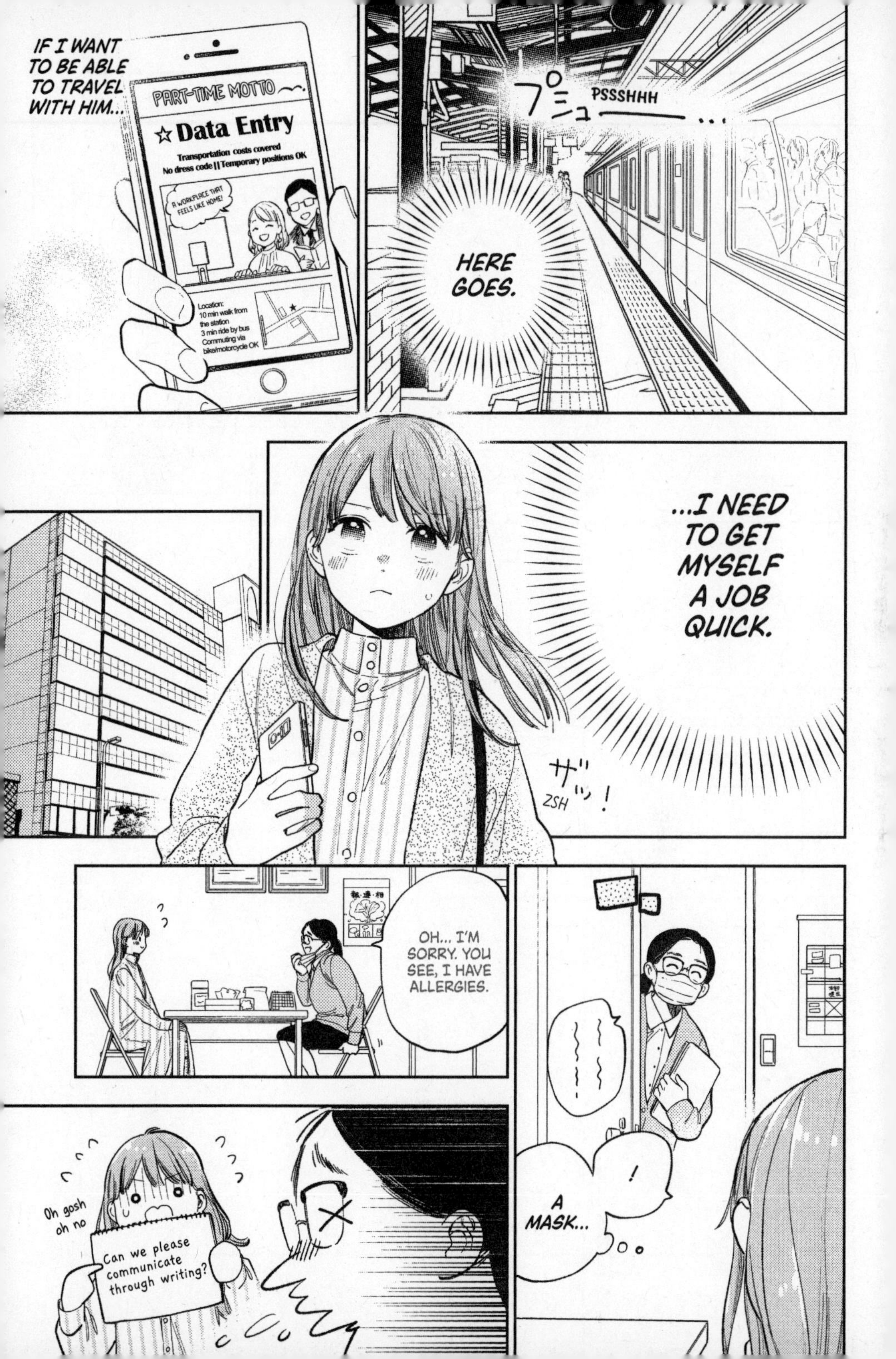

プシュー
PSSSHHH
...
HERE GOES.
IF I WANT TO BE ABLE TO TRAVEL WITH HIM...
PART-TIME MOTTO
☆ Data Entry
Transportation costs covered
No dress code || Temporary positions OK
A WORKPLACE THAT FEELS LIKE HOME!
Location: 10 min walk from the station 3 min ride by bus Commuting via bike/motorcycle OK
...I NEED TO GET MYSELF A JOB QUICK.
ザッ!
ZSH
!
A MASK...
OH... I'M SORRY. YOU SEE, I HAVE ALLERGIES.
Oh gosh oh no
Can we please communicate through writing?

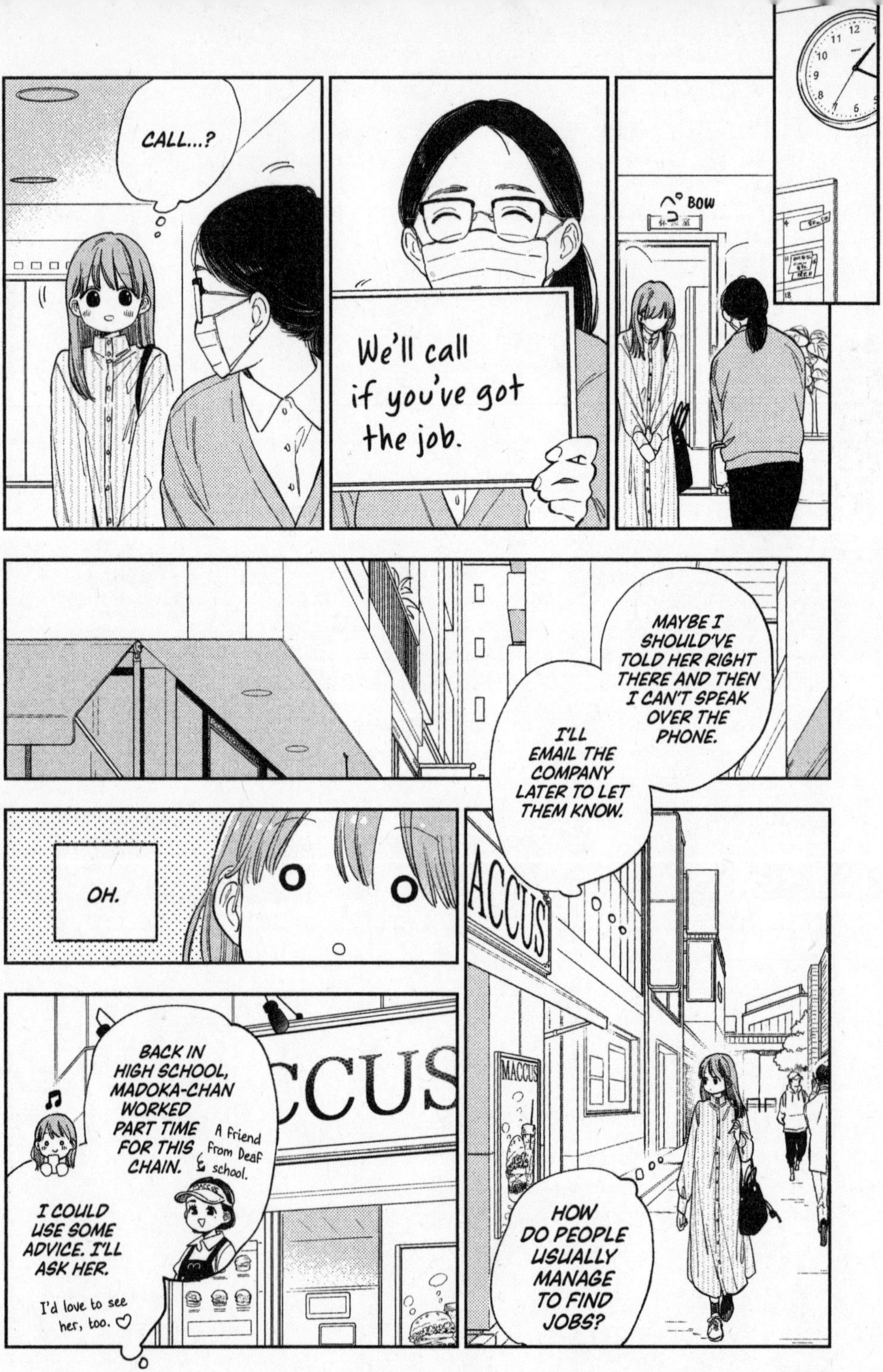
BOW
We'll call if you've got the job.
CALL...?
MAYBE I SHOULD'VE TOLD HER RIGHT THERE AND THEN I CAN'T SPEAK OVER THE PHONE.
I'LL EMAIL THE COMPANY LATER TO LET THEM KNOW.
ACCUS
MACCUS
HOW DO PEOPLE USUALLY MANAGE TO FIND JOBS?
OH.
CCUS
BACK IN HIGH SCHOOL, MADOKA-CHAN WORKED PART TIME FOR THIS CHAIN.
A Friend from Deaf school.
I COULD USE SOME ADVICE. I'LL ASK HER.
I'd love to see her, too. ♡

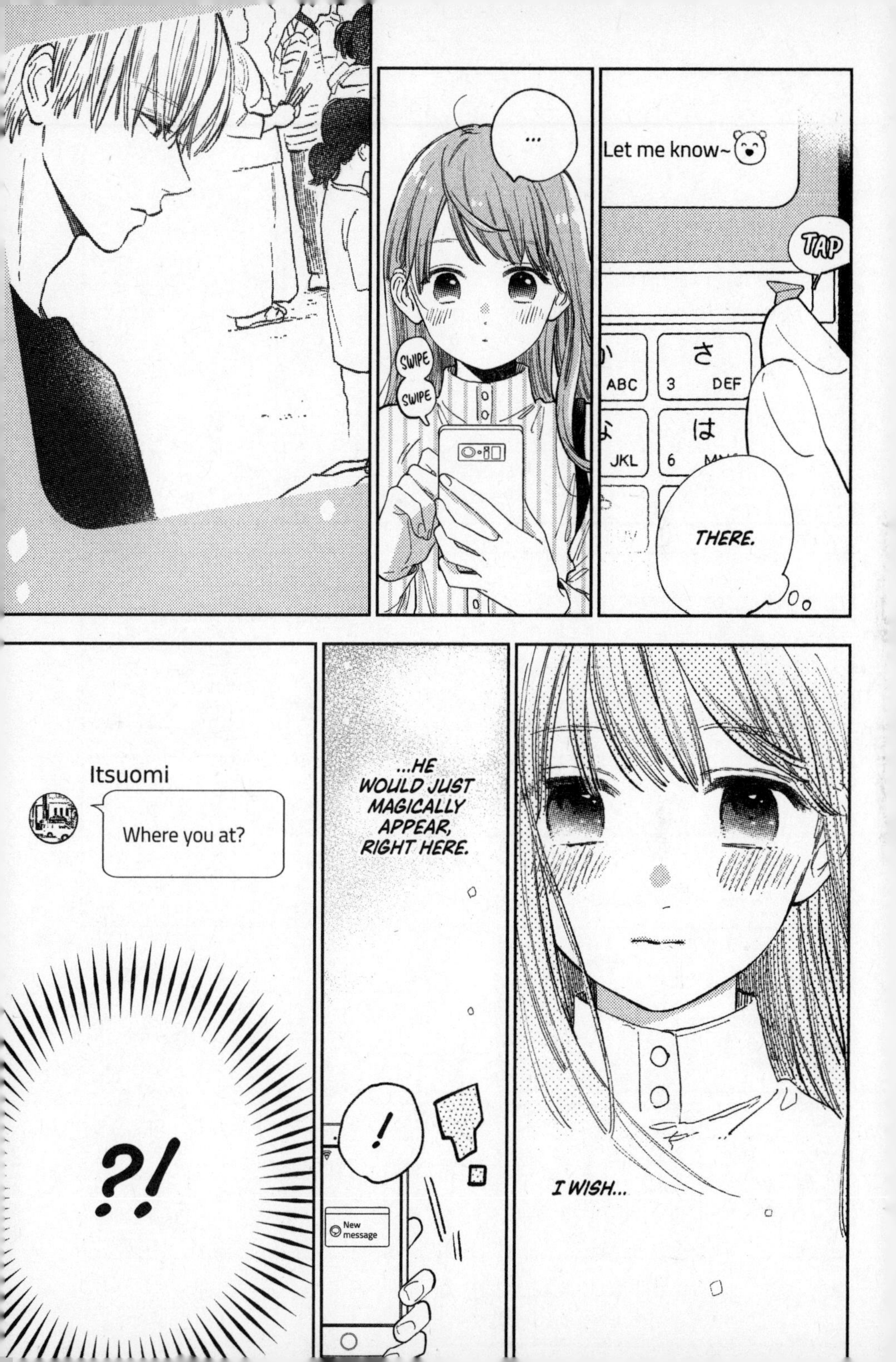
Let me know~
TAP
THERE.
...
SWIPE
SWIPE
I WISH...
...HE WOULD JUST MAGICALLY APPEAR, RIGHT HERE.
!
New message
Itsuomi
Where you at?
?!

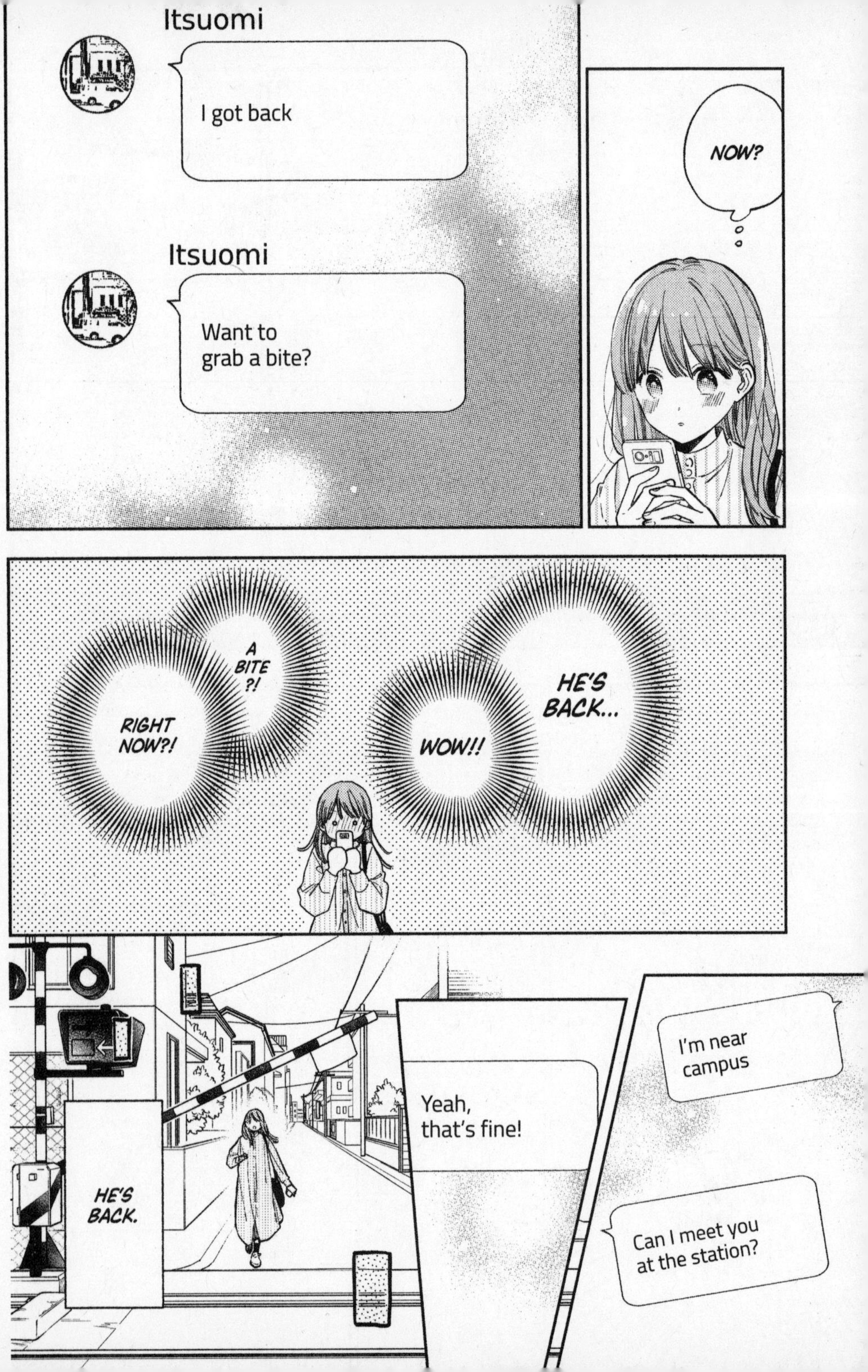
NOW?
Itsuomi
I got back
Itsuomi
Want to grab a bite?
HE'S BACK...
WOW!!
A BITE?!
RIGHT NOW?!
I'm near campus
Can I meet you at the station?
Yeah, that's fine!
HE'S BACK.

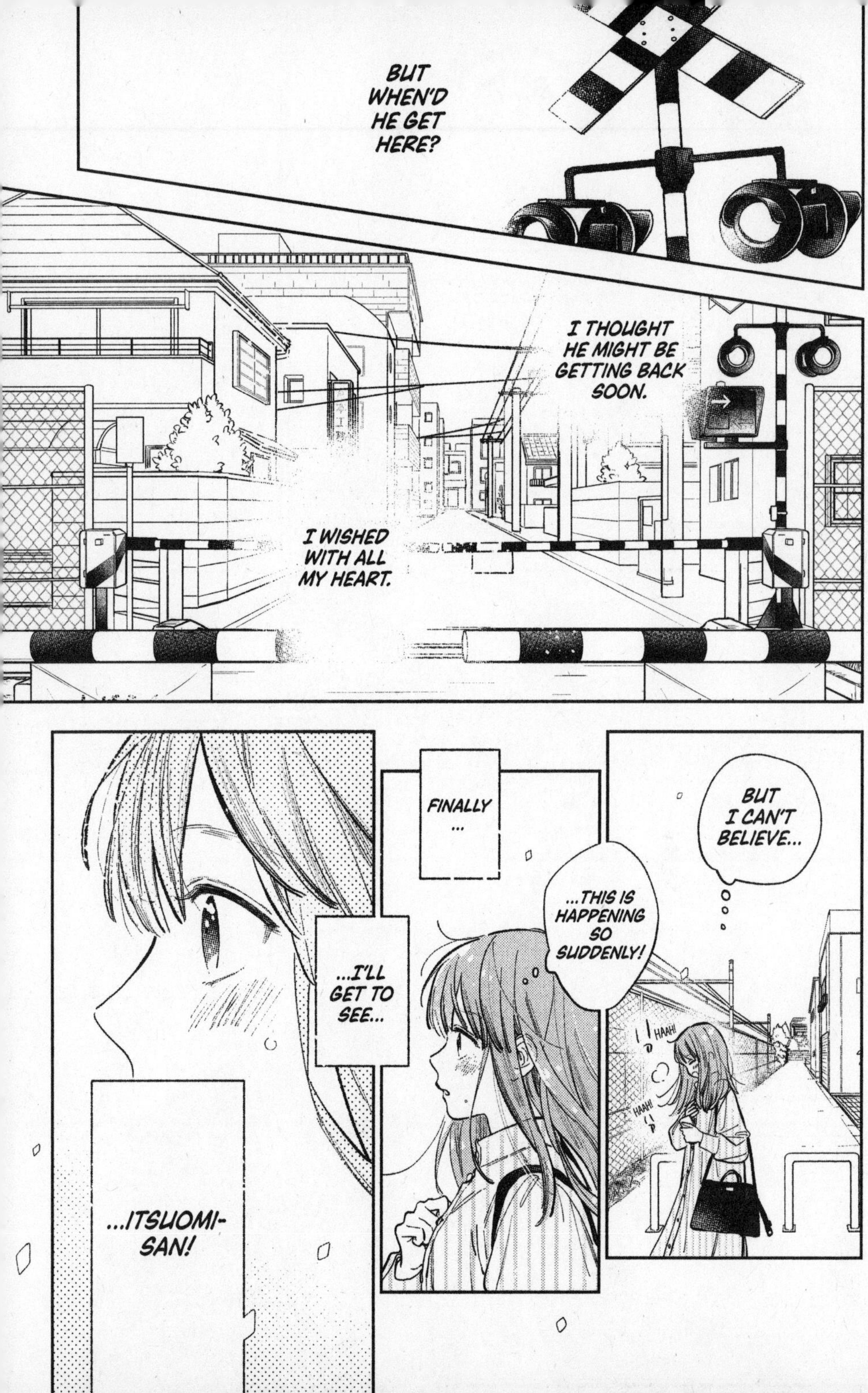
BUT WHEN'D HE GET HERE?
I THOUGHT HE MIGHT BE GETTING BACK SOON.
I WISHED WITH ALL MY HEART.
BUT I CAN'T BELIEVE...
...THIS IS HAPPENING SO SUDDENLY!
HAAH!
HAAH!
FINALLY ...
...I'LL GET TO SEE...
...ITSUOMI-SAN!

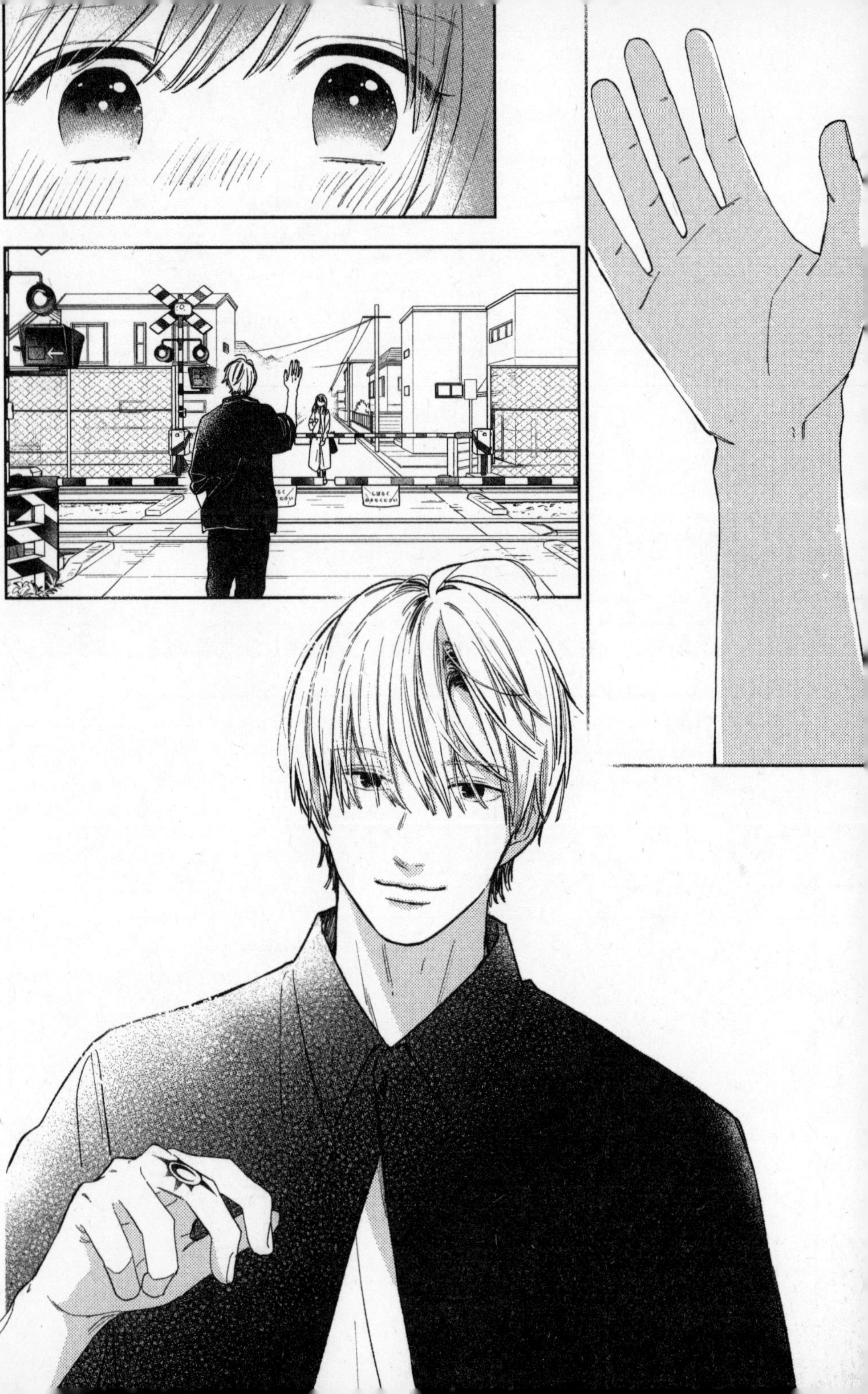

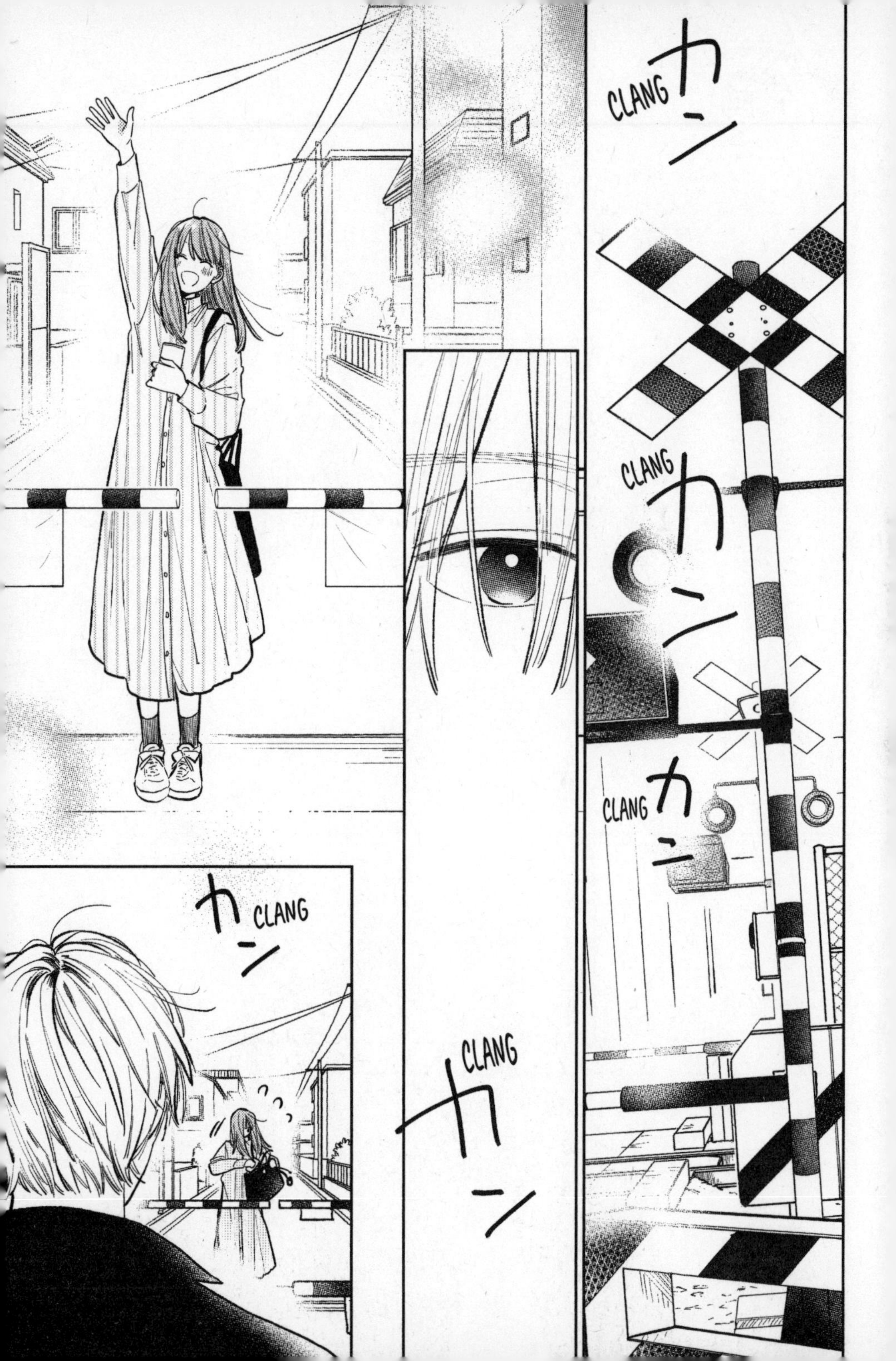

CLANG カーン
CLANG カーン
CLANG カン
CLANG カーン
カーン CLANG

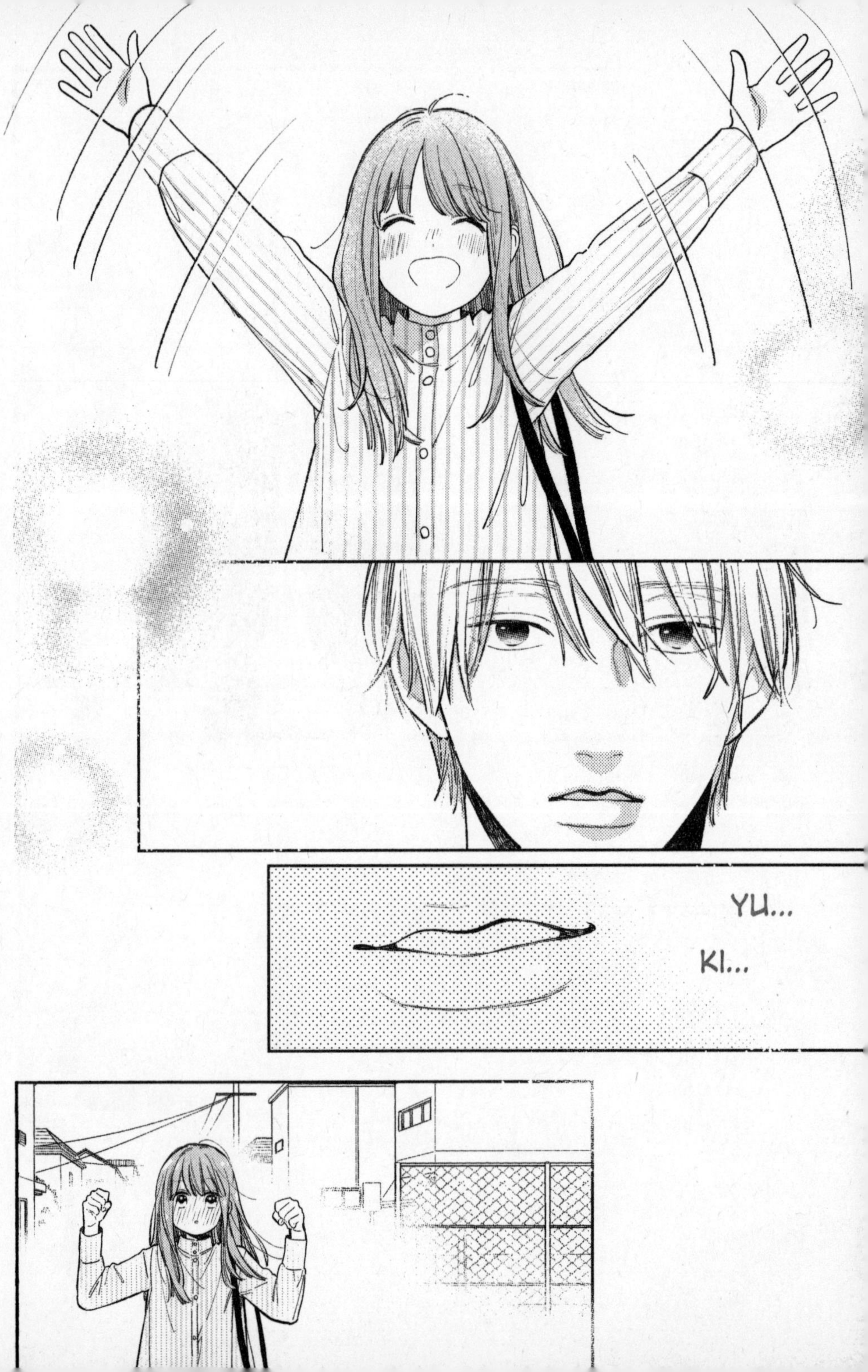
YU...
KI...

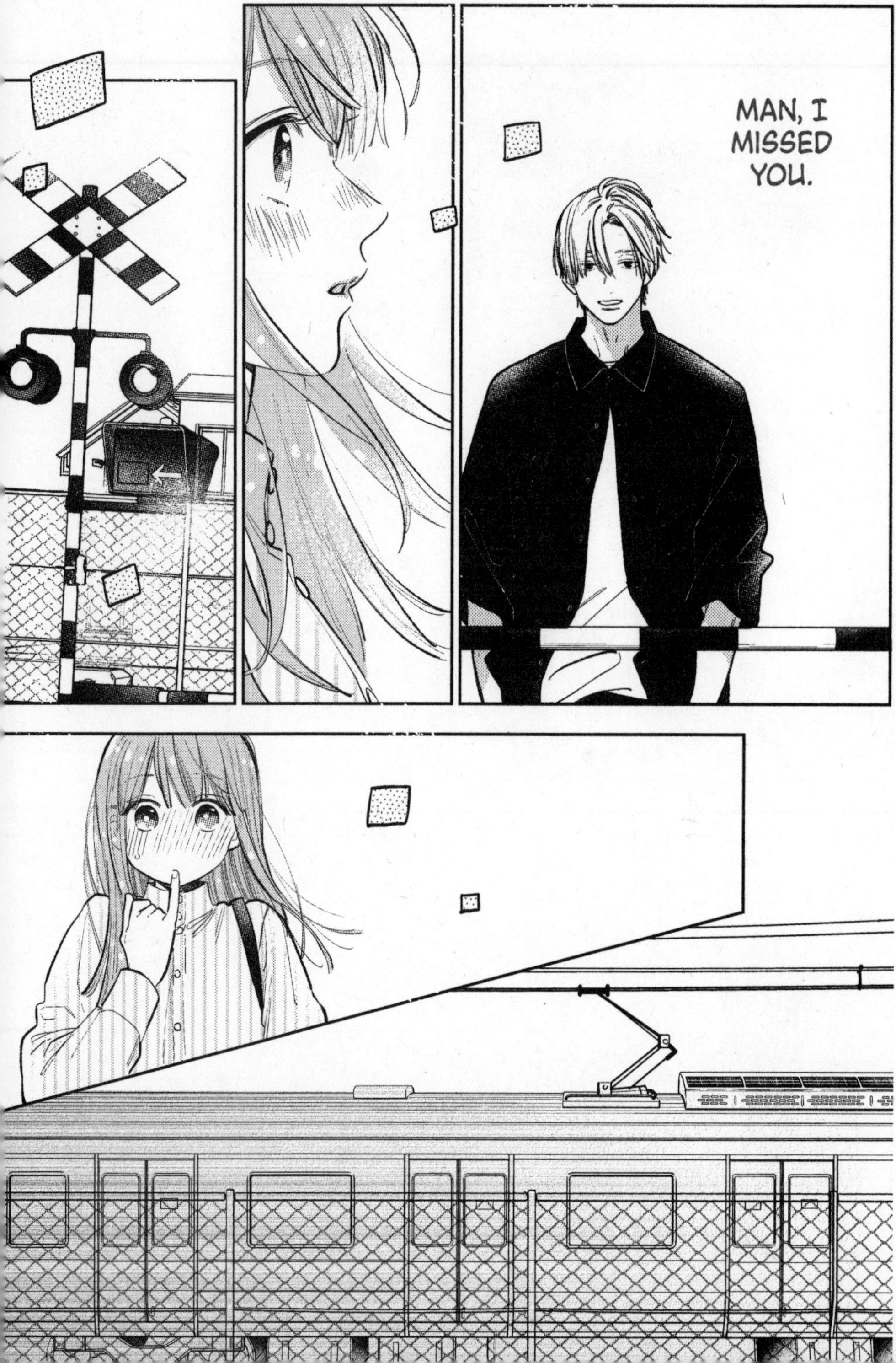
MAN, I
MISSED
YOU.

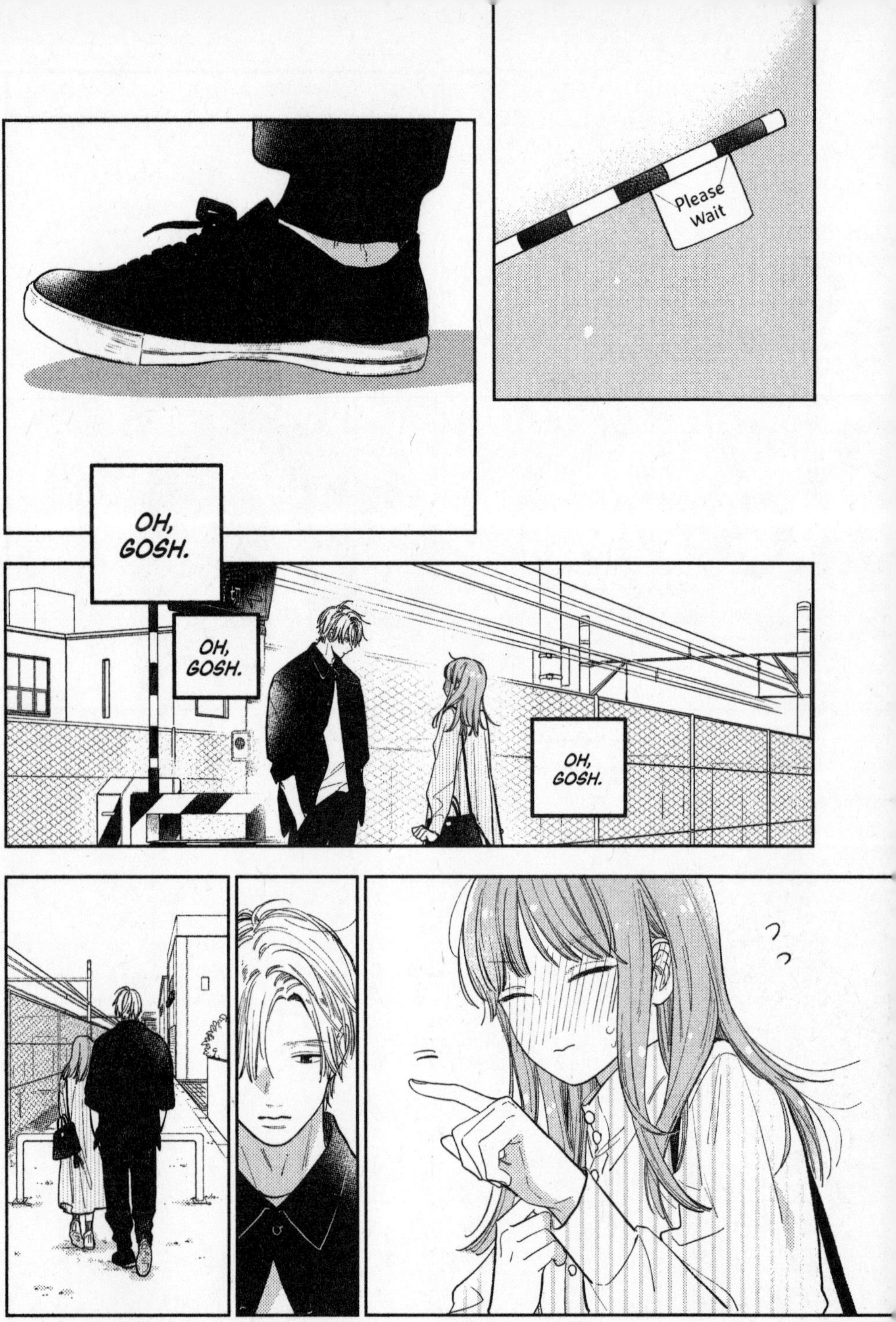
Please Wait
OH, GOSH.
OH, GOSH.
OH, GOSH.

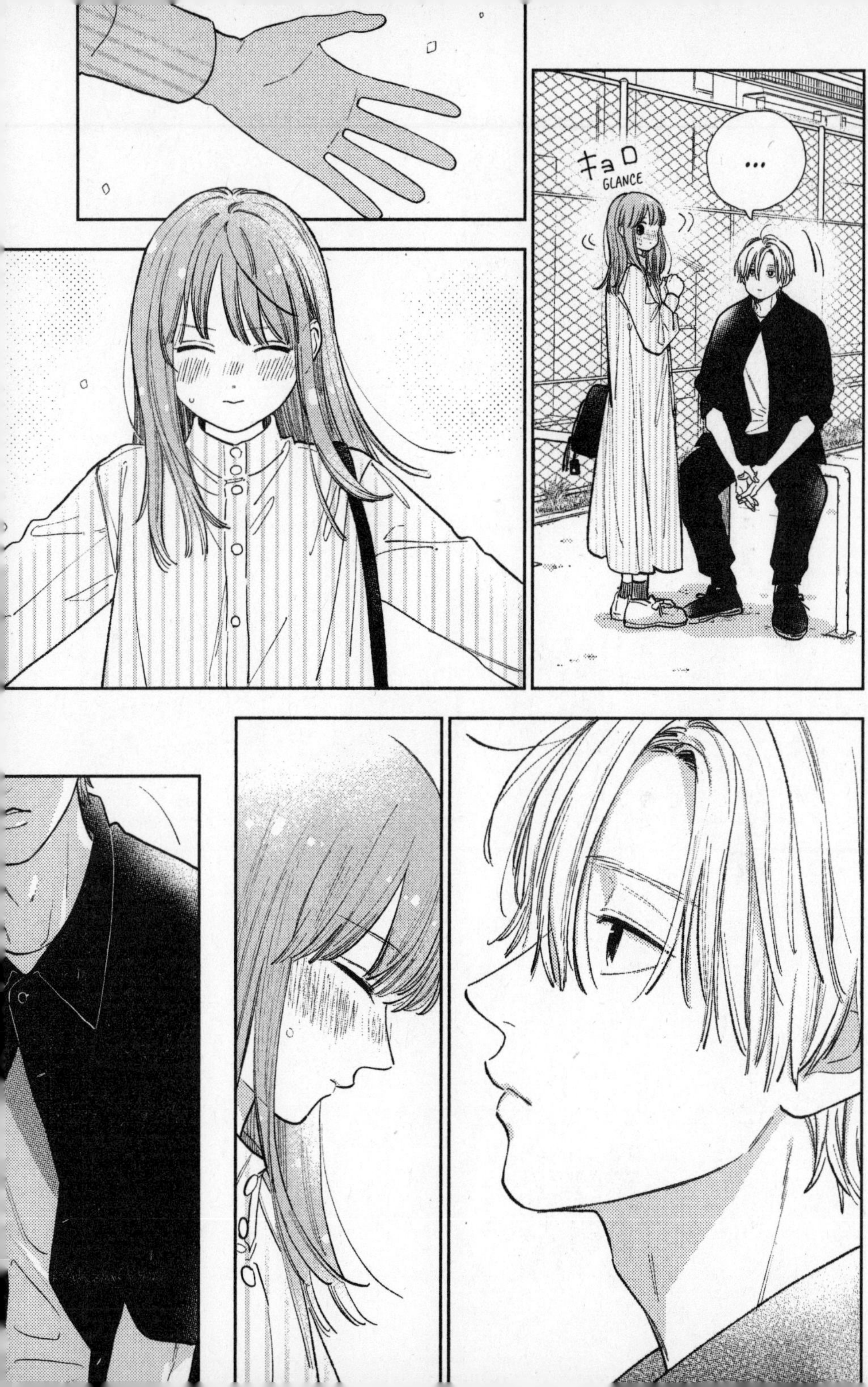
キョロ
GLANCE
...

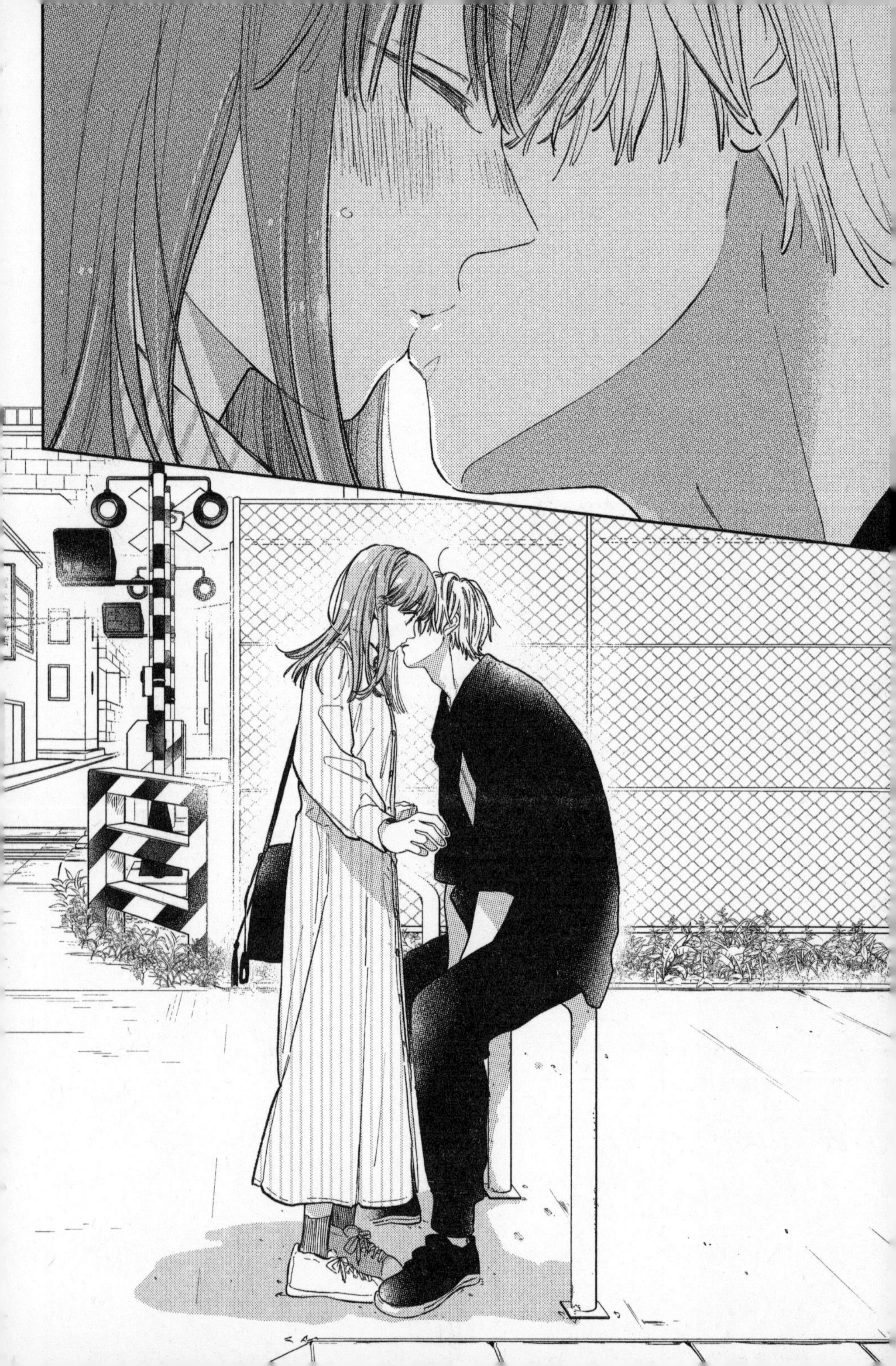

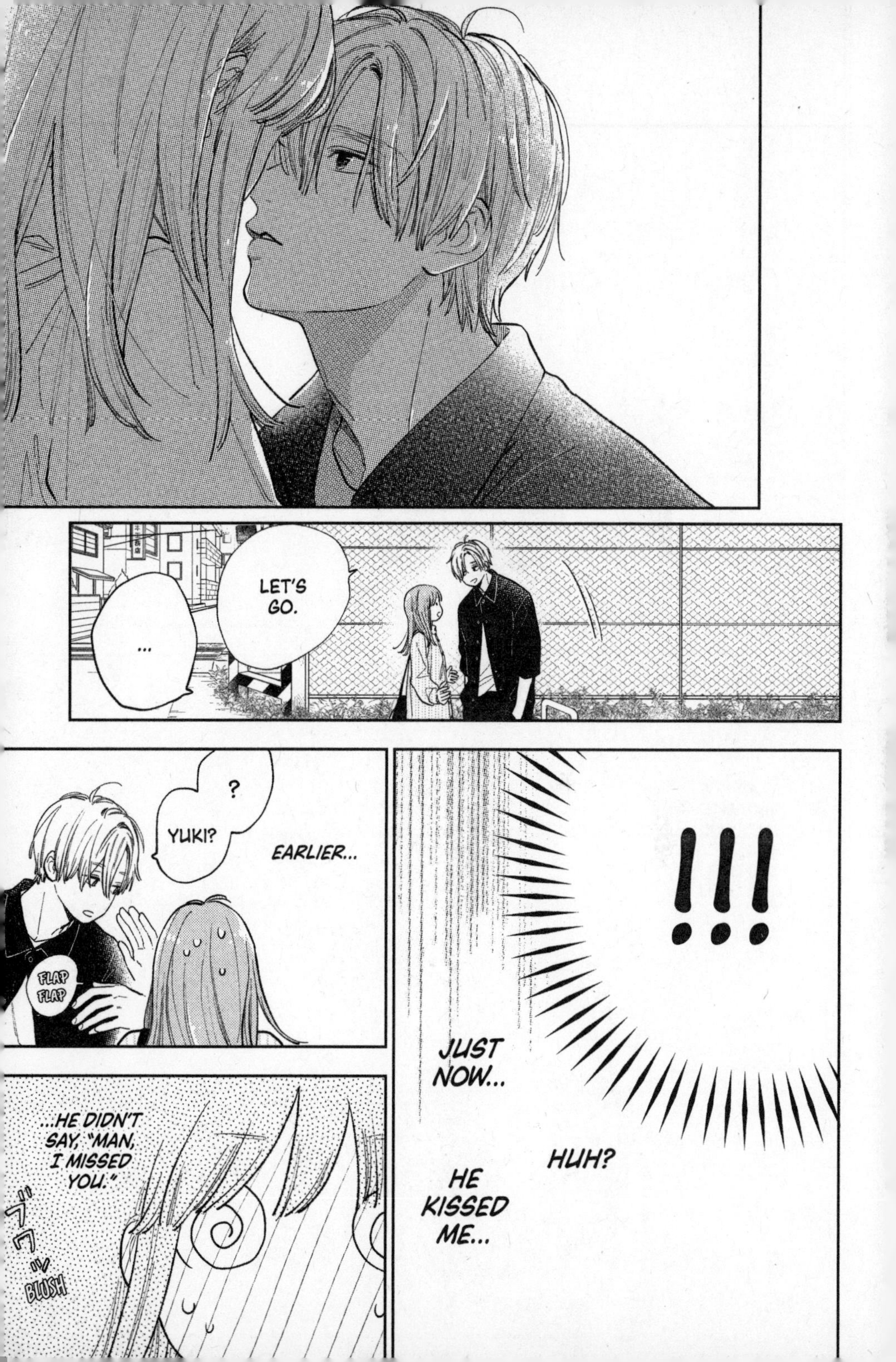
LET'S GO.
...
!!!
JUST NOW...
HUH?
HE KISSED ME...
?
YUKI?
EARLIER...
FLAP FLAP
...HE DIDN'T SAY, "MAN, I MISSED YOU."
BLUSH

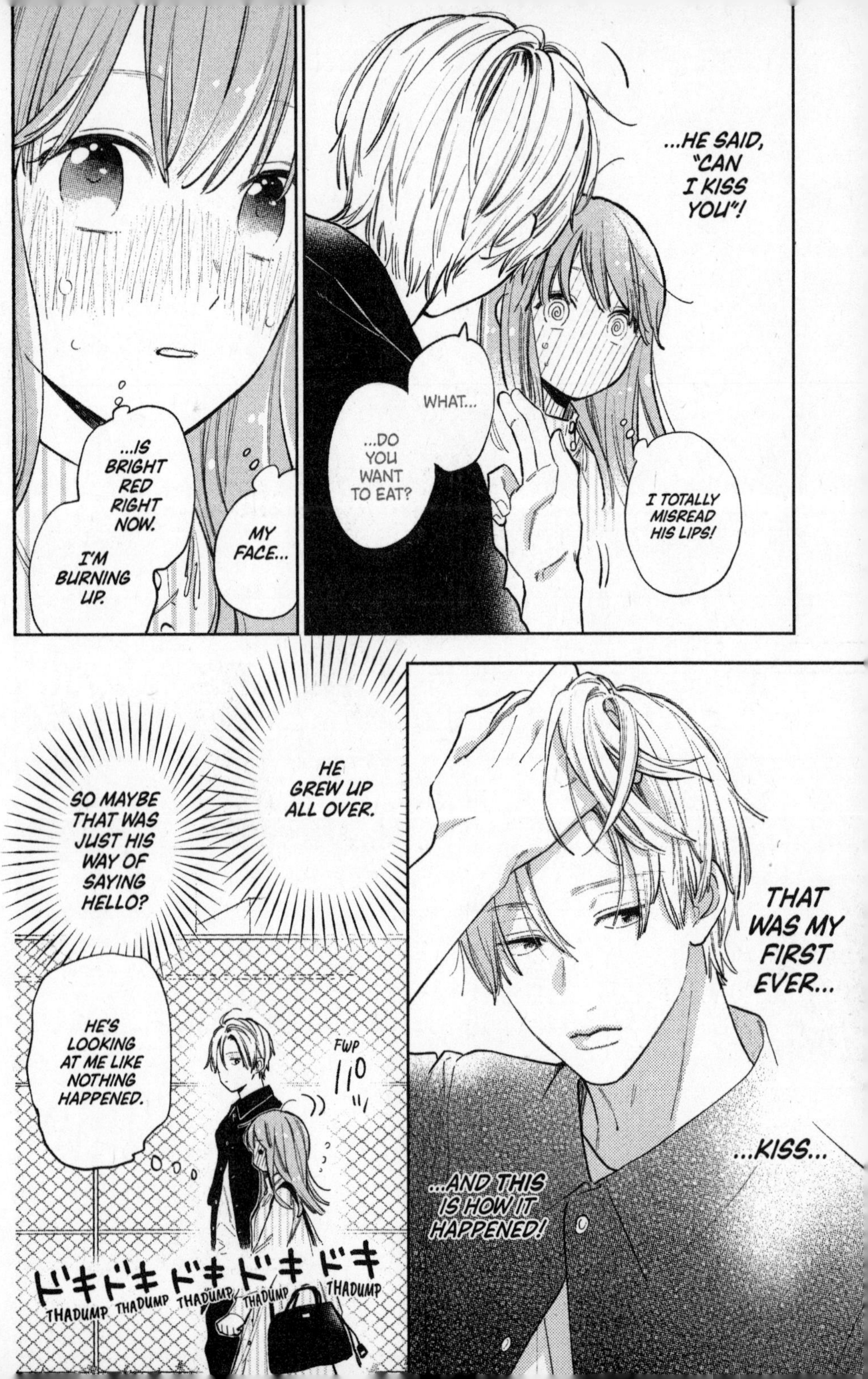
...HE SAID, "CAN I KISS YOU"!
WHAT...
...DO YOU WANT TO EAT?
I TOTALLY MISREAD HIS LIPS!
MY FACE...
...IS BRIGHT RED RIGHT NOW.
I'M BURNING UP.
THAT WAS MY FIRST EVER...
...KISS...
...AND THIS IS HOW IT HAPPENED!
HE GREW UP ALL OVER.
SO MAYBE THAT WAS JUST HIS WAY OF SAYING HELLO?
FWP
HE'S LOOKING AT ME LIKE NOTHING HAPPENED.
ドキドキドキドキドキ
THADUMP THADUMP THADUMP THADUMP THADUMP

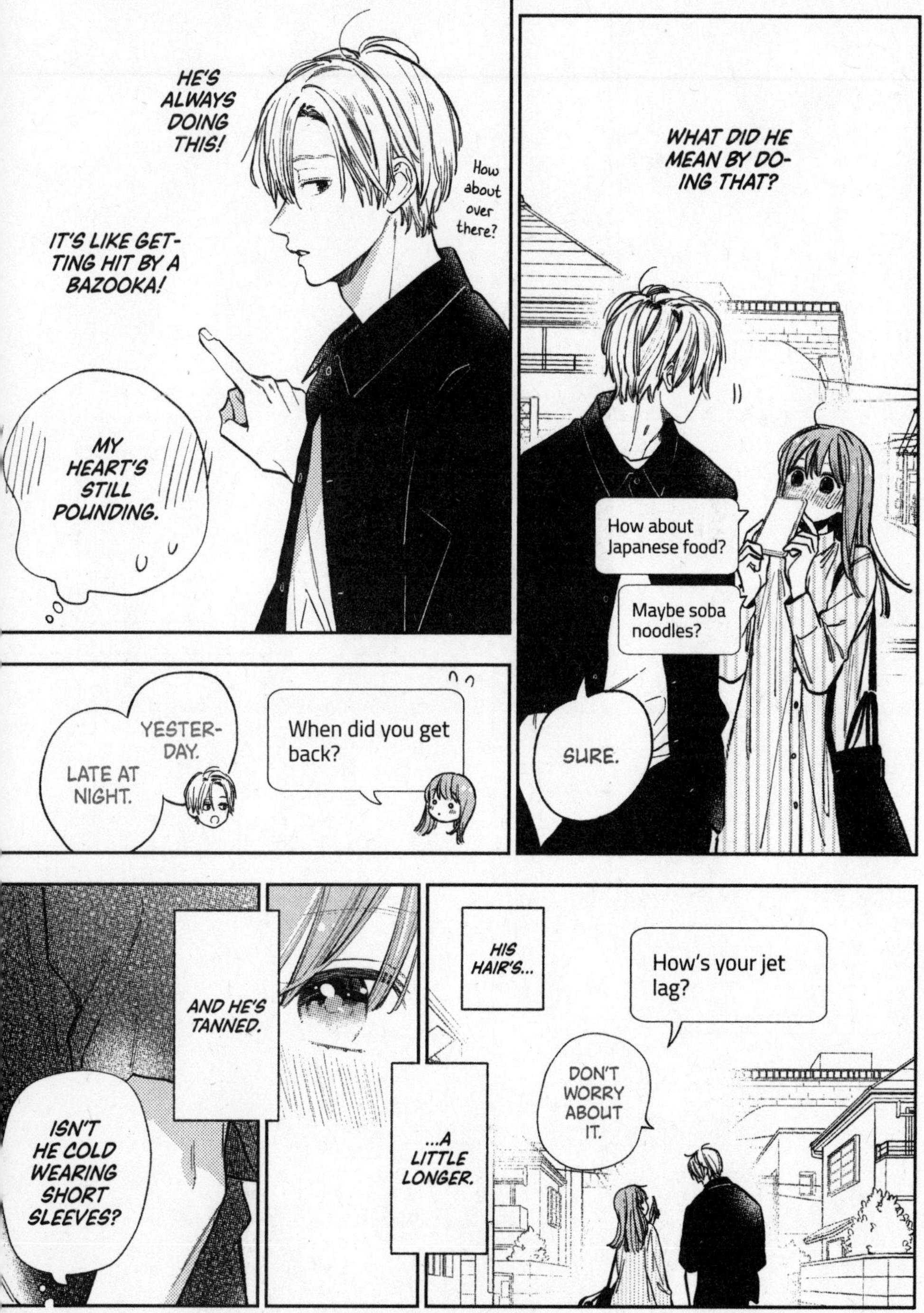
WHAT DID HE MEAN BY DOING THAT?
How about Japanese food?
Maybe soba noodles?
SURE.
How about over there?
HE'S ALWAYS DOING THIS!
IT'S LIKE GETTING HIT BY A BAZOOKA!
MY HEART'S STILL POUNDING.
When did you get back?
YESTERDAY. LATE AT NIGHT.
HIS HAIR'S...
How's your jet lag?
DON'T WORRY ABOUT IT.
...A LITTLE LONGER.
AND HE'S TANNED.
ISN'T HE COLD WEARING SHORT SLEEVES?

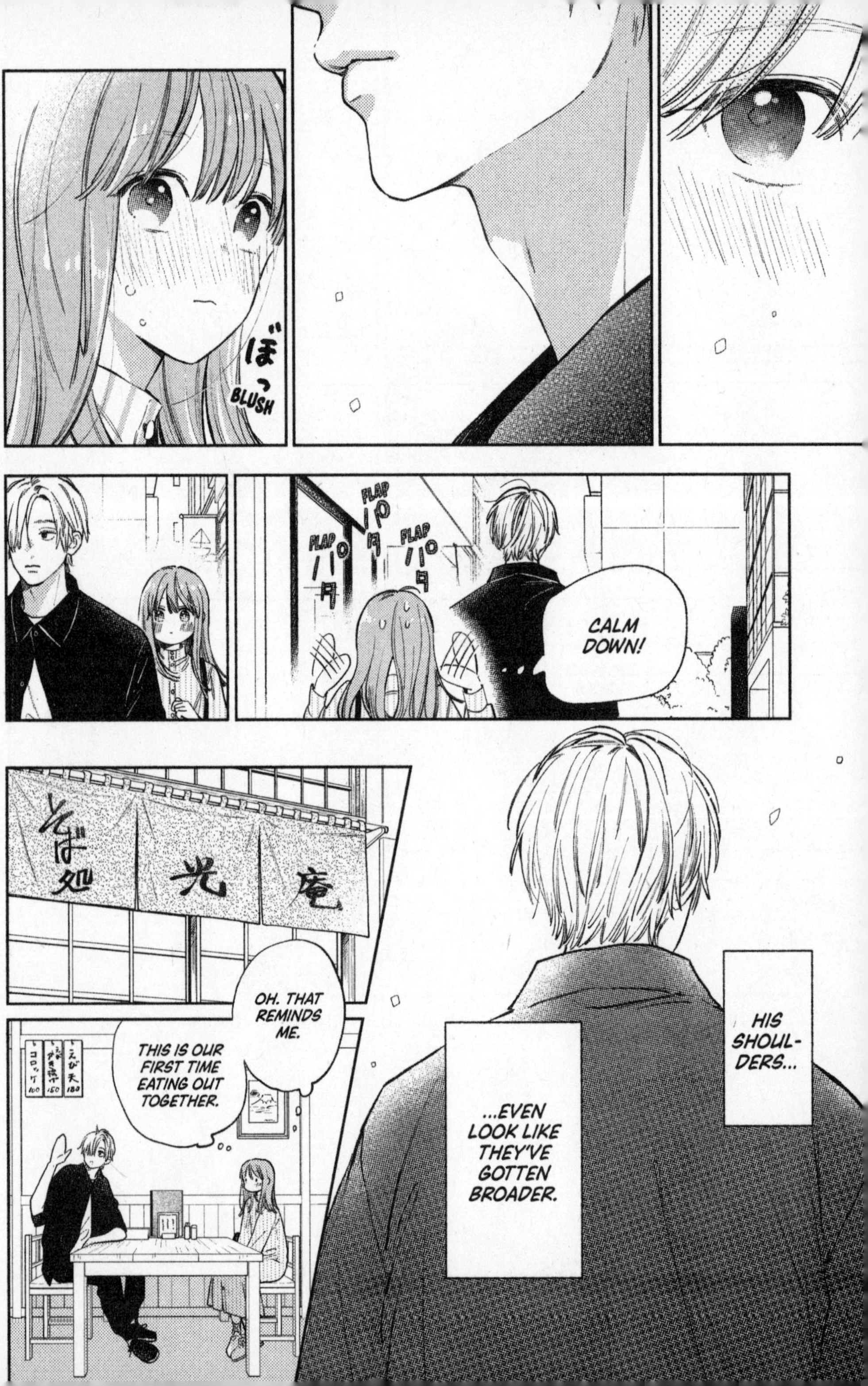
ぼっ
BLUSH
パタ FLAP
パタ FLAP
パタ FLAP
CALM DOWN!
HIS SHOULDERS...
...EVEN LOOK LIKE THEY'VE GOTTEN BROADER.
そば処 光庵
OH. THAT REMINDS ME.
THIS IS OUR FIRST TIME EATING OUT TOGETHER.

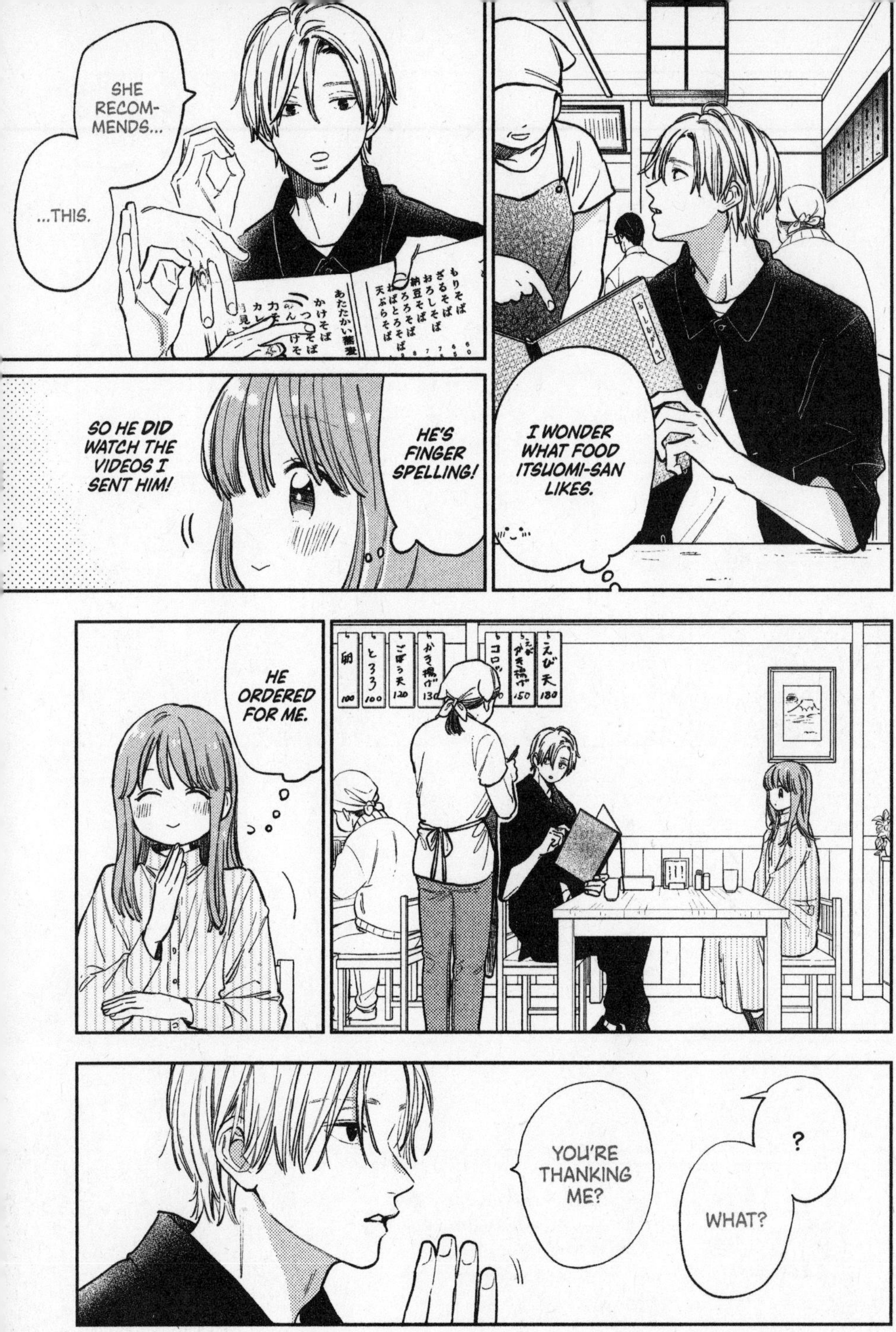
I WONDER WHAT FOOD ITSUOMI-SAN LIKES.
SHE RECOMMENDS...
...THIS.
HE'S FINGER SPELLING!
SO HE DID WATCH THE VIDEOS I SENT HIM!
卵 100
とろろ 100
ごぼう天 120
かき揚げ 130
えび天 180
HE ORDERED FOR ME.
?
WHAT?
YOU'RE THANKING ME?

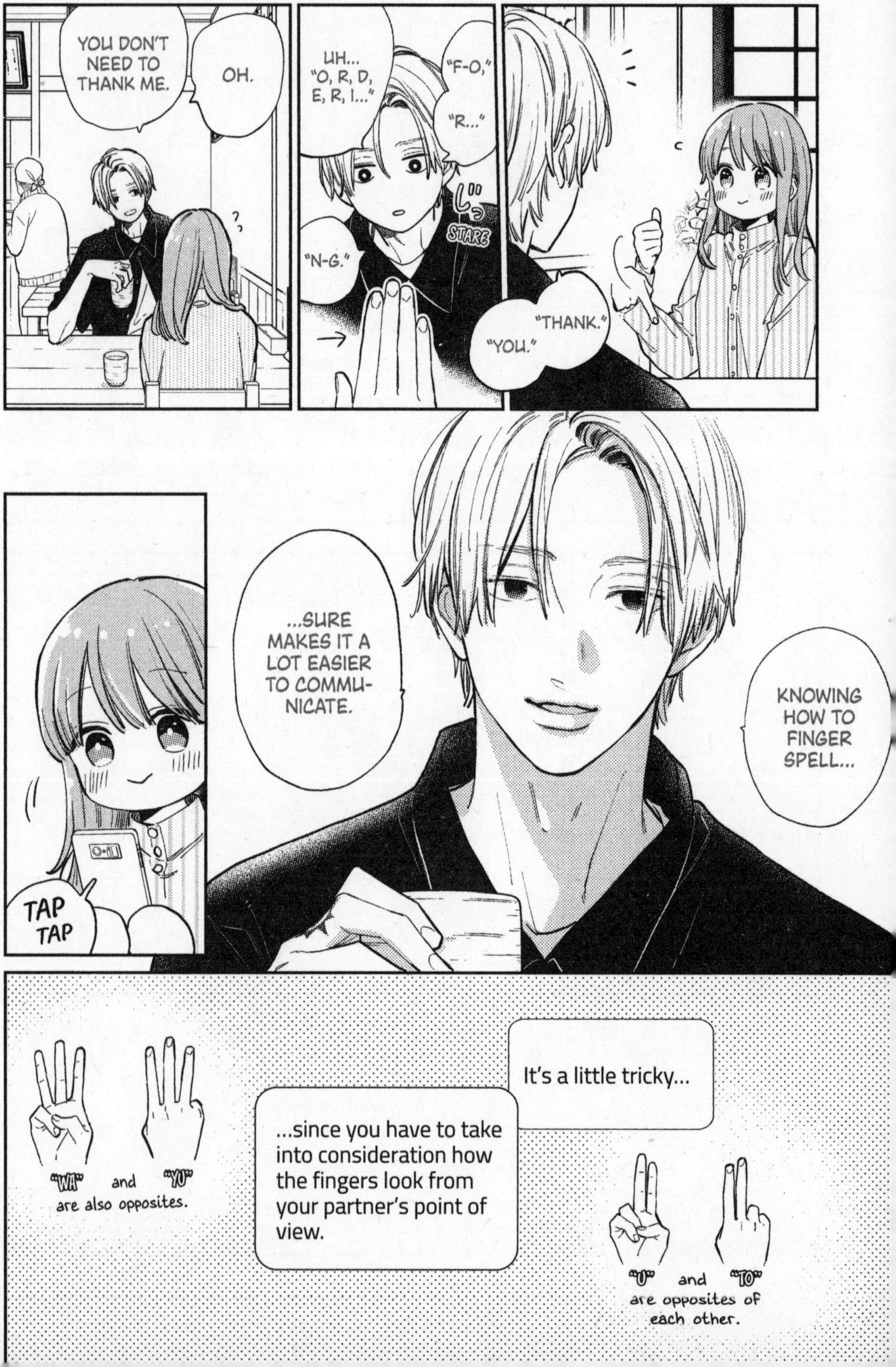
"THANK."
"YOU."
"F-O,"
"R..."
UH... "O, R, D, E, R, I..."
STARE
"N-G."
YOU DON'T NEED TO THANK ME.
OH.
KNOWING HOW TO FINGER SPELL...
...SURE MAKES IT A LOT EASIER TO COMMUNICATE.
TAP TAP
It's a little tricky...
...since you have to take into consideration how the fingers look from your partner's point of view.
"O" and "TO" are opposites of each other.
"WA" and "YU" are also opposites.

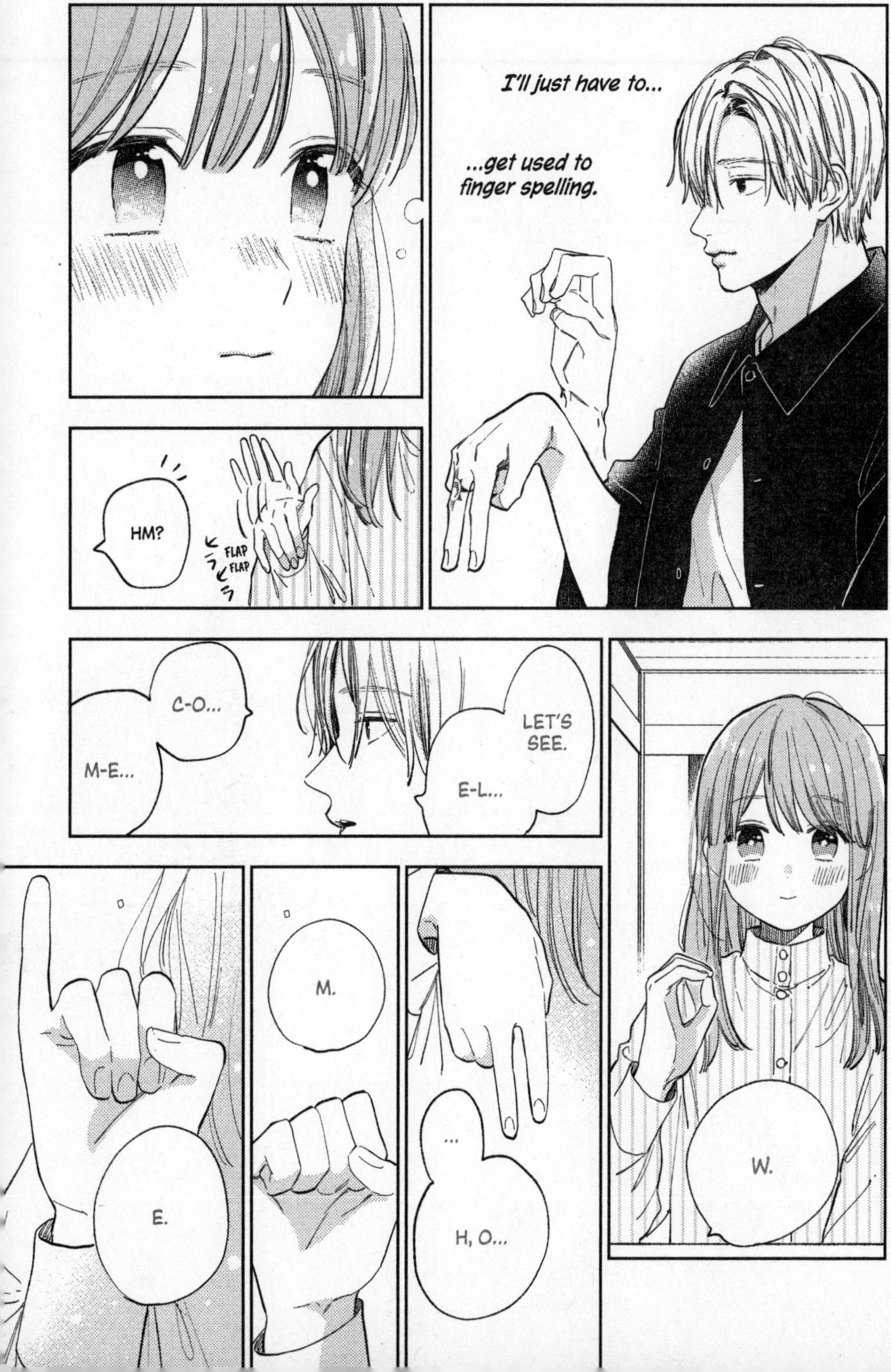
I'll just have to...
...get used to finger spelling.
HM?
FLAP FLAP
W.
LET'S SEE.
E-L...
C-O...
M-E...
...
H, O...
M.
E.

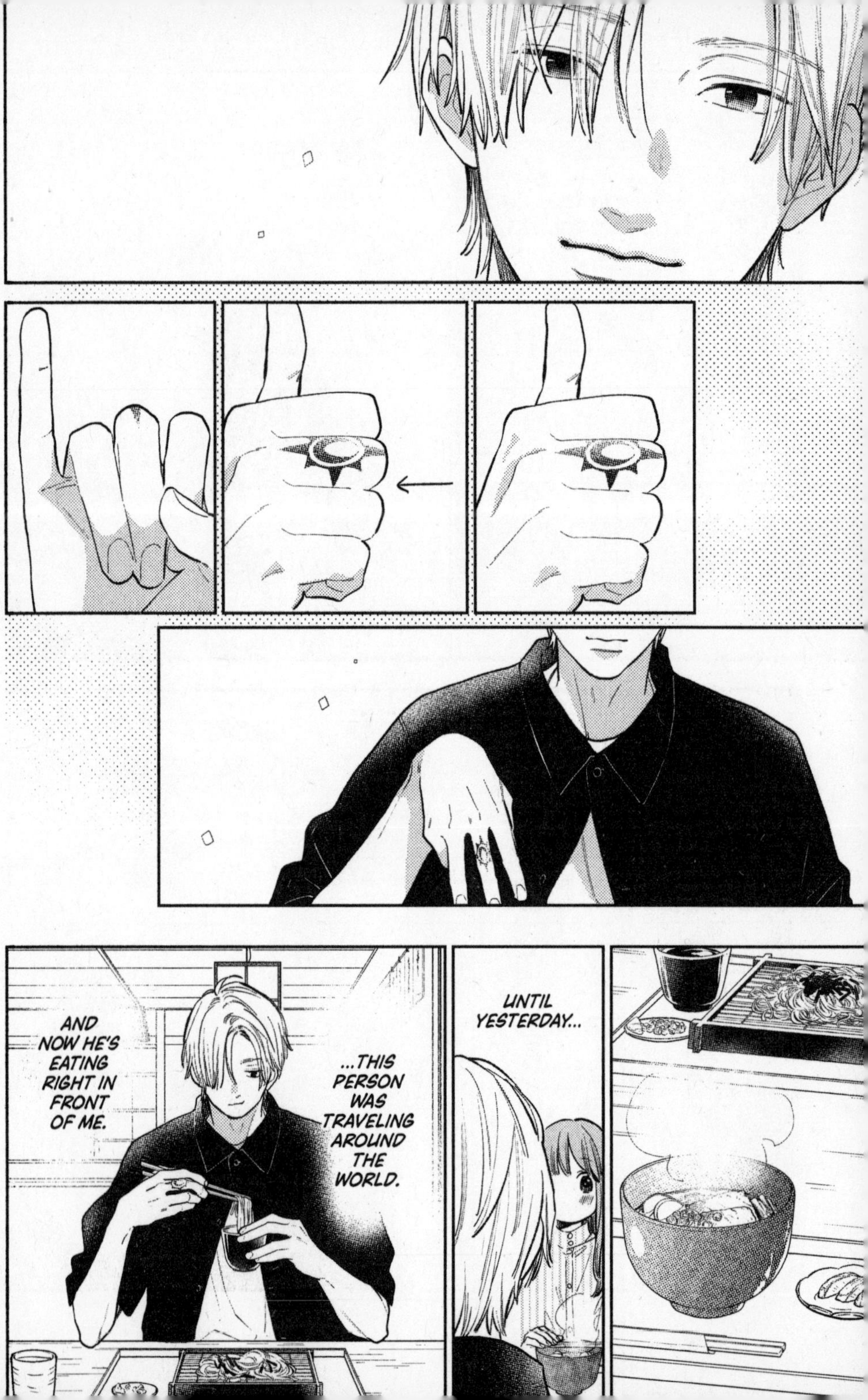
UNTIL YESTERDAY...
...THIS PERSON WAS TRAVELING AROUND THE WORLD.
AND NOW HE'S EATING RIGHT IN FRONT OF ME.

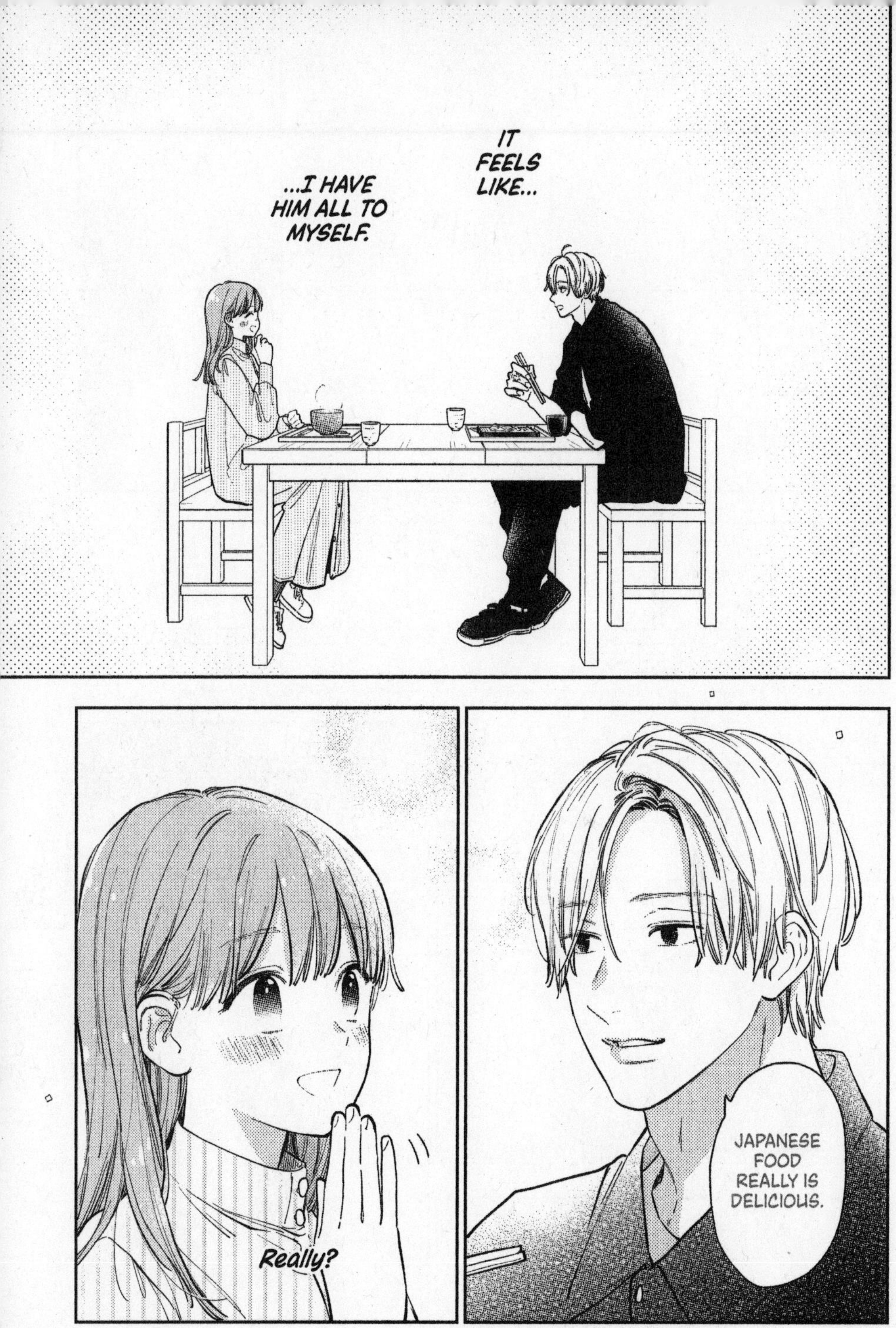
IT FEELS LIKE...
...I HAVE HIM ALL TO MYSELF.
JAPANESE FOOD REALLY IS DELICIOUS.
Really?

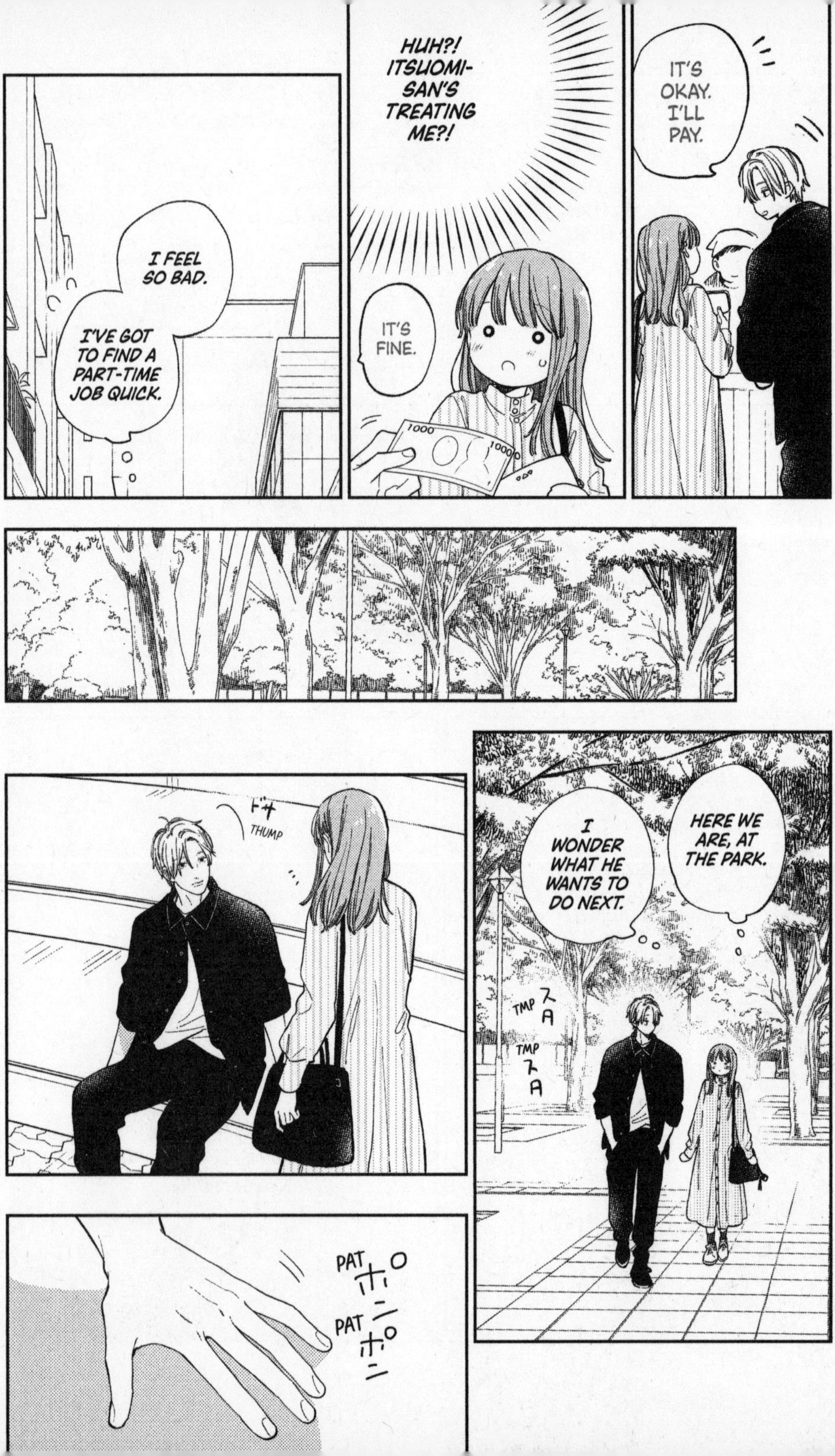
IT'S OKAY. I'LL PAY.
HUH?! ITSUOMI-SAN'S TREATING ME?!
IT'S FINE.
I FEEL SO BAD.
I'VE GOT TO FIND A PART-TIME JOB QUICK.
HERE WE ARE, AT THE PARK.
I WONDER WHAT HE WANTS TO DO NEXT.
TMP
TMP
THUMP
PAT
PAT

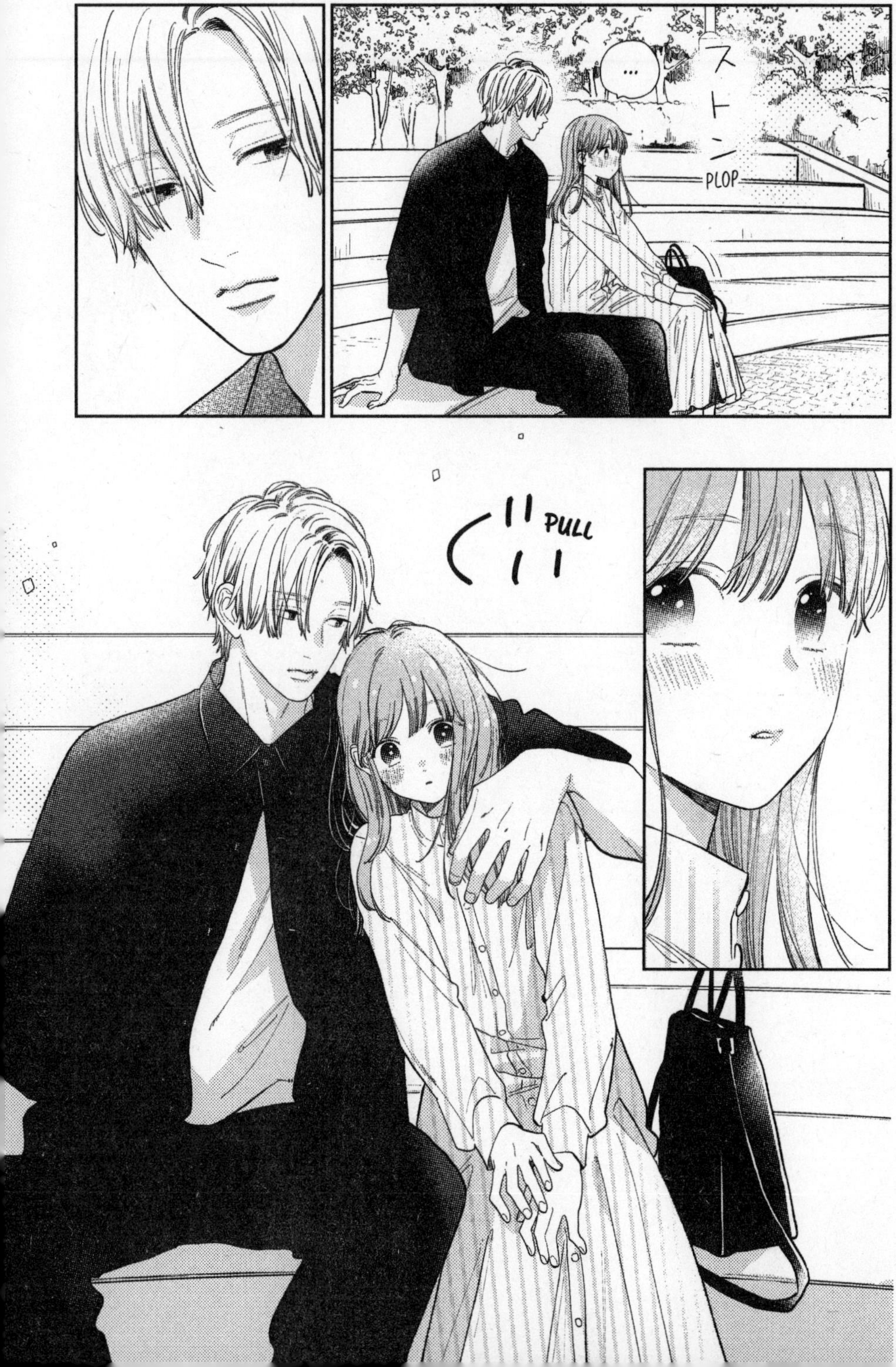
…
ストン
PLOP
PULL

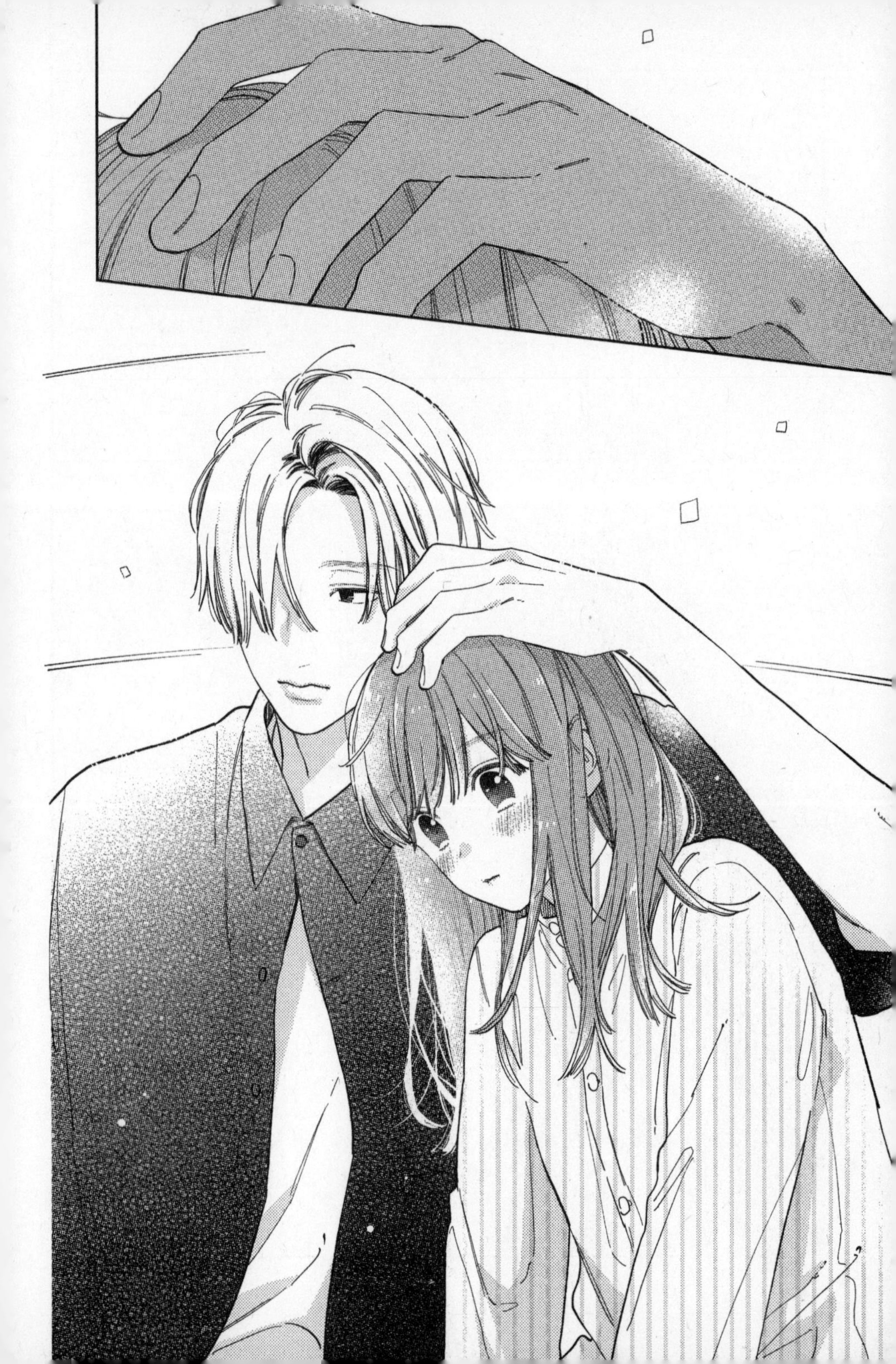

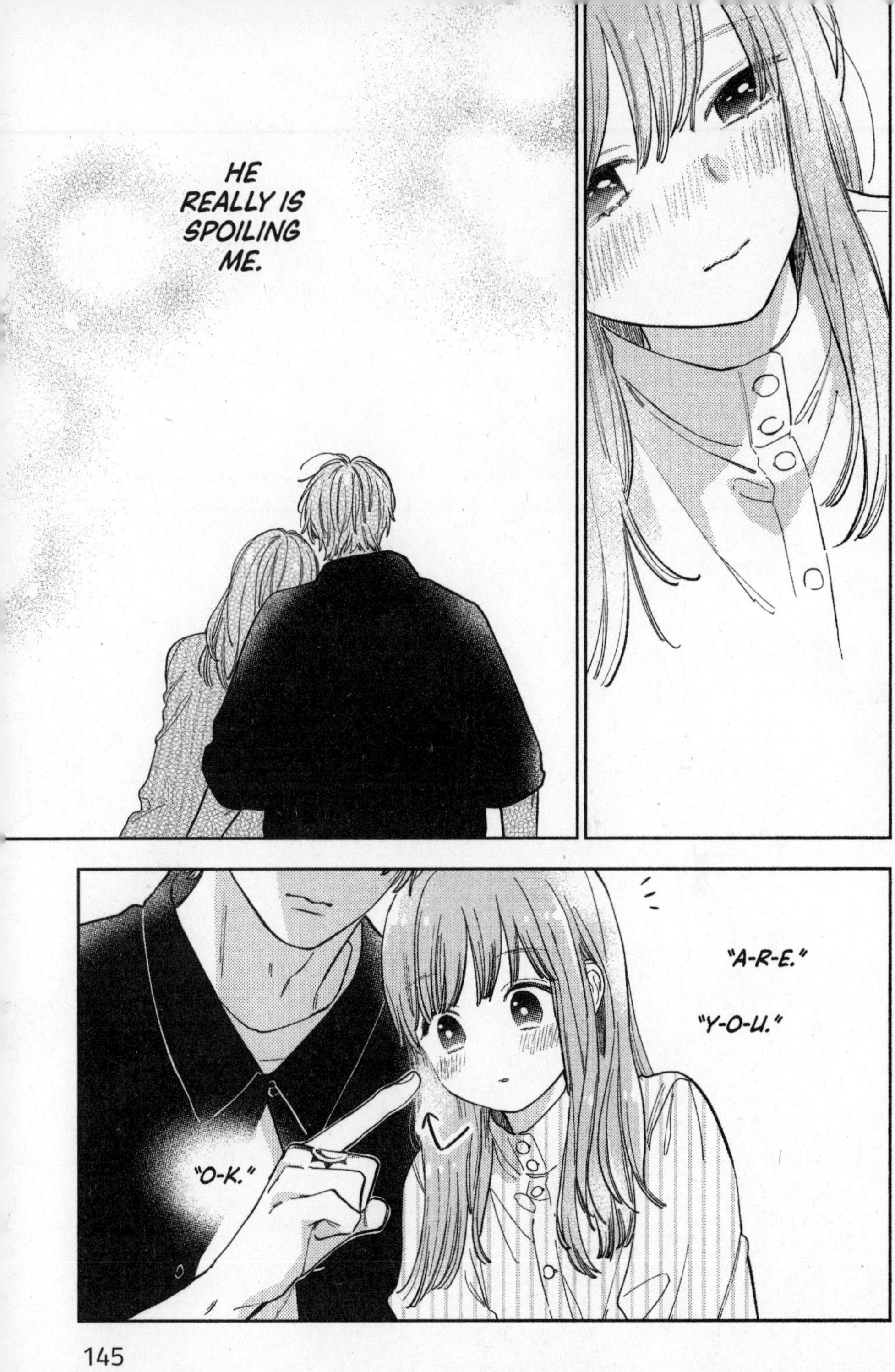
HE REALLY IS SPOILING ME.
"A-R-E."
"Y-O-U."
"O-K."

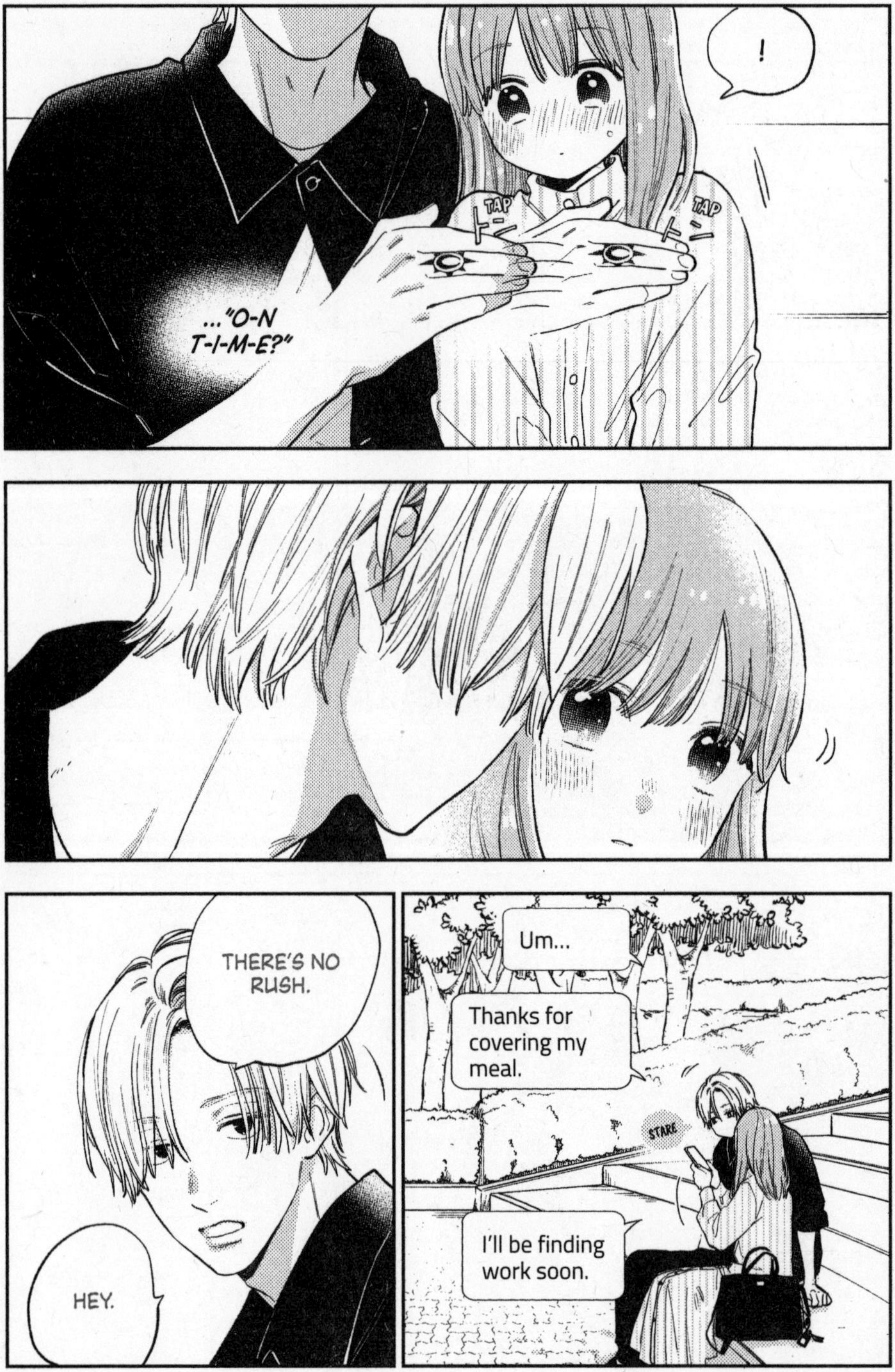
!
TAP
TAP
..."O-N T-I-M-E?"
Um...
Thanks for covering my meal.
STARE
I'll be finding work soon.
THERE'S NO RUSH.
HEY.

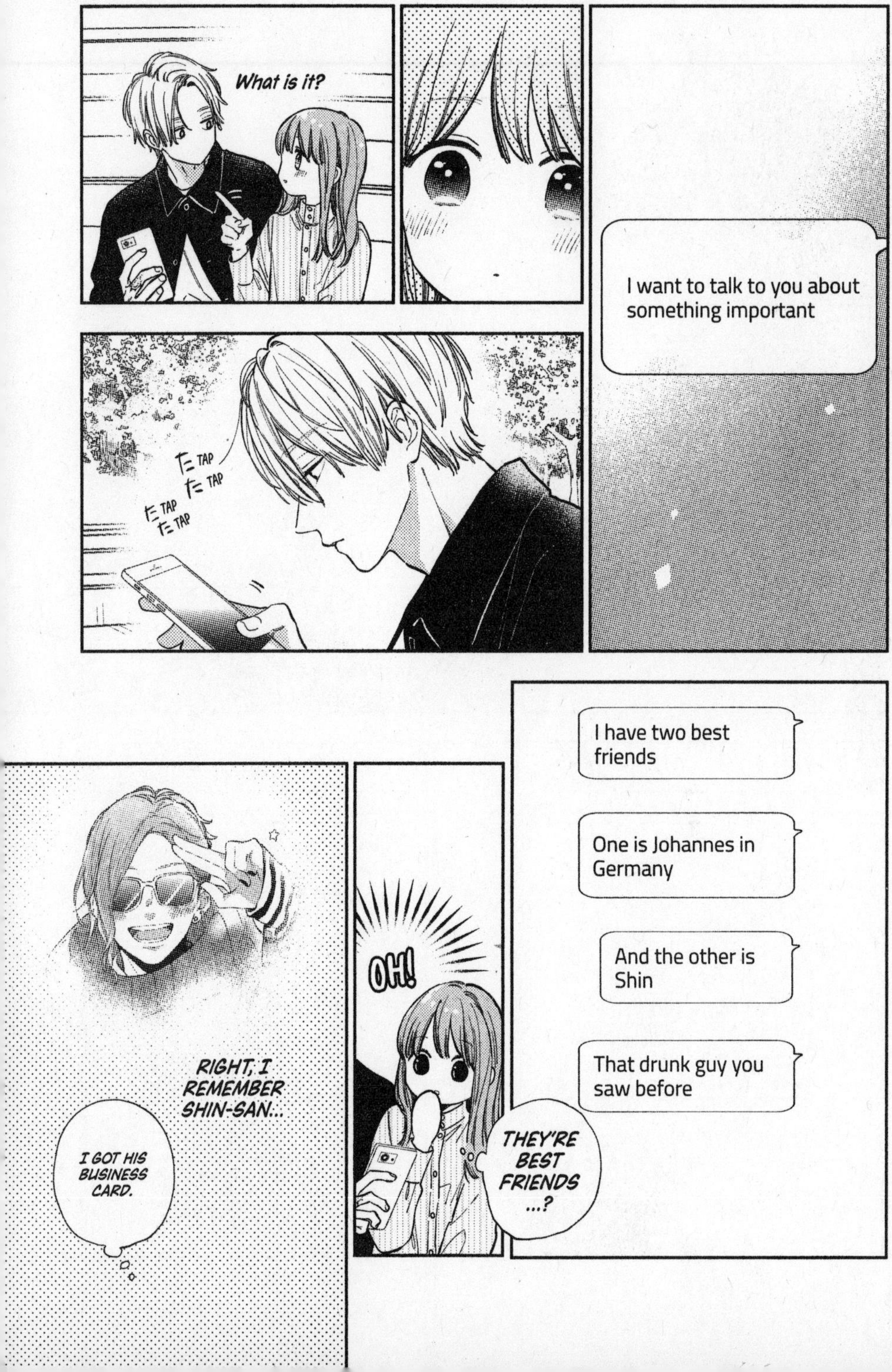
I want to talk to you about something important
What is it?
た TAP
た TAP
た TAP
た TAP
I have two best friends
One is Johannes in Germany
And the other is Shin
That drunk guy you saw before
OH!
THEY'RE BEST FRIENDS ...?
RIGHT, I REMEMBER SHIN-SAN...
I GOT HIS BUSINESS CARD.

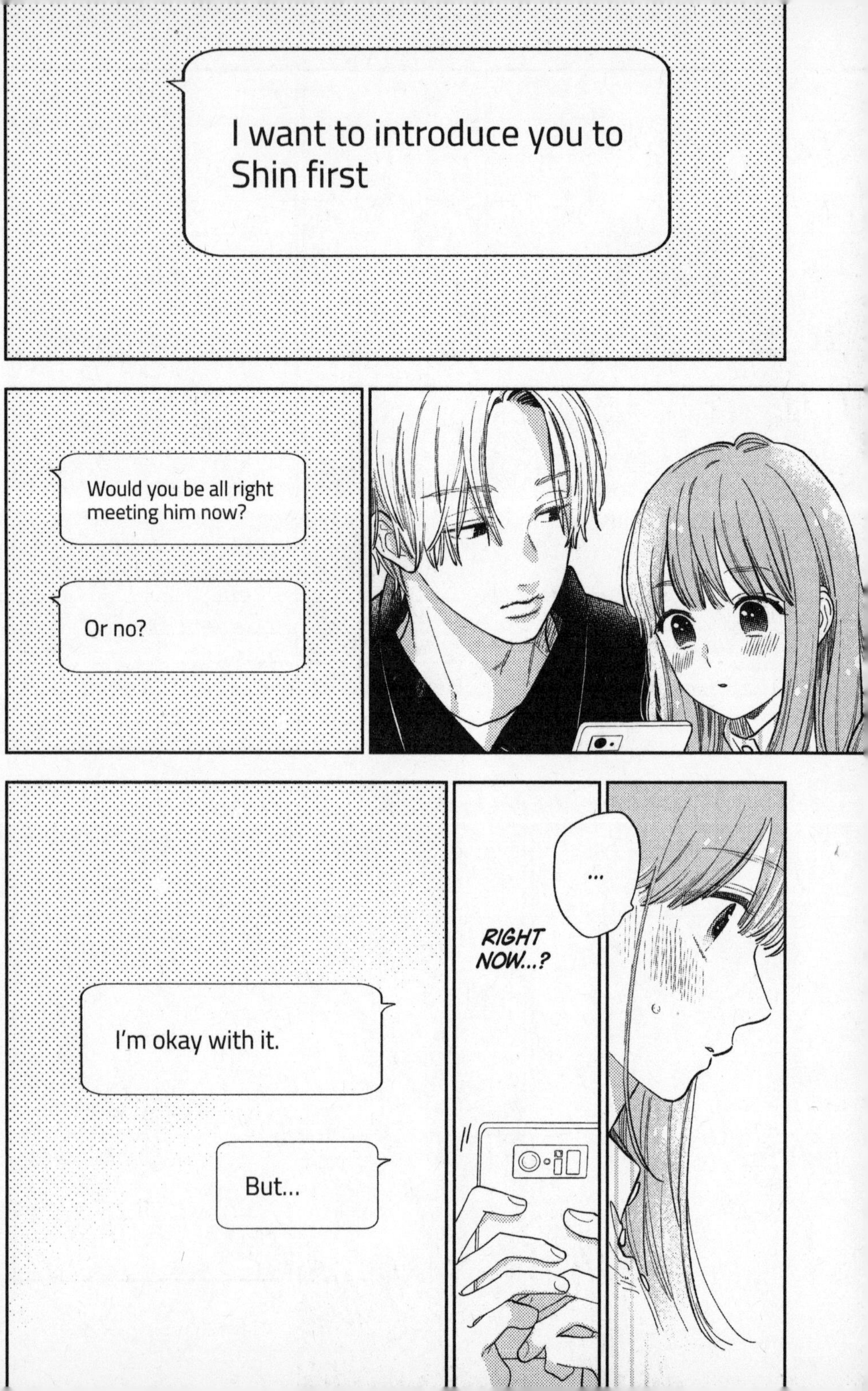
I want to introduce you to Shin first
Would you be all right meeting him now?
Or no?
...
RIGHT NOW...?
I'm okay with it.
But...

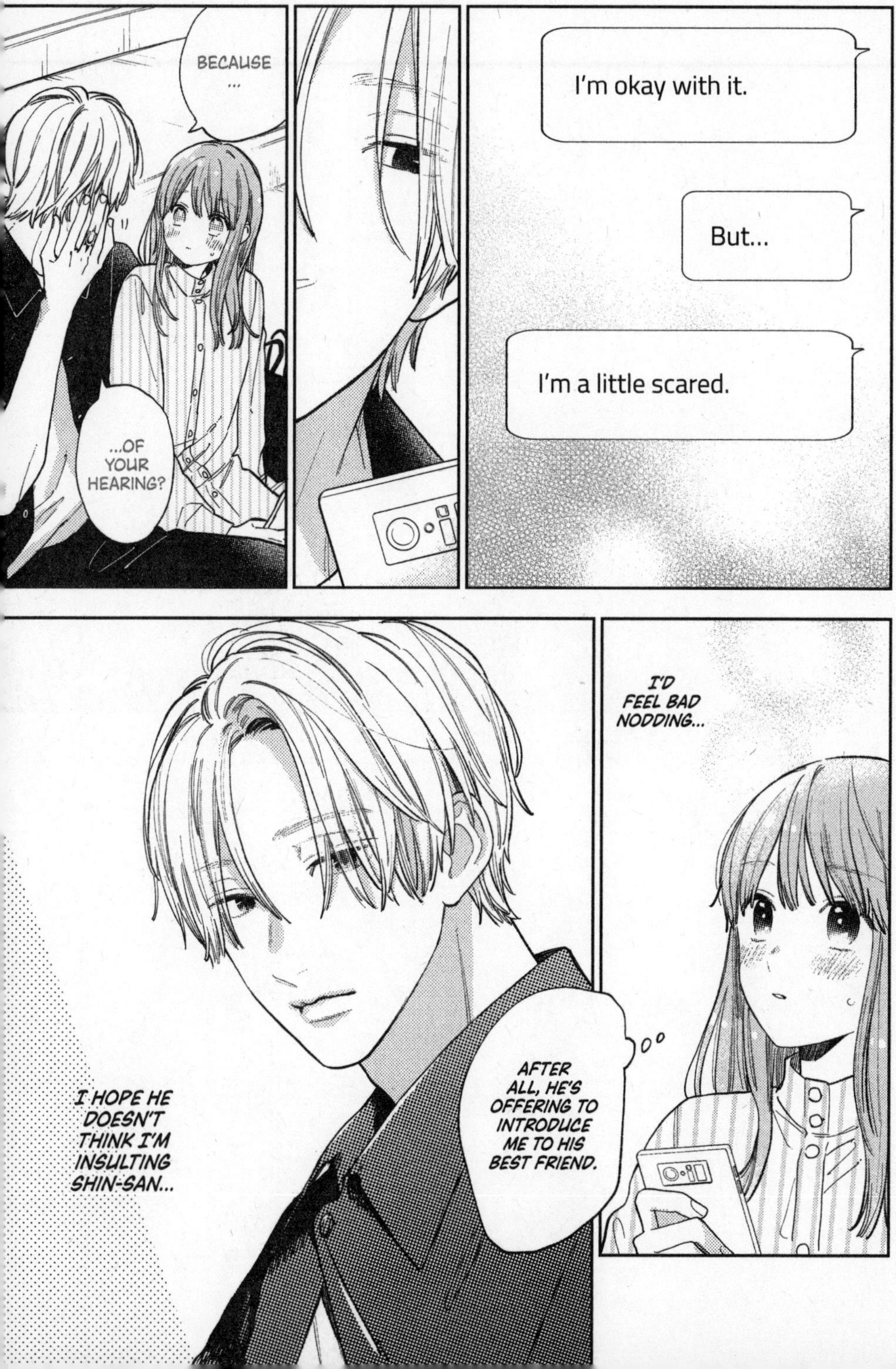
I'm okay with it.
But...
I'm a little scared.
BECAUSE ...
...OF YOUR HEARING?
I'D FEEL BAD NODDING...
AFTER ALL, HE'S OFFERING TO INTRODUCE ME TO HIS BEST FRIEND.
I HOPE HE DOESN'T THINK I'M INSULTING SHIN-SAN...

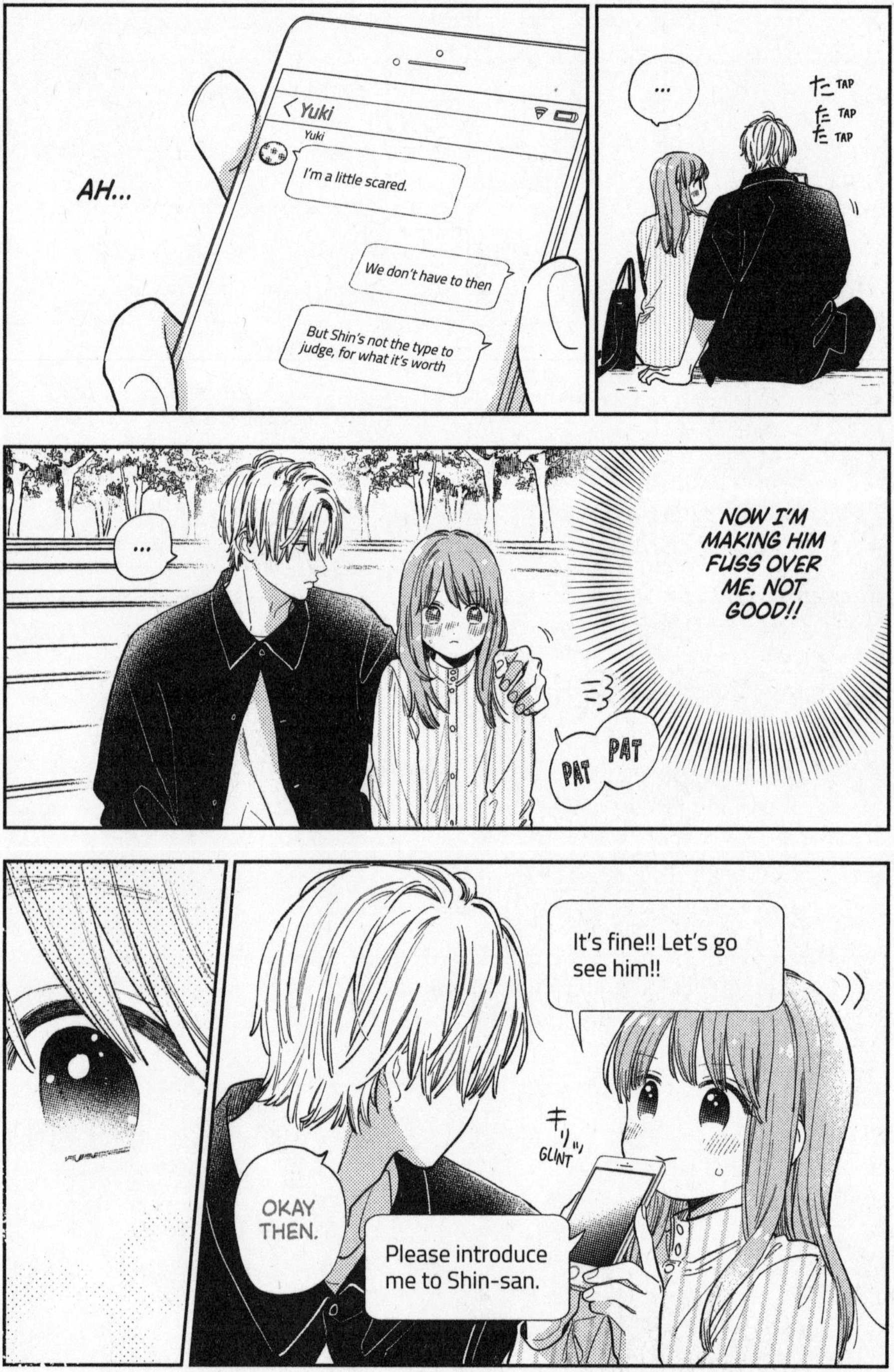
…
た TAP
た TAP
た TAP
< Yuki
Yuki
I'm a little scared.
We don't have to then
But Shin's not the type to judge, for what it's worth
AH…
NOW I'M MAKING HIM FUSS OVER ME. NOT GOOD!!
PAT PAT
…
It's fine!! Let's go see him!!
キリッ GLINT
Please introduce me to Shin-san.
OKAY THEN.

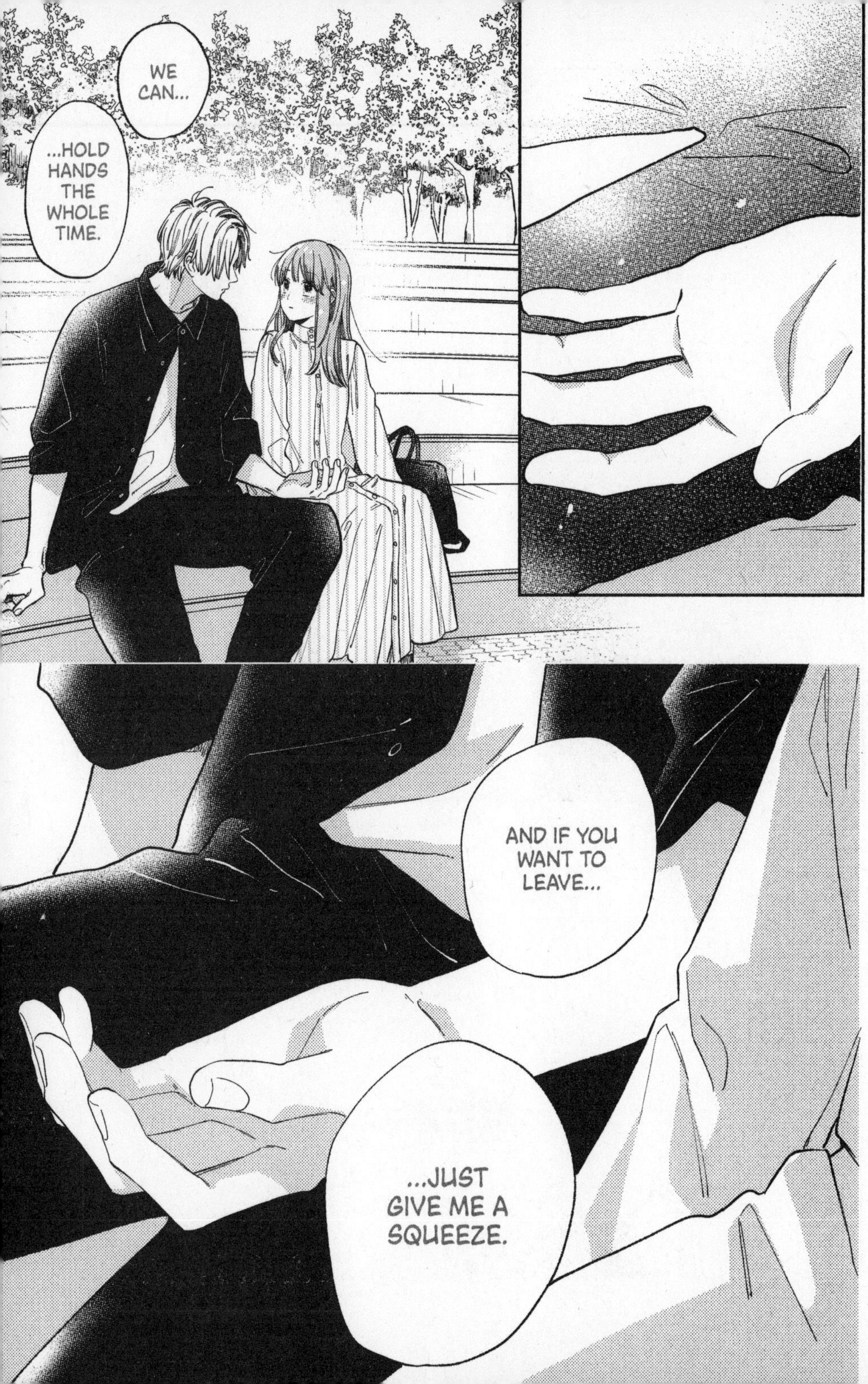
WE CAN...
...HOLD HANDS THE WHOLE TIME.
AND IF YOU WANT TO LEAVE...
...JUST GIVE ME A SQUEEZE.

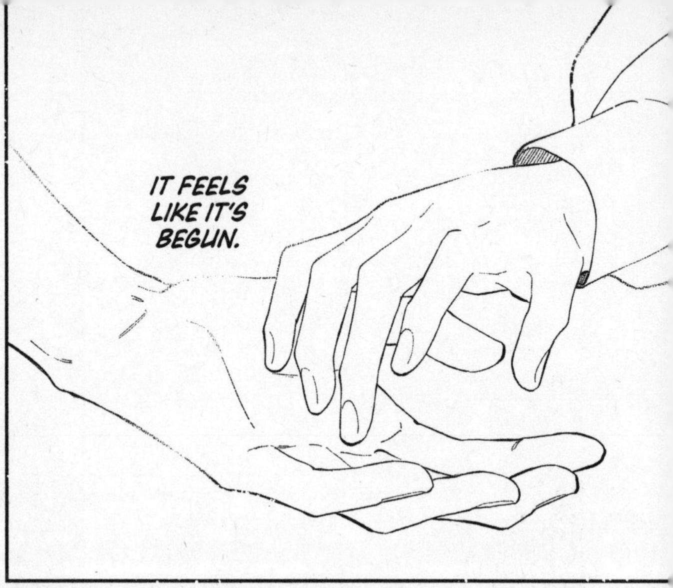
IT FEELS LIKE IT'S BEGUN.

I WANT TO BE TAKEN...

...INTO ITSUOMI-SAN'S WORLD.

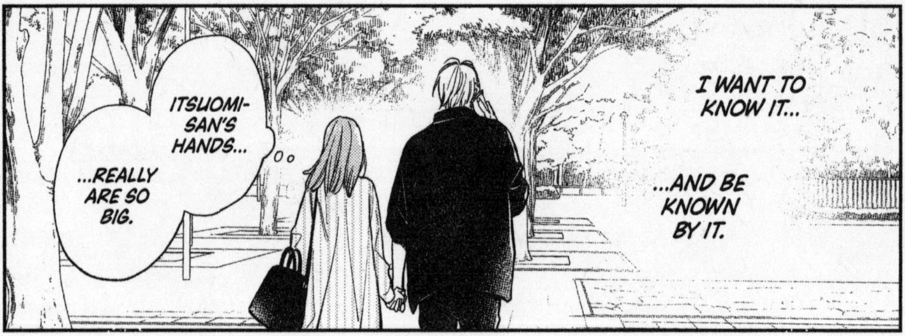
I WANT TO KNOW IT...
...AND BE KNOWN BY IT.
ITSUOMI-SAN'S HANDS...
...REALLY ARE SO BIG.

BUT...

...I DON'T WANT HIM TO REALIZE YET...

...HOW INCONVENIENT IT IS FOR ME TO HOLD HANDS.

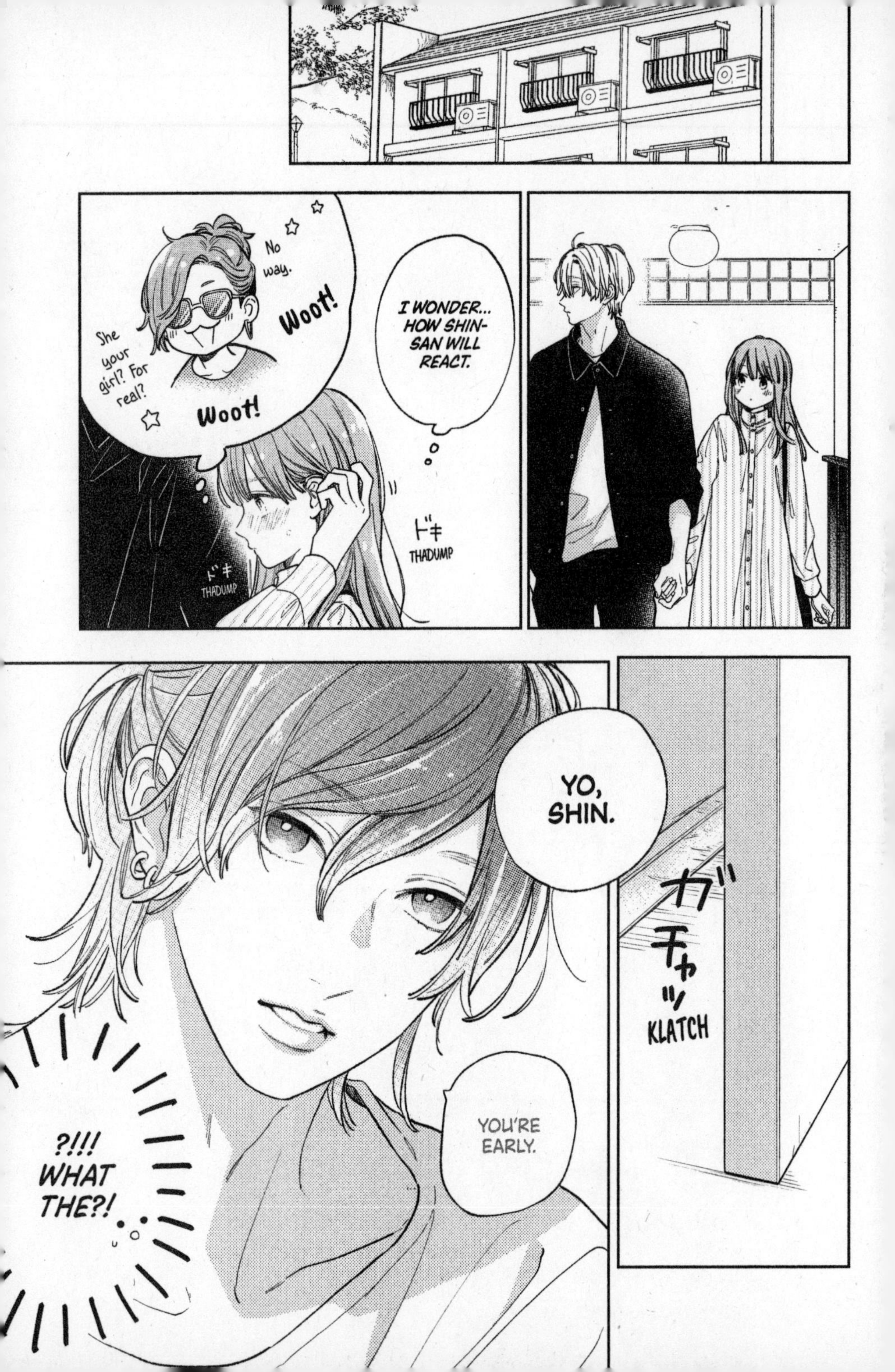
I WONDER... HOW SHIN-SAN WILL REACT.
No way.
Woot!
She your girl? For real?
Woot!
ドキ THADUMP
ドキ THADUMP
ガチャッ KLATCH
YO, SHIN.
YOU'RE EARLY.
?!!! WHAT THE?!

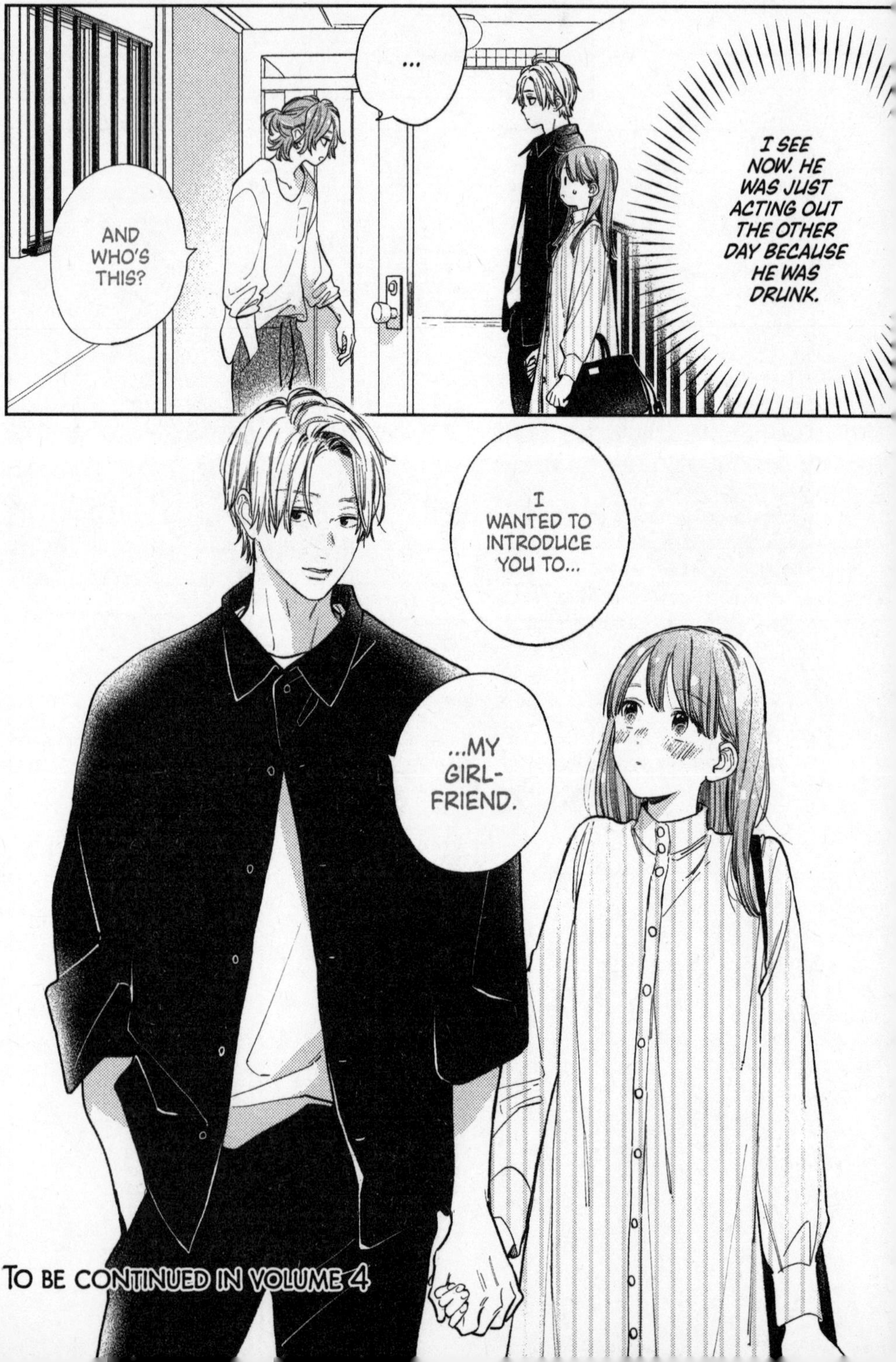
I SEE NOW. HE WAS JUST ACTING OUT THE OTHER DAY BECAUSE HE WAS DRUNK.
...
AND WHO'S THIS?
I WANTED TO INTRODUCE YOU TO...
...MY GIRL-FRIEND.
TO BE CONTINUED IN VOLUME 4

✿ Afterword ✿

Thank you very much for reading volume 3. I've been so happy to receive letters from readers telling me that they've started to learn sign language thanks to this story. Sign languages differ depending on the region, and signs go in and out of use depending on the times, so it's a constantly evolving language. In fact, even if you show sign language books to the Deaf, there will be signs that they don't use or even recognize. There may be instances of the sign language in this manga not matching what you're taught in sign language class, but I hope you will bear in mind that they're all legitimate forms of sign language. For the record, the sign that Itsuomi used with Yuki in this scene meant "go out with me."

(See chapter 10)

Well, I hope to see you again in volume 4.

suu Morishita

▶ Special Thanks ◀

▶ Editor: Shiigeru-san,

▶ Balcolony's Takeuchi-san, Ichiki-san

▶ Everyone at spica works

▶ The editorial staff of *Dessert*

▶ The international rights department

▶ Sign Language Collaborator: Yuki Miyazaki-chan
▶ Backgrounds Materials Collaborator: Rockin' Robin, Osu-sama

Research Help:
▶ Naomi Nishimiya-sama

▶ Sister Makiro

Staff ▶ Finishing Touches: Nao Hamaguchi-chan
▶ Backgrounds: Saya Aoi-san

▶ All of our readers! ◀

TRANSLATION NOTES

MAN, I MISSED YOU.

"Man, I missed you," page 129
In Japanese, Yuki thinks Itsuomi is saying, *"Gyuushite ii?"* or, "Can I hug you?" In fact, as she later finds out, he's saying, *"Chuushite ii?"* or, "Can I kiss you?" This is why Yuki is holding her arms out for a hug on page 131. The two words are similar in Japanese, a language with lots of homophones due to its relatively small number of vowel sounds.

Shin and *kokoro*, page 147
There is an interesting detail on this page in the Japanese version that is impossible to depict in English. Japanese is written using three alphabets: *hiragana*, *katakana*, and *kanji*. The first two are syllabic, meaning each letter is associated with the sound of a spoken syllable, but kanji is logographic, meaning its letters only represent words,

OH!

One is Johannes in Germany

And the other is Shin

That drunk guy you saw before

THEY'RE BEST FRIENDS ...?

and most kanji have multiple pronunciations. The kanji for Shin, 心, is also the word for "heart," in which context it's pronounced "kokoro." At the bottom of this page, Yuki is confused because she sees this kanji in Itsuomi's text messages and misreads it as "kokoro," not realizing he's referring to his friend Shin.

Sign language, page 155
Japanese Sign Language, spoken Japanese, spoken English, and American Sign Language are all different languages, so the written transcriptions of signs in this book are translations of translations. If this series has inspired you to learn more about American Sign Language, you may want to check out The ASL App, at theaslapp.com, or the ASL Connect: ASL for Free page at gallaudet.edu/asl-connect/asl-for-free/.

THE SWEET SCENT OF LOVE IS IN THE AIR! FOR FANS OF OFFBEAT ROMANCES LIKE *WOTAKOI*

VOL. 1

SWEAT AND SOAP

KINTETSU YAMADA

Sweat and Soap © Kintetsu Yamada / Kodansha Ltd.

In an office romance, there's a fine line between sexy and awkward... and that line is where Asako — a woman who sweats copiously — meets Koutarou — a perfume developer who can't get enough of Asako's, er, scent. Don't miss a romcom manga like no other!

KC KODANSHA COMICS

PERFECT WORLD

Rie Aruga

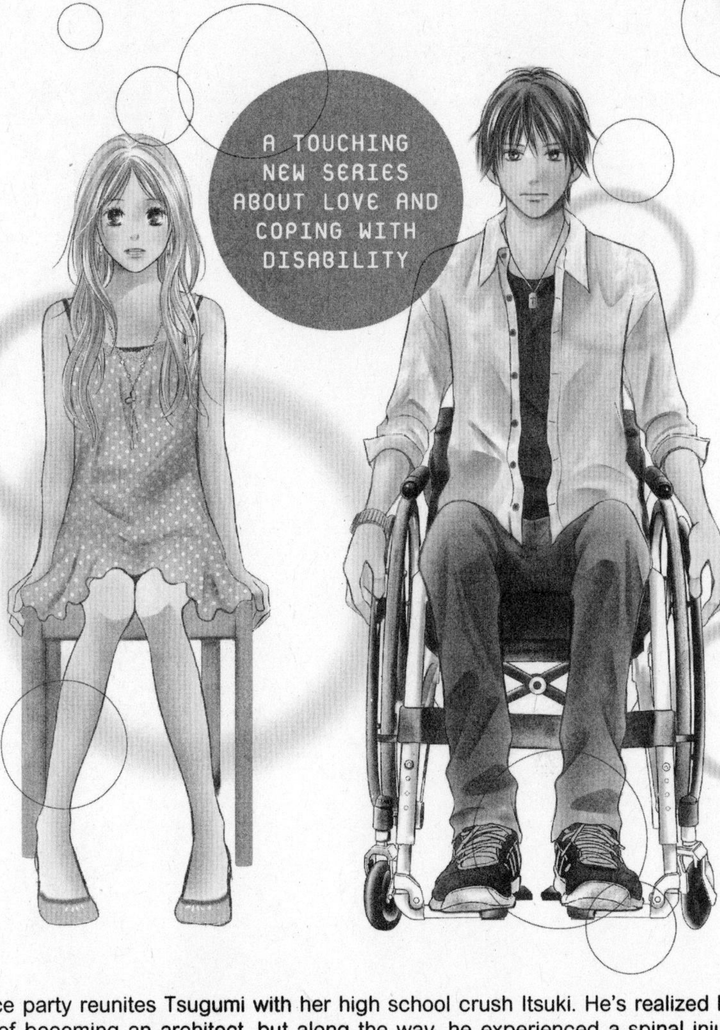

A TOUCHING NEW SERIES ABOUT LOVE AND COPING WITH DISABILITY

An office party reunites Tsugumi with her high school crush Itsuki. He's realized his dream of becoming an architect, but along the way, he experienced a spinal injury that put him in a wheelchair. Now Tsugumi's rekindled feelings will butt up against prejudices she never considered — and Itsuki will have to decide if he's ready to let someone into his heart...

"Depicts with great delicacy and courage the difficulties some with disabilities experience getting involved in romantic relationships... Rie Aruga refuses to romanticize, pushing her heroine to face the reality of disability. She invites her readers to the same tasks of empathy, knowledge and recognition."
—Slate.fr

"An important entry [in manga romance]... The emotional core of both plot and characters indicates thoughtfulness... [Aruga's] research is readily apparent in the text and artwork, making this feel like a real story."
—Anime News Network

KC
KODANSHA
COMICS

Knight of the ICE

Yayoi Ogawa

Knight of the Ice ©Yayoi Ogawa/Kodansha Ltd.

SKATING THRILLS AND ICY CHILLS WITH THIS NEW TINGLY ROMANCE SERIES!

A rom-com on ice, perfect for fans of *Princess Jellyfish* and *Wotakoi*. Kokoro is the talk of the figure-skating world, winning trophies and hearts. But little do they know... he's actually a huge nerd! From the beloved creator of *You're My Pet* (*Tramps Like Us*).

Chitose is a serious young woman, working for the health magazine *SASSO*. Or at least, she would be, if she wasn't constantly getting distracted by her childhood friend, international figure skating star Kokoro Kijinami! In the public eye and on the ice, Kokoro is a gallant, flawless knight, but behind his glittery costumes and breathtaking spins lies a secret: He's actually a hopelessly romantic otaku, who can only land his quad jumps when Chitose is on hand to recite a spell from his favorite magical girl anime!

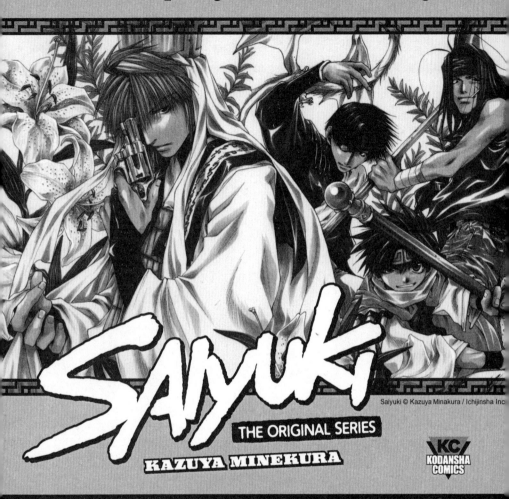

A SMART, NEW ROMANTIC COMEDY FOR FANS OF *SHORTCAKE CAKE* AND *TERRACE HOUSE*!

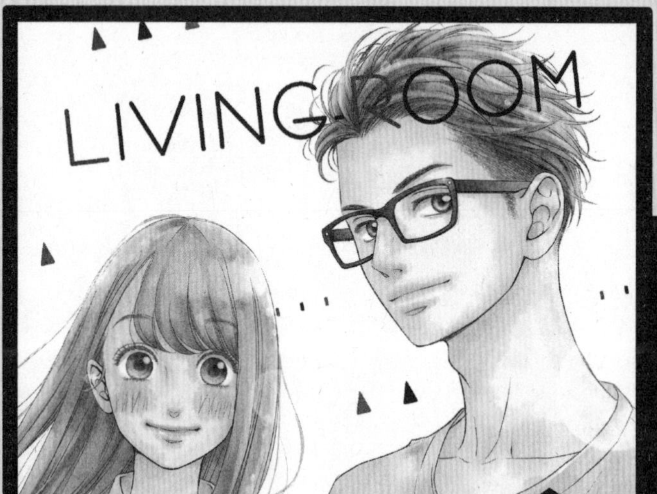
LIVING-ROOM
1
Keiko Iwashita
MATSUNAGA-SAN

A romance manga starring high school girl Meeko, who learns to live on her own in a boarding house whose living room is home to the odd (but handsome) Matsunaga-san. She begins to adjust to her new life away from her parents, but Meeko soon learns that no matter how far away from home she is, she's still a young girl at heart — especially when she finds herself falling for Matsunaga-san.

SAINT ☆ YOUNG MEN

A LONG AWAITED ARRIVAL IN PREMIUM 2-IN-1 HARDCOVER

After centuries of hard work, Jesus and Buddha take a break from their heavenly duties to relax among the people of Japan, and their adventures in this lighthearted buddy comedy are sure to bring mirth and merriment to all!

"Brilliant...the physical comedy and facial expressions will make you literally LOL."

—Sam Humphries
(host of *DC Daily*; writer, *Green Lanterns, Legendary Star-Lord*)

A Kodansha Comics Trade Paperback Original
A Sign of Affection 3 copyright © 2020 suu Morishita
English translation copyright © 2021 suu Morishita

Published in the United States by Kodansha Comics, an imprint of Kodansha USA Publishing, LLC, New York.

Publication rights for this English edition arranged through Kodansha Ltd., Tokyo.

First published in Japan in 2020 by Kodansha Ltd., Tokyo.

ISBN 978-1-64651-218-8

Original cover design by Sari Ichiki (Balcolony)

Printed in the United States of America.

www.kodansha.us

9 8 7 6 5 4
Translation: Christine Dashiell
Lettering: Carl Vanstiphout
Additional Lettering: Lys Blakeslee
Editing: Ben Applegate, William Flanagan
Kodansha Comics edition cover design by Adam Del Re

Publisher: Kiichiro Sugawara

Director of publishing services: Ben Applegate
Associate director of operations: Stephen Pakula
Publishing services managing editors: Alanna Ruse, Madison Salters
Production managers: Emi Lotto, Angela Zurlo
Logo and character art ©Kodansha USA Publishing, LLC